LIFE IN LETTERS OF WILLIAM DEAN HOWELLS

William Dean Howells in Columbus, 1860–1861

Life in Letters of
William Dean Howells

Edited by Mildred Howells

VOLUME ONE

Illustrated

Garden City, New York

DOUBLEDAY, DORAN & COMPANY, INC.

1928

PREFACE

IN PUTTING together these letters, a task far beyond me and one that I have attempted only because my father said that he would like me to write of him, I have remembered a letter to his sister Aurelia in which he says, "What would you think of my writing my autobiography? My published reminiscences have made a beginning, and it would forestall a biography, always a false and mistaken thing." Unfortunately, my father never carried his autobiography further than the *Years of My Youth,* but with his saying about biographies in my mind I have tried to let him tell his life himself in his letters, simply stringing them together on the slightest possible thread of explanation; and in the book, setting pride and affection aside, I have written of him as "Howells", in an effort to keep my shadow from falling between him and the reader.

Everyone, I hope, thinks his or her father the best, the wisest, and the greatest of men; so if I wrote of my father's virtues, the world might not find my testimony convincing, and I can only trust that from what he says—and does not say—in his letters, the public may be able to draw a true picture of him. Among my father's own letters I have included a number to him from his friends, which, besides adding to the interest of the book, say things of him that a daughter cannot well say.

My brother and I naturally wished to leave out all my father's personal references to his family, but we felt that without some touches of his tenderness towards it, the letters would not fairly represent him, and so we persuaded each other to let certain ones remain.

Having neither training nor experience to help me in

editing these letters I have had to use methods of my own, the apparent madness of which I should like to explain to the public, if they will give me leave.

Except for certain omissions the letters are printed as they were written, with all their native errors and inconsistencies, so that their human quality should not be lost.

The notes always refer to the letters following them.

Titles are given in italics, that they may be easily found.

As I have purposely refrained from all comment on the letters, so I have also purposely omitted openings to the chapters, in an effort to give the effect of a real life, which does not pause to sum up or explain itself as it goes.

Sometimes the letters have been cut, and where this has been done I have not put in asterisks because, with me, they seem to concentrate the mind more upon wondering what has been left out than upon reading what has been left in. Perhaps I wrong the reader by judging him in this matter from myself, and if so I will try to make amends by saying that only trivial and tiresome things have been taken out of the letters, and that where names have been omitted they have been those that would not add to the interest of the text. Permissions to reprint letters and quotations have kindly been given by D. Appleton & Company, The Century Co., Dodd, Mead & Company, Harper & Brothers, Houghton, Mifflin, Company, and G. P. Putnam's Sons.

MILDRED HOWELLS

CONTENTS

VOLUME I

CONTENTS

CONTENTS

CONTENTS

XIX
1886, 1887

XX
1888, 1889

LIST OF ILLUSTRATIONS

LIFE IN LETTERS OF WILLIAM DEAN HOWELLS

LIFE IN LETTERS OF
WILLIAM DEAN HOWELLS

I

1857, 1858, 1859

Ancestry and early years. At home in Jefferson. Editorial position on Ohio State Journal. Columbus *life and friends. First poem in* The Atlantic Monthly. *Anti-slavery enthusiasm.*

WILLIAM DEAN HOWELLS was born at Martin's Ferry, Ohio, on the first of March, 1837, in a little one-story brick house that it is said his father built with his own hands. He was the second child of his parents, Mary Dean and William Cooper Howells, his elder brother Joseph having been born some four years earlier at St. Clairsville, and he was followed by three sisters and three brothers, Victoria, Samuel, Aurelia, Anne, John, and Henry, so that he grew up surrounded by an affectionate and intelligent family that largely made up its own world.

His father was almost entirely Welsh, only one English great-grandmother breaking the Cymric strain, but it was through this Susannah Beesly that the love of reading and poetry is supposed to have come into the family. Her husband, Thomas Howells, came from the county of Radnor, and went with his brother William to London where they began life as watchmakers, and it was there that Thomas met and married his English wife. After his marriage Thomas returned to the little town of Hay, on the river Wye in Breconshire, where he engaged in making Welsh flannels, a trade he succeeded at so well that he finally owned three mills, one of which is still standing. During the Presidency of Washington, he made a journey to the States, taking a quantity of his flannels with him. He landed at Philadelphia, where he met the President, who advised him to settle in Virginia near the new city of Washington. He followed this advice to the extent of bargaining for a large tract of land near the Potomac for which he was to pay an English shilling an acre, but after returning to Wales, he gave it up. There is a legend in his family that on his way to the boat for his homeward voyage he wheeled before him a barrel of silver money, the proceeds of his enterprise in flannels.

Thomas Howells became a Quaker by convincement, as did also his son Joseph, but when Joseph married Anne Thomas, the orphaned daughter of a Welsh schoolmaster, she did not join the Society of Friends, and so he lost his membership in it. Joseph's son, William Cooper Howells, was a year old when his parents decided to emigrate to America, where the manufacture of wool was very profitable. There was then a law forbidding workmen skilled in certain crafts from leaving England, so Joseph Howells had to engage his passage as a "gentleman," but in spite of this precaution he was arrested at Gravesend and sent back to London. As there was, however, no evidence of his having served an apprenticeship, he was allowed to sail with his wife and child to Boston.

He came with letters to various Quakers and went about among them helping to set up woolen mills, but though he brought a considerable sum of money with him, it was not large enough for him to live upon, and delays and disappointments in his business used it up. He wandered from Boston to Virginia, and then over the Alleghanies in a road wagon to Ohio, where he made several disastrous attempts at farming, in one of which he sank a legacy from his father of three hundred pounds.

Although Joseph was no longer a member of the Society of Friends, William Cooper Howells was brought up as a Quaker and wore a "shad-bellied" coat that made him the butt of the boys at Steubenville, Ohio, when he arrived there. He was under a constant injunction from his father never to strike anyone, but in his memoir he confesses that he compromised by kicking his tormentors' shins until they left him in peace. He always loved letters and politics, and after helping in his father's unsuccessful farming ventures until he grew up, he became a printer and journalist and published a small weekly of his own called the *Eclectic Observer,* which died at the end of six months. He then secured a place as foreman in the printing office of the *National Historian* at St. Clairsville, Ohio. It was at this time that he married Mary Dean of Wheeling, West Virginia, who was Irish on her father's side, and, through her mother's family, the Docks of Harrisburg, Pennsylvania, of German descent. Her brothers were pilots, captains, and owners of river boats, and though they were democrats, and had grown up in a slave state, when in later years an abolition lecturer was denied public hearing at Martin's Ferry, they said he should speak at their mother's house. It was during this lecture that their smallest nephew, William Dean Howells, sitting in his mother's lap, was nearly hit by a stone which some objector hurled through the window.

As Howells's grandfather was an abolitionist, his father a Henry Clay Whig or constitutional anti-slavery man, and his Dean uncles were converted to the Whig party, he grew up in a strong anti-slavery atmosphere. This, with perhaps the fact that his parents had become Swedenborgians, separated his family somewhat from their neighbors, for in Southern Ohio there was strong pro-slavery feeling.

When Howells was three years old, his father moved to Hamilton, Ohio, the scene of *A Boy's Town,* where he took charge of a Whig newspaper. It was in his father's printing office there that Howells first learned his letters from the

type, and then learned to set up type, when he was so small
that he had to stand upon a chair to do it. In telling of the
family life in Hamilton, he says:

"The fortunes of a Whig editor in a place so democratic
as the Boy's Town were not such as could have warranted
his living in a palace; and he must have been poor as the
world goes now. But the family always lived in abundance,
and in their way they belonged to the employing class; that
is, the father had men to work for him. On the other hand,
he worked with them; and the boys, as they grew old
enough, were taught to work with them, too. My boy grew
old enough very young; and was put to use in the printing
office before he was ten years of age. This was not altogether because he was needed there, I dare say, but because
it was part of his father's Swedenborgian philosophy that
everyone should fulfil a use.

"If his mother did her own work, with help only now
and then from a hired girl, that was the custom of the time
and country. She was always the best and tenderest mother,
and her love had the heavenly art of making each child feel
the most important, while she was partial to none. In spite
of her busy days she followed their father in his religion
and literature, and at night, when her long toil was over,
she sat with the children and listened while he read aloud."

There was always reading going on in the family, and
this, with the printing office, formed the greater part of
Howells's education. He went to a variety of schools in
Hamilton, all of which he liked, and out of school he lived
a boy's life of swimming, hunting, fishing, skating, playing
with other boys, and also fighting with them, although this
was forbidden as against the Quaker tradition of his family.
It must have been in Hamilton that he read Goldsmith's
Greece, and Irving's *Conquest of Granada;* there also his
father introduced him to *Don Quixote,* which remained a

passion with him all his life. He wrote verses and even plays, but of literature as an art he had no conception until, at the age of ten, he wrote a novel on Hamlet el Zigri, the last of the Moorish kings, in such time as he could spare between play and school.

When Howells was twelve, his father sold the paper in Hamilton and went to Dayton, where he undertook to buy another newspaper by a sort of progressive purchase, but never succeeded in quite paying for it. Howells and his eldest brother had to leave school to work in the printing office, and it was a hard time for them all. In the *Years of My Youth* Howells says of his part in it:

"Until eleven o'clock I helped put the telegraphic despatches (then a new and proud thing with us) into type, and between four and five o'clock in the morning I was up carrying papers to our subscribers. The stress in my father's affairs must have been very sore for him to allow this, and I dare say it did not last long, but while it lasted it was suffering which must make me forever tender of those who overwork, especially children who overwork. The suffering was such that when my brother, who had not gone to bed much later, woke me after my five or six hours' sleep, I do not know how I got myself together for going to the printing office for the papers and making my rounds in the keen morning air."

But in spite of all their labor the business failed and for a while Howells and his brother worked in a German printing office, where he learned the German type.

Then came a plan made by his father and three of his Howells uncles for taking over a grist mill and a saw mill on the Little Miami River near Xenia, and turning them into paper mills, around which they hoped to gather a sort of communal settlement of suitable people. One of the uncles was to supply the capital, and they were all to bring their families there when the community was started, while in the meantime his father was to take charge of the mills and run them until they were turned into paper mills. The fact that he knew nothing of mills seems not to have discouraged them, and he himself was ready to undertake almost anything to support his family.

The only house near the mills was a log cabin that Howells described in *My Year in a Log Cabin* and in *New Leaf Mills*. Into this cabin the family moved, the children with delight and their mother with reluctance. It was a hard and primitive life for her, with few available neighbors, and far from her own people, to whom she was always devoted; but she faced the change bravely, and her husband and children delighted in the adventure. The cabin was of squared logs papered with newspapers in an effort to make it more comfortable, but all the cooking had to be done at the big fireplace, and the snow drifted in through the cracks in the roof on the boys sleeping in the loft. It was in this loft that Howells discovered in a barrel of paper-covered books which his father had stowed away there, a copy of Longfellow's poems, and for a time he fitfully studied an old Spanish grammar under the influence of *The Spanish Student*. The boys led a free and joyous life in the fields and woods, and especially on, and in, the river. There was a school two miles away through the woods, but it had little to teach them, so they were not kept at it.

A printer at Xenia offered Howells work in his office, and to help the family resources he tried it, but the despairing homesickness that he had inherited from his mother made him rejoice when, at the end of a week, an older man was found for the place. Soon afterwards the mills were given up and the family went to Columbus, where his father was to report the proceedings of the Legislature for the *Ohio State Journal*. For this reporting he received ten dollars a week, while Howells worked as a compositor on the same paper for four, and his brother Joseph as a clerk in a grocery for three. With this they were able to live comfortably in a small brick house that they hired for ten dollars a month.

After his work in the printing office was over, Howells wrote verse in imitation of Pope and Goldsmith, or walked and talked with his father, who was his chief companion. The first poem he ever had printed appeared during this winter in the paper he worked for, and was copied in a New York paper and in the Cincinnati *Gazette.* He was soon changed from the newspaper room of the *State Journal* to the book room, where he worked and frolicked with another boy, John J. Piatt, with whom he afterwards published the *Poems of Two Friends;* but Howells's mind was then so full of literature that he had no time to play with other boys.

At the end of the winter William Cooper Howells started another newspaper enterprise, taking over the Ashtabula *Sentinel,* which he and his sons bought with their work, for they had no money. After a little while he moved the paper from Ashtabula to the county seat at Jefferson, where the family realized their ideal of living in a village. Jefferson was in the Western Reserve, that had been settled almost entirely by New Englanders, and the *Sentinel* represented the Freesoil sentiments of the country.

In Jefferson, at fifteen, Howells taught himself Spanish in his devotion to *Don Quixote,* and worked in the office of the *Sentinel,* which was one of the social centres of the town, the village girls coming in to help fold and address the papers, and the young men following them. There was always talk going on there, and it was mostly of the merits of different authors. When his work, which began at about seven, was finished early in the afternoon, Howells, after doing a man's labor at printing, devoted himself to studying four or five languages by himself, for, besides writing prose and verse, he was reading everything he could find. He worked far into the night at his studies, and became so nervously exhausted that he fell a prey to hypochondria, and having been bitten by a dog in his childhood, it took the form of a fear of hydrophobia. This horror haunted him for years, and he could never bear to keep a dog, although dogs always adopted him with a determined devotion. Owing to this illness he had to give up work in the printing office and spend most of his time in driving about on political and business errands with his father, who tried to help him by telling him of his own youthful hypochondria and assuring him that all evil from the dog bite was long outdated. With rest and an open-air life Howells's nerves regained their tone, and he was able to go back to his work and studies; at the same time he was composing sketches and poems that he set up in type for his father's paper without first having written them.

There was on the *Sentinel* a young printer of Howells's own age and tastes, who lived with the family as well as worked in the office, and they became great friends. Jim Williams was a blithe spirit with a smooth, girlish face and an ambition to become a professor in some Western college, and in following this ambition, which he realized before he was killed in the Civil War, he shared Howells's studies in Latin, Greek, German, and Spanish. The languages they pursued together only with the purpose of reading them, for they did not try to write or speak them. Williams was a leader in the simple village gaieties into which he sometimes lured Howells who had become exiled from them in his devotion to literature. When Williams left Jefferson, Howells made friends with two older men; one of them was an Englishman three times his age, who built organs for country churches and adored Dickens, and the other was a New England dealer in jewellery. There is a daguerreotype of the three taken together, with Howells, a slender youth of eighteen, seated between the two older men.

It must have been at about this time that Howells tried studying law in the office of Senator Benjamin Wade, who lived in Jefferson. He knew that if he became a lawyer it would be a great help to his family, so he dutifully read on at the law for a month until he found that Blackstone said the law was a jealous mistress that permitted no other interest, and realizing that his heart was in writing, he went back to the printing office.

The whole village was proud of his studies, and a neighboring Scotch farmer offered to be one of three or four persons to send him to Harvard, while Howells himself was eager to go to an academy in a town near Jefferson; but though his father could have spared him to study law, which would have brought an immediate return, his work could not be spared, for the sake of abstract learning, from the effort the family was making to buy their house. Howells often felt his lack of schooling, and in an outline of his life that he wrote when he was editing the *Atlantic* he says: "It is and always will be a deep regret with me that I have had so little regular education—I mean in the way of schools and colleges. What I could do to supply the lack, I have done. I have always liked study, and have always loved reading."

Howells and his oldest sister, Victoria, were beginning to grow impatient of the village life in their longing to see something of the outer world, and when their father, who had been chosen for one of the House clerks in the State Legislature at Columbus, went to take up his duties there, they went with him. He had arranged to furnish, with his son, a daily letter for the Cincinnati *Gazette* and other newspapers on the Legislative proceedings, a letter that his son mainly wrote from the material given him. They were afraid that the papers might not care for reports written by a boy of nineteen, but after the letter had found favor with the editors, William Cooper Howells withdrew from the work after telling them who was doing it. In Columbus Howells had the free range of the State Library, where he read with avidity, discovering De Quincey and steeping himself in Tennyson.

At the end of the winter his letters had pleased the Cincinnati *Gazette* so well that he was asked to become the city editor of that paper, and he went to Cincinnati to see what the work would be. He tried reporting on the paper to fit himself for the position, but one night's rounds of the police stations with the other reporters convinced him that he was not meant for the place, and after several home-sick weeks he went back to Jefferson, where in his enthusiasm for Heine he took up German again, studying it with an old German bookbinder.

His father's clerkship in the Legislature had ended, so in the autumn of 1856 Howells applied for the correspondence of the Cincinnati *Gazette* and the Cleveland *Herald* for himself, and, securing them, he went back to Columbus; but during the summer he had been ill with a rheumatic fever, and almost as soon as he began writing his letters his health failed and his father had to take over the correspondence. Howells dragged drearily through the winter, helping his father when he was able, but nothing could stop the vertigo that tormented him, and at last he went home to Jefferson, where, being too ill to work at printing, he spent his days tramping about the woods. In the spring he grew stronger and was able to go back to the *Sentinel* office, where he worked all the summer, feeling very discouraged about his future, and it is at this period of his life that his letters begin. But as there is no description in them of his wife or her family, it might be well to say something of them before commencing his letters.

Elinor Gertrude Mead was the oldest daughter in a family of nine children, with three brothers older than herself, and three brothers and two sisters younger. Her father, Larkin G. Mead, was a lawyer in Brattleboro, Vermont. He was known as "Squire Mead," and started the first bank

Between two older friends, 1856

and library in the town. Her mother, Mary Noyes, was the sister of John Humphrey Noyes, who founded the Oneida Community. She and her brother Horatio were the only ones of his brothers and sisters who did not join the Community. Through her father Elinor Mead was descended from the Meads of Lexington, Massachusetts, who had married into the Munroe and Converse families there, and through her mother she was a descendant of Parson Russell of Old Hadley, and of the Reverend James Noyes of Newburyport.

All of Elinor Mead's brothers and sisters had a distinct artistic gift. John Noyes Mead, the oldest of the family, who died while he was still at Harvard, drew and painted well; Larkin G. Mead, Jr., was a sculptor and made the statue of Lincoln at Springfield, Illinois, and the one of Ethan Allen in the Capitol at Washington; William Rutherford Mead became a partner in the architectural firm of McKim, Mead and White, and Elinor Mead was herself an artist. On the table of their sitting room in Brattleboro there lay a piece of gamboge, a cake of Prussian blue, and one of crimson lake, so that any member of the family could pause in passing through the room to do a little painting, and when they wished to describe anything very clearly to each other, they always drew it.

Brattleboro was one of the first summer resorts in New England because of the water cure established there by Dr. Robert Wesselhoeft, a political refugee from Germany. In the season it was full of people from New York and Boston, and before the Civil War several Southern families used to come there, bringing their slaves with them. There were also some foreigners, one of whom, a Russian count, taught the Brattleboro girls to smoke cigarettes, and, rising early, picked the best flowers in the village gardens, which later in the day he made into bouquets and presented to their astonished owners. In these surroundings Elinor Mead grew up, knowing something of the world, and observing her native town with keen intelligence. In person she was slight with fair colouring and light brown hair, and as quick and graceful in her movements as in her mind.

It was during the winter she spent with her cousin Laura Platt in Columbus that she met Howells, and it was after he had gone as consul to Venice that they became engaged. As he could not leave his post long enough to come home to be married, she went out to France with her brother Larkin, who was on his way to study sculpture in Italy, and was married at the American Legation in Paris. Owing to the Civil War there were very few Americans in Venice during the first year of the young couple's marriage, and because of the Austrian occupation there was no social life among the Italians, so Howells and his wife were left almost entirely to themselves, and she told him all about everyone and everything in Brattleboro. It was this intensive view of New England that made Howells able to understand it so clearly when he went there to live, and it was his wife's vivid powers of observation and her gift for criticism that made her such a great help to him in his work. She had a wonderfully true sense of proportion both in art and literature, and though she could never argue them out, her intuitive criticisms of books or pictures were almost unerring.

1857

This first letter from Howells, with its self-taught German and Latin, is to his sister, Victoria Mellor Howells, of whom he says in *Years of My Youth:*

"I had grown more and more into intellectual companionship with the eldest of my sisters, who was only a little more than a year younger than myself. It was laid upon me to try solitarily for the things I had no help in doing, and I seldom admitted anyone to the results until that sister of mine somehow passed my ungracious reserves. I do not know just how this happened; but perhaps it was through our confiding to each other, brokenly, almost unspokenly, our discontent with the village limit of our lives. Within our home we had the great world, at least as we knew it in books, with us, but outside of it, our social experience dwindled to the measure of the place. I have tried to say how uncommon the place was intellectually, but we disabled it on that side because it did not realize the impossible dreams of that great world of wealth, of fashion, of haughtily and dazzlingly, blindingly brilliant society, which we did not inconveniently consider we were altogether unfit for."

The letter was written on his return to Jefferson after his first winter in Columbus, where he went with his father and his sister Victoria on a journalistic venture, as he explains:

"We were to furnish, my father and I, as I have already told in *My Literary Passions,* a daily letter giving an account of the legislative proceedings, which I was to mainly write from material he helped me get together. My sister of course had no part in the enterprise, and for her our adventure was pure pleasure, the pleasure we both took in our escape from the village, and the pleasure I did not understand then that she had in witnessing my literary hopes and labors."

These notes refer, as do all other notes, to the letter following them.

To Miss Victoria M. Howells

Jefferson, Oct. 27, 1857.

MEIN LIEBES SCHWESTERCHEN:

I'm in such a state of mind, not to say sin and misery, as hardly to be able to write. In the morning I get up in a stew, and boil and simmer all day, and go to bed sodden, and ferociously misanthropical. An hundred times a day, I give myself to the devil for having come back to Jefferson, when neither sickness nor starvation drove me; and as often I take myself to task for a discontented fool. For I know very well that had I remained in Cincinnati or Cleveland, I would have discovered as clearly as I have here, that I was in the worst possible situation, the most uncomfortable, the most unprofitable and unpromising. It's a taint of the blood. Here I am, *at home,*—to me the dearest of all places on earth—to begin with. I have books—the best friends. I have time—the most precious thing. No one molests me nor makes me afraid. I sit under my own vine and fig tree (figurative) and cock up my feet on my own secretary (reality). Yet I am not happy. I am not reasonable. They are fools or humbugs who say man reasons. Gammon! He wishes for, he grumbles at. The horse who shakes himself free of the wrinkles and recollections of his harness, and gratefully crops the grass, *reasons* more.

The present question with me, for instance, is, how am I to make a living? I bore myself continually about it, conjuring up possible unpleasant predicaments, and give myself no rest. I am proud, vain, and poor. I want to make money, and be rich and grand. But I don't know that I shall live an hour—a minute! O, it was the loftiest and holiest wisdom that bade us take no thought for the morrow and to consider the lilies of the field! If a man were to pray for the *summum bonum,* he would pray: Give me heart to enjoy this hour. Alas for me! Here I might be happy, yet here I am wretched. I want to be out in the world, though I know that I am not formed to battle with life. I want to succeed, yet I am of too indolent a nature to begin. I want to be admired and looked up to, when I might be loved.—I know myself, and I speak by the card, when I pronounce myself a mistake.

This is chiefly sermon. Don't be bored, Vic. It has cleared my mind a good deal to write all this trash.

Your affectionate brother,
WILL.

1858

It must have been soon after Howells's letter of October 27th that the summons to write for the *Ohio State Journal* came, for in *Years of My Youth* he writes:

"I was at home that autumn, as I had been all the summer, eating my heart out (as I should have said in those days) when the call to a place on the *Journal's* editorial staff incredibly, impossibly came, and I forgot my ills, and eagerly responded. I hardly know now how to justify my inconsistency when I explain that this place was the same which I had rejected at twice the salary on the Cincinnati *Gazette*. Perhaps I accepted it now because I could no longer endure the disappointment and inaction of my life."

He went back to Columbus and lived at the Medical College, then abandoned by medicine and used as a boarding house, where he roomed with a fellow poet, Thomas Fullerton, who became a lifelong friend, and of whom he says, "My own room-mate was a poet, even more actual than myself, though not meaning so much as I to be always a poet; he was reading law and meaning to practise it, but he contributed two poems to the *Atlantic Monthly* before any of mine had been printed there."

"John" was his youngest brother, John Butler Howells, always especially dear to him, of whose future he had great hopes.

To Miss Victoria M. Howells

Columbus, Dec. 26, 1858.

DEAR SISTER VIC:

I wish you were here with me to-day, sitting with your eyes upon the cheerful coal fire, and listening to the rain dropping from tower to tower, with musical irregularity. I am in the most charming state of animal comfort. I have just eaten the heartiest dinner, have accomplished without disaster three flights of stairs, and am embraced by the arms of a great split-bottom chair. It is entirely dismal out of doors, and its dismalness makes it more pleasant indoors. Directly, when I have finished this letter, my room-mate Fullerton will drop in, and we will chat away the time over some favorite author, with frequent reading of select passages aloud; or else we will throw ourselves upon the beds, and let the rain sing us to sleep. In the evening, I will go up to old Jones's room, and we will make our Sunday call at our German friend's house. But is there no shadow in this bright picture? Assuredly. There is a shadow and a skeleton. I have an abominably sore nose, which to my diseased imagination and impracticable vision seems monstrous. As nearly as I can describe it, it appears about the size of a sugar-bowl, and is of dull mahogany color. Could you see it, I am sure you would find it quite a consolation. What can ail the unfortunate feature, I am at a loss to know.

I got father's letter this morning, though a short note had previously relieved my mind in regard to John. You can well imagine, I think, how much trouble my dream gave me. I dream most every night something about home. But so long as I continue to improve in health, I shall not be homesick. I am going to send some presents home, for New Year's. I am sorry about that watch business; but sometime it will be made all right. I am going to write for the Odd-Fellows *Casket*, to which I have been invited to contribute, and anything I can make in that outside way, shall not be used selfishly. The *Casket* pays $2.00 a page. I think I can save eight or ten dollars in that way every month. Benedict of the Cleveland *Herald* said he would copy my things and designate me as the author, and Coggshall will also help to bring me out. I am not satisfied with the New Year's address I have written, but I will suffer it to be printed anyway.

"Dr. Smith's," was the house of Dr. S. M. Smith, who, when Howells was going to Venice, asked him what provision he had made for the chances before him.

"I told him and whether he thought it not enough in that war-time when personal risks were doubled by the national risks, he said, 'Well, I am not a rich man, but if you think you need something more, I can let you have it.' I had been keeping my misgivings to myself, but now I owned them and borrowed the two hundred dollars which he seemed to have there with him, as if in expectation of my need."

This kindness was never forgotten, and was repaid in kindness long after the money was returned.

Mrs. Carter was another Columbus friend, and he says of her:

"My world had been very small, and it has never since been of the greatest, but I think yet, as I divined then, that she was of a social genius which would have made her in any great-worldier capital the leader she was in ours. Her house expressed her, so that when her home finally changed to another the new house obeyed the magic of her taste and put on the semblance of the first, with a conservatory breathing through it the odor of her flowers and the murmur of the dove that lived among them: herself a flower-like and bird-like presence, delicate, elegant, such as might have been fancied of some fine, old-world condition in a new-world reading of it."

"Joe" was his elder brother, Joseph A. Howells.

To Miss Victoria M. Howells

[1858 or 1859]

JOURNAL FOR VIC

Monday 25. The usual nothing occurred at the office. In the afternoon, I carried home to Madame R. a volume of Heine I had borrowed several months ago. I thought to be received with coolness and reproaches for not having come to see her for so long a time (she is the German lady at whose house I used to visit so much with Jones when I first came to Columbus), but instead of this, she treated me with the greatest cordiality, and complimented my German immensely.

In the evening, I called upon Miss Wing, a *Dickens*-girl, with whom I spent an hour in very pleasant talk. I like her, for her freedom and heartiness put me in mind of my dear sister. When I rose to go, she said, "Don't go, Mr. Howells, I'm about to sing for you, though you haven't asked me." She is a glorious singer. I had heard her at Dr. Smith's, where she sang "Excelsior" in a manner that made my heart ache. I ought to have remembered to ask her to sing, but I really didn't think. I excused this, and declared that I should be delighted to hear her. So she sat down, and sang "Morning, Noon and Night," "Here's a double health to thee, Tom Moore," (a beautiful thing that Dunie was perpetually humming last spring when I was at Pittsburgh,) "Kathleen Mavourneen," and Schubert's "Serenade." I was charmed, and exceedingly provoked when two young fellows came and interrupted us. Wasn't this a different way of spending an evening from that of Jefferson, where the girls are so stiff and constrained that a call

is painful to them and everybody else? It was then nine
o'clock, so went and got a book which I had promised to
Miss Carter, and carried it to her. Sat down and had an
hour's chat—pleasant, of course—about books and people.
The Misses Carter had been spending the evening at Bald-
win's. Mrs. Carter came in, and the talk centering upon
religion (she is a very devout Swedenborgian) she said
that she did hope that Mr. Howells would never do anything bad to make her dislike him. Is it possible for a fellow with such friends to be wicked? Came home, and read
till twelve. Sleep.

Sunday, May 1st. I have, to-day, a whole week's work to
bring up. The coming of dear Joe broke in upon the regu-
larity of my habits, and I have neglected the journal until
to-day. I enjoyed Joe's visit so much, but he seemed "kinder
not to take no interest." Why I don't know, but I felt so
dissatisfied and disappointed when he went away that if I
had been a girl, I suppose I should have taken "a good
cry."

The same evening that Joe came, after he had imbedded
himself, I went to a party at Judge Swan's, where I had a
very desolate time. Fate consorted me with a very young
lady, whose talk was of the thrilling and momentous occurrences of school life. I wanted to spread myself and
flirt a little, but it was impossible to do so under the circumstances. I said a number of stupid things to numbers of
people, and came away gnashing my teeth. Afterwards I
learned from Mrs. Dr. Smith that I ought to feel immensely flattered at being asked there, as no young gentlemen but those of the first-chop-est description were invited,
and that the party was extremely aristocratic. I was presented to Mrs. Parsons, who, I am told, affects the *bon*-est
possible *ton;* but who was certainly gracious to me.

Joe went home Thursday morning, and that evening, I
called at Dr. Smith's, and had a long and delightful chat
with madame and with Miss Anthony, whom I regard with

the deepest respect. I don't know—everybody, even those
who have been mentioned as entirely different, seem to me
single hearted and sincere—perhaps because I am so myself.

Last night I walked the twilight up, and was about
lounging in at the college post, when I heard a flutter and
twitter, and was aware that Mrs. Carter was at her gate.
She was going to call upon Miss Lillie Swain. Would I go
with her? I pleaded dusty boots, but she said, nobody would
look at my boots, I was so agreeable—that the dress of
stupid people was alone subjected to criticism. I knew that
not so, but I went with her. Fortunately Miss L. was at
home, and she showed me some books on German literature
that she had been reading, and our talk fortunately for me
fell in that channel. She is extremely lively and *picturesque*,
and so I enjoyed myself mightily, and Mrs. Carter was
obliged to say twice that she was sorry to hurry me away,
before I consented to move.

I came to my room and read *Wahlverwandtschaften*,
after which I made an unsuccessful attempt to write some
poetry, and then went to bed.

The weather to-day is indescribably glorious. Everything
is so beautiful that my heart aches with a *höchst angenehmer
Schmerz*. There is no news. Dearest love to all. Will write
during the week to father and mother.

Affectionately,
WILL.

1859

The next letter is to Howells's dearly loved elder brother,
who stayed in Jefferson to help on the family newspaper,
the Ashtabula *Sentinel,* of which he became, and remained
for many years, the editor.

To Joseph A. Howells

Columbus, Aug. 14, 1859.

DEAR JOE:

As the lady justly remarks in the play, "How swift the time flies!" It is mid-August, and the summer is nearly wasted away. I have been sitting at my window, (having lately risen from a delightful postprandial nap,) and looking out on the sweep of land-and-chimney-scape it commands. All afternoon the sun has been bland and warm, and the summer wind has borne innumerable thistle down through the soft light. In the vacant lot on the east of the college, the thistles grow luxuriantly, and the place is forever haunted by twittering yellow birds—do you mind them, in the old "Dayton Lane"? And so the autumn comes, and fills my heart as it always does with a passionate pain that is sweeter in its sourness than pleasure—in other words, a psychological lemonade.

> Tears, idle tears, I know not what they mean,
> Tears from the depth of some divine despair,
> Rise in the heart and gather to the eyes,
> When looking on the happy autumn-fields,
> And thinking of the days that are no more.

Do you remember one August afternoon, near the close of a grasshopper-eaten summer, when you and I rode to Rock Creek, and I repeated these lines?—I don't know why, but I think of many things that happened to you and me; and I am happy in believing that as we have grown to be men, we have not grown apart. As boys, and members of the great evil brotherhood of boys, we had many fights and quarrels; the first are now become impossible, and the latter, I hope we have left behind us forever. It seems a foolish superfluity to write this, but I have never yet told my brother in words how dear he was to me.

I feel particularly light-hearted to-day. For two months, my familiar devil, Hypochondria, had tormented me, so that I sometimes thought that death would be a relief. Yesterday, I could bear it no longer, and went to Dr. Smith, telling him my trouble, and receiving for answer that there was nothing the matter with me.—You may mention this to father.

I hope that you and father will keep me posted in regard to politics. Remember that my anxiety is just as lively as your own. I notice by the *Telegraph* that Krum declines to be a candidate for the Board of Equalization. How will that affect matters?

If you send a package of quoins here, of course they will be noticed. I will attend to it myself.

I believe there is nothing more to write. Only take that small nephew and kiss him on both eyes, after his uncle's favorite method. My love to Eliza, and all at home. Tell Vic I will write to her during the week.

Affectionately,
WILL.

John J. Piatt was an old friend of Howells, who had romped and scuffled with him when, as boys, they set up the House and Senate Bills in the book room of the *Ohio State Journal.* He joined Howells in publishing a book of verse, *Poems of Two Friends,* which was printed in 1860 by Follett, Foster & Company of Columbus.

"The governor" was Governor Chase of Ohio, and "your *Journal"* was the Louisville *Journal.*

To J. J. Piatt

Columbus, March 4, 1859.

MY DEAR PIATT:

When I got your letter this morning, I upbraided myself that I had neglected you. But you know how I live—in a

continual strife with time and fate, and always being beaten
—and I think you can forgive me.

As often as we have published your poems, I have sent
you copies of the paper. With regard to the ms. I have still
unpublished, I will do as you ask. I was so glad and proud
that you had got into the *Atlantic,* though a mean little
pang of envy was felt at first. I "noticed" the fact of *The
Morning Street* being from your pen. Ah! if I only could
write something worthy of the *Atlantic!* To whom did you
send your poem, and who replied announcing its acceptance, and—do tell me all about it.

I have not latterly done a great deal of scribbling for
the *Journal*—running chiefly to translations and news. I do
not understand what story you refer to as being a decided
case of falling in love. I have seen a very charming sonnet
of yours to certain beautiful-eyed Indiana cousins. *Hab'
acht!* Cousins are very dangerous. I've tried it.

Dear old Jones is gone to Cincinnati, and I don't haunt
the Neil House any more. It is quite lonesome without him.
He promised to write me, but hasn't.

Had I bought Schiller before you left? I got that pretty
edition we looked at in Randall's. I am not so much in love
with him as with Heine. Ah! dear, wicked Heine! I have
read *Das Lied von der Glocke*—the Bell Song, you know.
Of course it has *gefallen* me, but I can't say anything very
rapturous about it, which is not to my credit, I suppose.

I have not been at the governor's house since you were
here; but am going to call shortly. The governor lent me a
curious book, *Future Life,* by the author of *Peter Schlemihl
in America.* I read it and could not give any opinion of it.
He says he wants to convert me, and has asked me to call
some evening. He expressed himself to Jones as much
pleased with your poetical success *Atlantic*-ward. You lucky
boy!

I have just been reading a foolish life of Sir Philip Sidney by a silly woman. If you want to laugh, read it—a new

book, Boston published. A lady friend lent it me, with the expectation that I would admire it. Dear heaven!

If you should ever find any German Volksbücher, read them. I have newly finished one. They are very poetical, and so simple in diction that the poorest Germanicist shall understand them.

I am writing more than you want to read. Here are two poemlings. I send them in manuscript because I would rather have them printed in your *Journal* than ours. "Should you think them worthy," please say they are by me, giving the *National Era* credit of original publication. Will you?

Yours always,

WILL. D. HOWELLS.

The poem that the *Atlantic* was so long in publishing was *Andenken,* which appeared in the January *Atlantic* of 1860 and later in Howells's *Poems* under the title of *Pleasure Pain.* It was probably this poem that, as Lowell told Howells years after, was held for some time to make sure it was not a translation from Heine, so strong was that poet's influence in it. *The Poet's Friends,* by Howells, followed in the February *Atlantic* of the same year. It was these poems that helped Laura Platt of Columbus, when her New England cousin, Elinor Mead, exclaimed, "Why, have you got the *Atlantic* out here!" to answer proudly, "There are several contributors to the *Atlantic* in Columbus." During the winter of 1860, which she spent with her cousin in Columbus, Elinor Gertrude Mead met the one of these "contributors" whom she afterwards married.

To William Cooper Howells

Columbus, Oct. 26, 1859.

MY DEAR FATHER:

I have just spoken to Mr. Cooke about the Senate Clerkship; and he tells me that so far he has heard of no applications for that post. Many apply for searg. at arms-ships, and one man from Newark wants an assistant clerkship. The field seems to be open, and you know what to do. Cooke thinks the best plan would be to get the Western Reserve Senators pledged, as there might be some Corwin prejudice against you. Parish, of Sandusky City, is an old Freesoiler. I will make inquiries from time to time in regard to this matter and write you. Meanwhile, you'd better pitch in at once.—I got Sam's and Vic's letter this morning. I am sorry that I can't help you in money-wise. There is nearly $100 coming to me, of which I can't get a cent. O dear!—Foster will get out my poems in about a month. I don't suppose I shall make anything out of them.—I am heartsick with waiting and disappointment. Dear heaven! the way is *so* rough and hard.—The *Atlantic* has not published my poem yet. I don't know what to think. I'm afraid it won't at all.—Tell dear mother I'll write to her soon, and I'll go home as soon as I can raise the money to do so. Good-bye.

Your affectionate son,
WILL.

The "Old Gid" of the following letter was Congressman for the nineteenth district of Ohio. "He was that Joshua R. Giddings, early one of the paladins of anti-slavery in a series of pro-slavery Congresses, where he represented and distinguished his district for twenty years after his resignation under a vote of censure and his overwhelming reëlection." This letter gives some idea of the enthusiasm of anti-slavery youth for John Brown. "Only those that lived in that time can know the feeling which filled the hearts of those who beheld in John Brown the agent of the divine purposes of destroying slavery." On November 25th Howells wrote his poem *Old Brown* which was printed in the *Ohio State Journal* for the next day.

To William Cooper Howells

Columbus, Nov. 6, 1859.

DEAR FATHER:

I had a talk with Russell about your clerkship, and he thinks you can get it without any great trouble. He did not make any suggestions of value—that is, beyond what you are already doing. Your opposition to Corwin and your extreme anti-slavery views will not injure you. He said that if you got a few Senators who would go for nobody but you, the case was pretty safe, but you know that, already.

My life drags on here in the accustomed way, and there is little to tell you. Old John Brown is the prevailing thought and talk. Everybody—nearly—deprecates, while he sympathizes.

I send you to hand to young John Brown a copy of Wendell Phillips' glorious lecture. Mr. Reed and I desire to be remembered to him in the heartiest sympathy.—He comes of a noble stock. If I were not your son, I would desire to be Old John Brown's—God bless him!

I did hope to see something violent in the *Sentinel* on the subject of Harper's Ferry. I trust that old Gid stands firm. There was something in his speech I didn't like; and I was glad when a Boston man in a lecture hit him for it. He had said: "The history of this event will occupy but a brief page in the history of the country." "If this be true," said Thoreau, (he is author of *Walden,* by the way,) "how long will be the paragraph that records the history of the Republican party?"—Brown has become an idea, a thousand times purer and better and loftier than the Republican idea, which I'm afraid is not an idea at all.

The weather here is beautiful—genuine Indian summer, days of dream, that lose themselves in delicious nights.

I don't know what to write. I think Brown all the time.

Give my dear love to all at home. I don't know how long it will be till I see you.

Good-night, with love.
WILL.

II

1860, 1861

First visit to New England. Campaign Life of Lincoln. Appointed Venetian Consul. Journey to Venice.

THE following fragment is all that remains of Howells's letters home telling of his first visit to New England and of a dinner made for him by Lowell during his few days in Boston. He describes it in *Literary Friends and Acquaintance*:

"The dinner was at the old-fashioned hour of two, and the table was laid for four people in some little upper room at Parker's, which I was never afterwards able to make sure of. Lowell was already there when I came, and he presented me, to my inexpressible delight and surprise, to Dr. Holmes, who was with him. * * * A little while after, Fields came in, and then my pleasure was complete. Nothing else so richly satisfactory, indeed, as the whole affair could have happened to a like youth at such a point in his career; and when I sat down with Doctor Holmes and Mr. Fields, on Lowell's right, I felt through and through the dramatic perfection of the event."

To William Cooper Howells

Well we all met at Parker's, and had a glorious time. I think I never heard so much delicious wit and wisdom and drollery, as when Lowell and the Autocrat got started. I was only too glad to sit still and do the laughing, on which I come out strong.

The dinner lasted four hours, from three till seven, and

involved an intoxication to me, as entire as that of Rhine wine. Lowell and Holmes both seemed to take me by the hand, and the Autocrat, about the time coffee came in, began to talk about the apostolic succession. To-morrow evening I am to take tea with him; and next day I am off for the White Mountains.

Good-bye.

Affectionately,
WILL.

Mr. Fields, who was afterwards to offer him the editorship of the *Atlantic*, must either have advised Howells about trying for a place on the New York *Post*, or must have given him a letter to Mr. Bigelow—it is impossible now to know which—and this letter is to report the results of his venture.

The Pilot's Story was a long poem in hexameters by Howells, in which a slave mother is gambled away by the white father of her child. It was first printed in the September *Atlantic* of 1860.

To James T. Fields

Jefferson, O., August 22, 1860.

MY DEAR MR. FIELDS:

I ought to have written you from New York, that my application to Mr. Bigelow was not entirely successful. He objected to my youth, and rather deferred the decision of the matter, giving me some writing to do. I was obliged, however, to come home at once, and could not finish the work. So he said that I should drop him a letter from Columbus, occasionally, and we should keep our eyes upon each other. That was about the result. So I am now at my father's, and shall leave for Columbus this afternoon. I do not know exactly what lies before me there, but I shall do, for the present, whatever I can find to do. My regret at not getting the place on the *Post* was softened by the fact that the more I saw of New York, the more I did not like it.

"Better fifty years of Boston than a cycle of New York," if one may so dilapidate *Locksley Hall*. The truth is, there is no place quite so good as Boston—God bless it! and I look forward to living there some day—being possibly the linchpin in the hub. I wonder if I could not find enough writing there, on different journals, literary and otherwise, to employ me, and support me in comfortable poverty? I know that the pen is a feeble instrument with which to keep the wolf from the door, but then, what will not youth dare—to hope?

I am very glad the correction was made in the poem, and I trust the expense did not fall altogether upon the publishers. Have you seen what the N. Y. *World* said about *The Pilot's Story?* The *World* is a journal of taste. If possibly in looking at the notices you received you should send me some (if there are any) that are favorable, I would be very glad.

I will write up the story of which I spoke to you, and submit it to the *Atlantic* as soon as possible.

Regards to Mr. Ticknor, to the dear "Professor" and to Mr. Lowell. Pray remember me to Mrs. Fields, and please do write me a line at Columbus, if you can think of anything comforting to say.

Very sincerely yours,
W. D. HOWELLS.

The introduction from Lowell to Hawthorne led to one from Hawthorne to Emerson, written on the back of Hawthorne's card and saying briefly, "I find this young man worthy."

To James Russell Lowell

Columbus, August 31, 1860.

DEAR MR. LOWELL:

I have yet to thank you for making me acquainted with Mr. Hawthorne, whom I liked very much, and came nearer to, than I at first believed possible. I was two days in old Concord; and look back to the time I spent there with a pleasure only less hearty than that with which I remember Boston. At New York, I spent four days, and was glad to come away. Indeed, the metropolis disappointed me— which was sad for the metropolis, and annoying to me.

Finally, I am not sorry to be again in Columbus—for I find myself willing and able to work, which is only another locution for willingness and ability to be happy. To the young poet at least, a little immediate applause is grateful, if not necessary, and I get this in Columbus. The whole dear town seemed glad to see me; and one of my particular triumphs was that an acquaintance, a violent pro-slavery physician, (the worst possible combination, you know,) should stop me, to shake hands and tell me that he thought my *Pilot's Story* was very good. The poem has been copied into a Cincinnati paper at length, and the praise of the Boston papers has found its echo here.

Well, it was not wholly of myself that I meant to speak. Indeed, the volume which this accompanies will suggest that I had something else to mention. A glance at the title-page will reveal the nature of the book, and a glance at the preface will make known its peculiar constitution. It is only your attention to the work that I write to secure; for I have neither the wish nor the space to tell you all my own feeling in regard to it. It is the work of a very industrious littera-teur, and an enthusiastic believer in the merits and sufferings of Western poets. For myself, I believe that so far as Western Poetry has deserved recognition, it has received it. The sad error has been on the part of its friends, the belief that cockle and cheat with sufficient cultivation will turn to grain, and they have delved and dug about in fields, that would never have yielded anything but weeds, whether upon the Ohio or the Charles. Nevertheless I fondly believe that there is some poetry in this book, and that it will have its uses. There are dreary wastes of trash in it which I would not have set down in the map of Western Literature; but the purpose of the editor was candor and fidelity to all that existed; and the historical nature of the book is not to be forgotten.

I hope, Mr. Lowell, that you will understand me only to direct your attention to the book. It is foolish, I think, to deprecate just criticism; for nothing is finally so mischievous. It is the wish of the publisher and editor alike, I believe, to submit through me the volume to you, that it shall be judged according to the merits of the plan—but after all this is only impertinence, for you will know how to judge, and we have confidence that you will be just.

Very sincerely yours,
W. D. HOWELLS.

1861

In this fragment of a letter to his sister, Victoria, Howells gives a picture of Columbus at the beginning of the Civil War as seen with the eyes of his Quaker descent, and in *Years of My Youth* is this further glimpse of it:

"Our first camp was in our pretty Goodale Park, where I used to walk and talk with the sculptor Ward, and try the athletic feats in which he easily beat me. Now the pine sheds covered the long tables, spread with pork and beans, and the rude bunks filled with straw, and here and there a boy volunteer frowzily drowsing in them.

"I have sometimes thought that I would write a novel, with its scene in our capital at that supreme moment when the volunteering began. Instantly the town was inundated from all the towns of the state and from the farms between as with a tidal wave of youth; for most of those who flooded our streets were boys of eighteen and twenty, and they came in the wild hilarity of their young vision, singing by day and by night, one sad inconsequent song, that filled the whole air, and that fills my senses yet as I think of them:

> "Oh, nebber mind the weather, but git ober double trouble,
> For we're bound for the happy land of Canaan."

"The sculptor Ward" was J. Q. A. Ward, a lifelong friend of Howells.

To Miss Victoria M. Howells

Columbus, April 21, 1861.

MY DEAR SISTER:

Your reproach that I neglect you at home is hardly deserved. The past week I have been so very busy, I really could not write, if the excitement had permitted me to write anything. I knew that father was writing, and I thought that would do, until I got time.

Everything is in an uproar here, and the war feeling is on the increase, if possible. There has been a sort of calm to-day in the city, but down at the camp the carpenters were busy building barracks, and the troops were drilling and the mad and blind devil of war was spreading himself generally. The volunteers seemed to be in very good spirits, and to look upon campaigning as something of a frolic. A good many of them are young boys—not over eighteen; but some are men past their prime. Poor fellows!

To Mrs. William Cooper Howells

Columbus, May 5, 1861.

DEAR MOTHER:

I didn't think I would have to write again before coming to see you, and that's why I have left Vic's letter unanswered so long. On Wednesday night I had packed my carpet bag ready to start, and father had laid in some candy and oranges for the children. But I was in extremely low spirits about money matters and about what I was to do in the future, and remembering how many visits home my stupid melancholy had spoiled—I advised with father, and we concluded it was best for me to remain here until I should know something definite, and be able to go home in a more cheerful frame of mind. You see, Cooke, who is my employer, is about to leave the *State Journal* and the chances of my being retained on the paper are somewhat remote. Hunt wishes to retain me, and will, unless his future partner should be also an editor—in which case of course I shouldn't be needed. But this is not the only thing. Cooke owes me something over two hundred dollars, and I have had doubts whether I shall be able to get the money. I think he would pay me if he could, but I don't believe he can at present. I may be all in error about this, and I sincerely hope that I am, but I can't tell. He's now absent and I shall not see him for two weeks. *Then* I'll have a settlement. Of course, dear mother, if I get this money, I will buy that carpet for you, and will I hope be able to make you other presents.—I am almost sick when I think of my labor being wasted, and of the disappointment you will feel in hearing of this. But I thought it best to explain the whole matter to you, for I know you would rather think me unlucky, than unkind, or grudging with my money.

This war business deranges all my literary plans of course; and the future is all confusion to me. I guess, however, things will straighten out and I shall get through.

Father was very well when he left here, and I am well.
Don't let this gloomy letter discourage you, mother, about
me. I wouldn't have written anything at all of this, but for
the reason I gave.

My love to all. I'll write soon to Vic.

Your affectionate son,
WILL.

Not being able to get the money for making his intended
tour of the Western cities must have been a bitter disappointment to Howells, who was anxious to write of them
for the *Atlantic*.

To Ticknor and Fields

Columbus, June 10, 1861.

MESSRS. TICKNOR & FIELDS:

The want of means has prevented me from making the
tour of the Western cities, this spring, and has defeated
the plan of the articles proposed to be made for the
Atlantic. I should have informed you of this before, that
you could have been able to procure similar articles elsewhere, but I still hoped to meet my engagement—and now
announce my inability to do so, only at the last moment.

If at some future time—in the autumn, or next spring—
it should seem desirable to have me go on and make the
articles, or sketches, as I proposed—I should be very glad,
but for the present, it is impossible. I regret the impossi-
bility profoundly enough on my own account. I trust that
I may not have to add to this regret, the fact that I have
disappointed in any great degree.

Respectfully,
W. D. HOWELLS.

In *Years of My Youth* Howells says of his not meeting
Hay in Columbus:

"In my greater devotion to literature I omitted to make the calls which were necessary to keep one in society even in a place so unexacting as our capital. Somewhat to my surprise, somewhat more to my pain, I found that society knew how to make reprisals for such neglect; I heard of parties which I was not asked to, and though I might not have gone to them, I suffered from not being asked. Only in one case did I regret my loss very keenly, and that was at a house where Lincoln's young private secretaries, Hay and Nicolay, passing through to Washington before the inauguration, had asked for me. They knew me as the author of 'The Pilot's Story' and my other poems in the *Atlantic Monthly,* as well as that campaign life of Lincoln which I should not have prided myself on so much; but I had been justly ignored by the hostess in her invitations, and they asked in vain."

Of his campaign life of Lincoln, he says:

"This was the life of Abraham Lincoln, printed with his speeches in the same volume with the life and speeches of Hannibal Hamlin, who was nominated with him on the Presidential ticket at the Republican Convention in 1860. It was the expectation that I would go to Springfield, Illinois, and gather the material for the work from Lincoln himself, and from his friends and neighbors. But this part of the project was distasteful to me, was impossible; I would not go, and I missed the greatest chance of my life in its kind, though I am not sure I was wholly wrong, for I might not have been equal to that chance; I might not have seemed to the man I would not go to see, the person to report him to the world in a campaign life. What we did was to commission a young law-student of those I knew, to go to Springfield and get the material for me. When he brought it back, I felt the charm of the material; the wild poetry of its reality was not unknown to me; I was at home with it, for I had known the belated backwoods of a certain region in Ohio; I had almost lived the pioneer; and I wrote the little book with none of the reluctance I felt from studying its sources."

To John Hay

Columbus, O., June 10, 1861.

DEAR SIR:

I hardly know how to address you on the business of this letter—and I must trust to the inspirations of an office-seeking impudence. Let me the first thing, however, ask that you will pardon the boldness of one personally unknown to you, in venturing to address you at all; and then perhaps you will have clemency enough to forgive even the offence of addressing you on a subject in which you are nowise interested.

I have been an applicant for the consulship of Munich, and my application was filed some two months ago. I believe it consisted of the usual certificates of good moral character, uncommon appropriateness for the place, and ended perhaps with the statement that I was acquainted with the language of the country, to which I wished to be sent. It was signed by all the office-holding virtue of this State, and was couched in language so laudatory, that I could not more than glance at it.

I have not seen that any appointment for the place has ever been made, and it has occurred to me (in the dismantled condition of my fortunes,) that possibly the President might yet name me for it, if I could be named to him. Indeed, I should be most sorry to think that he would neglect so much biographical merit, if his attention could be for a moment drawn to it.

So I write to you—knowing that you see him; and trusting you will forgive the liberty I take with you, if you cannot do anything more.

It would have given me great pleasure to have met you

when you were in Columbus, and I hope that we may yet some day see each other—if only that I may have the opportunity of apologizing for the absurdity of this letter.

Very respectfully,

W. D. HOWELLS.

Howells had written in an earlier letter to his father:

"I have received an appointment as United States Consul to Rome (in Italy, not Ashtabula,) and shall set off for that memorable place as soon as I can arrange things. One thing which concerned me very much, I have made inquiries about. The income of the consulate is in fees, and not in the shape of a salary. I have written to Piatt, who is in the Treasury Department, to look at the accounts of the Roman consulate, and give me the aggregate of the annual income. As soon as I hear from him, I shall notify the dep't of my acceptance—if the amount is large enough to support me. Mr. Cooke thinks the place is worth from twelve to fifteen hundred a year. Even if the income were not quite a thousand, I think I should accept the place."

But the income at Rome proved only five hundred dollars, so Howells gave it up and applied for Venice.

It was in leaving the office of the President's private secretaries, secure of his appointment as consul at Venice, that Howells saw Lincoln:

"That day or another, as I left my friends, I met him in the corridor without, and he looked at the space I was part of with his ineffably melancholy eyes. . . . I faltered a moment in my longing to address him, and then I decided that every one who forebore to speak needlessly to him, or to shake his hand, did him a kindness. . . . He walked up to the water-cooler that stood in the corner and drew himself a full goblet from it, which he poured down his throat with a backward tilt of his head, and then went wearily within doors. The whole affair, so simple, has always remained one of certain pathos in my memory, and I would rather have seen Lincoln in that unconscious moment than on some statlier occasion.

"Within no very long time past my old friend Piatt (he of the *Poems of Two Friends*) has told me that Lincoln then meant me to speak to him, as I might very fitly have done, in thanking him for my appointment, and that he had followed me out from the secretaries' room to let me do so. But without doubting my friend, I doubt the fact; neither Hay nor Nicolay ever mentioned the matter to me in our many talks of Lincoln; and I cannot flatter myself that I missed another greatest chance of my life."

To William Cooper Howells

Washington, Sept. 7, 1861.

DEAR FATHER:

I suppose you are anxious to hear from me, and my success in office-seeking. After spending a day and a half in New York, I came on to this city, and arrived in a rain that sank my heart into my boots—it was so dismal. But I set to work at once. I found that the law did not permit the increase of the pay of any but seaport consulates, and I found that Rome was worth but a trifle over $500, and very uncertain at that. So I went to see Mr. Nicolay, the President's private secretary. He said he would see if the Consulate at Venice were vacant. I should call again next day. I called, the place was vacant, he thought I could have it. I am told by him that the President has signed my commission, and that it only awaits some formality at the State Department. Nicolay thinks I will get it on Monday. Venice is now worth $750 a year—*in salary,* and N. says, that being a seaport can be raised to $1000. I am pleased with my luck, and consider the change a fortunate one.

When I get my commission in my pocket, I shall feel perfectly satisfied.

I am well and full of hope. I have seen poor Hinton, who is neither, and in truth Washington is a most heart-sickening place—the Disappointed throng the streets like uneasy ghosts, and refuse to believe themselves hopeless. —There is nothing to make a letter about for the paper. The place is dull and quiet, and you hear nothing of war.

I don't know exactly when I'll be home, but soon I hope. I'm staying with Piatt, and am managing cheaply. Love to all.

Affectionately,
WILL.

Bowling Green, Ohio, was where Howells's Welsh grandmother, Anne Thomas Howells, lived with her daughter. It was his affection for this grandmother that made him regret, when he was a little boy, that he would have to grow into an old man, and that he could never become an old lady, like her.

To William Cooper Howells

Parker House, Boston, Sept. 11, 1861.

DEAR FATHER:

I received my appointment as Consul at Venice on Monday, and left Washington the same afternoon. I suppose— yes, I am quite certain—that I will be at Ashtabula on Saturday night. If Johnny could meet me at that time, I'd be very glad. Having a new bond to make out, it is necessary to hurry things through. Annie must be ready to start to Bowling Green with me by the early train Tuesday morning.

I'll be more full in my explanations when I reach home.

Affectionately,
WILL.

Howells sailed for England on the *Glasgow* on November 9, 1861, on his way to Venice.

During his "excessively cold" journey over the mountains to Italy, Howells travelled with an Englishman who reversed the temperatures they passed through by becoming a steadily warmer friend as the cold increased, even to sharing Howells's flask and rug with him, but gradually cooling off to bare civility again as they descended to the milder air of Italy.

To William Cooper Howells and His Family

Venice, December 7, 1861.

DEAR FOLKS AT HOME:

At last, I am arrived in this wonder-city to which it seems as if I had been coming all my life, so long, so wearisome has been the journey. Don't let the map of Europe deceive you. If the Continent is small, the railroads are slow, and one spends as much time in traversing a little German state as it takes to go from home to New York.

I wrote you the last from London, where I stopped three days, and then pushed on to Paris. I intended indeed to have written you from each point on my route, but I found myself often without the leisure, and often without the humor, for I knew that you did not want a *short* letter, and I could write no other. Making very brief pauses, where I halted at all, I was naturally eager to see the most that I could of each place, and I would be so tired after sight-seeing that I had not energy to take up a pen.

Let me tell you now of my travel, and you can make out the route on the map, if you like. From London, I went to a little seaboard town called Folkestone, arriving at eleven in the evening, and waiting three or four hours for the little steamer which was to take me to France. About five o'clock in the morning, we landed at Boulogne-sur-Mer, and were immediately boarded by some twenty frantic little old women, who in Boulogne-sur-Mer are the porters. They furiously possessed themselves of our luggage, and rushed up to the custom-house, where the officers scanned my modest traps with an eagle eye, and passed them unopened. (Note well that here in Boulogne, I got my first cup of French coffee, which is the most delicious drink in the world, and is successfully imitated by the German and Italian coffee. It is quadroon-colored, rich as Crœsus, and bland as June.) I had the good fortune to be in company with some English people, who could speak French, and went with them to their hotel in Paris, where I bought a day's experience of Paris for eleven francs. (Don't expect me to tell you of cities, and that sort of thing. This is merely a little selfish record for your perusal alone.) Of course Paris is wonderful—I'm going to write about it for the *State Journal.* I left that city at eight o'clock in the evening, and instead of going to Marseilles, as I first intended, I went to Strasbourg, and so pursued my journey hither, overland. We stopped about an hour only at Strasbourg, and I made no other halt until I reached Stuttgart, the capital of Württemberg. I had on my way the company of a little old lady from London, who got in at Paris, and who was so delighted at my speaking English to her that she executed a little comical *pas seul* in the car. She was going to Heidelberg to see her son, who was sick there, and she told me nearly all her family history. I was equally confiding, and the dear old creature took pity on me so far from home, and was as tender of me as could be. And when we got to the German frontier, where I could use the honest, good *sprache,* then I was at home, and managed magnificently for the old lady, settling her route, and doing everything for her. I got to Stuttgart at ten o'clock, Friday night, and intended to go on the next day at four P. M., but calling on our consul there, I found him a gentleman from Cincinnati, living in such good American fashion with his mother and sisters that I couldn't resist staying three days in Stuttgart. It is quite a wonderful little city, full of palaces, full of pictures, and I saw everything—even the little village where Schiller was born. Leaving these good friends on Monday afternoon, I went so far as Munich, where I stayed all night. The next morning at ten, I took the cars for Vienna, which city I reached Wednesday morning at 5 o'clock. Here I stopped two days, leaving Thursday. At Vienna, too, I enjoyed myself greatly, for there I found the consul a German from Illinois, and he went all about with me, and was extremely kind and good. I took supper at his house, and he went with me to restaurants, where they have the most delicious coffee imaginable. And good beefsteak. It was excessively cold, travelling from Vienna to this place, until we reached the south side of the mountains, when the most surprising change of temperature took place. On Thursday night the frost stood on our window-panes nearly one half inch thick, but Friday night there was none. It was five o'clock Saturday morning when I reached Venice. There at the depot, I took a gondola, and glided up the Grand Canal, with its sad old palaces on either side, and through an hundred secret, winding streets of water, to the door of the Hotel Danieli. You cannot imagine how weird and strange this little ride was. A perfect silence reigned, except for the starlit-silvered dip of the oars, and the groaning of the gondoliers. The lofty houses, white and grand, lifted on either side, and the lamps burning at intervals only made the night more solemn and mysterious. I confess to you that I did not feel altogether comfortable. I had a little money about me, and my gay gondoliers might have dipped me into the water, and let me stay there, without my being able to make anybody understand the facts of the situation. However, they didn't, and I went to bed at the hotel, and slept till ten o'clock.

Now you know, I have just arrived in Venice, and I write you without being able to enter into particulars; but I can tell you that the city is as beautiful as ever it was dreamed, and that my heart if beauty could satisfy it, would be at peace. But exile is so sad, and my foolish heart yearns for America. Ah! come abroad, anybody that wants to know what a dear country Americans have! We tremble here, the outgoing Consul and I, lest there should be a war with England, which would be most disastrous in every respect. God avert it!

En passant, this ex-consul has acted in the kindest manner, and does everything to assist me in learning the way to do things. But for his protection, I should already have been grievously cheated in one hundred ways.

If you like, you can send this letter to Mrs. Carter, to whom I'm going to write before long. Good-bye. I hope to hear soon from home, for I have as yet received no letter. Dearest love to every one.

Most affectionately,
WILL.

Mrs. W. B. Kinney was the mother of Edmund Clarence Stedman, with whom Howells had made friends in Washington just before leaving for Venice, as he says in *Literary Friends and Acquaintance.*

"I had already met, in my first sojourn at the capital, a young journalist who had given hostages to poetry, and whom I was very glad to see and proud to know. Of course I liked him, and I thought him very handsome and fine, with a full beard cut in the fashion he has always worn it, and with poet's eyes lighting an aquiline profile."

To Mrs. W. B. Kinney

Venice, December 8th, 1861.

Some friends, who are going from Venice to Florence, give me the opportunity to send to you a copy of the poems of your son. I would have been only too glad to have given the book into your hands myself,—for to see you would, I feel, be something like seeing my friend Stedman again. I also enclose the letter which he gave me to you—hoping that sometime, either in Florence or in Venice, we may be known to each other. Permit me in the meanwhile to say that any friends of yours who may be coming to this city will be cordially welcomed by me, on your introduction.

It is but a few weeks (since the 9th of November,) that I have left America, and it was only ten days before I left that I saw your son in Washington. We met for the first time, but my heart went out to him at once, and I am not only very glad, but very proud to think we are friends, for I greatly admire him. I am sure you will acquit me of design to flatter, when I say that I think Mr. Stedman the best of our young American poets—it costs so much to say this that it is certainly not done idly.

When I saw him, your son was well, and most actively engaged in writing contemporaneously the history, which our poor country is now so rapidly making. His letters to the New Y. *World* are great successes, and altogether the best accounts of the war.

Pardon me, unknown to you personally, for saying so much in a letter which should merely have announced to you a book. I forgive myself only when I think how glad my own mother would be to have any one write so much of her son.

I renew the expression of my wish to serve you in any possible way at Venice, and the hope that we may soon be acquainted.

It is through the kindness of Mr. Sturgis, of Chicago, that I am enabled to send you the accompanying volume.

Very respectfully,
W. D. HOWELLS.

III

1862

Venetian Friends. Marriage in Paris.

"THE Emperor" referred to at the close of the next letter was Franz Josef, Venice being then under the Austrians. As no Italians would go to the opera during the Austrian occupation the Emperor had only Germans to look at.

To Miss Victoria M. Howells

Venice, January 18, 1862.

DEAR SISTER VIC:

I've just read through your letter, which the postman brought to me ten minutes ago. I answer while the impression is yet fresh upon my mind—an impression only less delightful than that I should receive from hearing you talk all that you wrote. I think your letter was too short—that's all; and I do not see why all the family do not send something each time. As for my own letters, I do not think you have to complain of their brevity; for since I have been in Venice, I have not only written you folks at home long letters, but have given you the benefit of numerous enclosures to other people. There are two in the present letter: one for "Richard H. Stoddard, corner 10th street and 4th avenue, N. Y." and the other for "Mr. John Swinton, Care of the *Scottish American Journal* or N. Y. *Times*, N. Y." I wish you'd send them, Vic, and accept the accompanying photographs as a slight token of my gratitude and a faint illustration of the glorious things I see in Venice

46

every day. As for describing the place, and its novelties, the task is simply hopeless; it's as much as anyone can do to enjoy them. Only you may well believe that Venice is as wonderful and beautiful as it is "cracked up to be." By this time, you will have read accounts of my London sensations in the *State Journal,* if they publish my letters, and I do not know that I can say anything more than I have said about England. You know that I was only there three days, and had not more than twelve hours daylight, put it altogether. Besides, I felt so bitter toward the English that I was glad to get out of England, where I was constantly insulted by the most brutal exultation of our national misfortunes. I tell you, Vic, no one knows how much better than the whole world America is until he tries some other part of the world. Our people are manlier and purer than any in Europe; and though I hope to stay here my full four years, and know I shall profit by my experience and enjoy it, I still hope to go back and engage in the strife and combat, which make America so glorious a land for individuals. Not but what I like the Italians and the Germans with their gentle and amiable ways. You would like them even better, and would undoubtedly pronounce them preferable to the best of Yankees.

Last night I attended a lecture at the Schiller Casino (an Austrian club, here,) and met again the Russian gentleman of whom I spoke in my letter to Mrs. Carter. We fell into the pleasantest chat,—as Americans and Russians always do—and watched the people dancing, after the lecture was over. Your being present at a dance in Europe is sufficient warrant that you are a proper person; and a gentleman does not require an introduction before asking a lady to dance; but though I was greatly tempted to dance, I refrained, for I was in my frock coat, and had only dark gloves. People are so punctilious here about such matters; and in order to stamp myself as respectable, I've been obliged to buy and wear a "plug" hat, and have my boots blacked in the most regular manner. This latter service is performed for me at 25 soldi (about 10 cents) a week, by the most filthy and fascinating old wretch imaginable. It is a part of Venetian nature to cheat, and this excellent man tried to have me pay him in advance, urging a large, interesting, and suffering family in justification. I affected extremest indignation, and declared that he could either do what I said, or leave my boots. Then he complied, and now every morning takes off his greasy old cap, and calls himself my servant, with a brazen humility that is worth twenty times the money I give him. Of course beggars abound, but if you do not give, you say simply, *"Altra volta"* (another time), when they bless you all the same, and you save a soldo. The gondoliers are a droll race, much decenter than hackmen (to whom they correspond) in other cities. They have a charming vein of swindling and romance in their nature, and still cheat the *Inglesi* and chant the songs of Tasso. I have mustered enough Italian to talk to them, when I have business to do, but I cannot wander about the city, seeking such leads and unique conversation as I would like to do, for nothing on the part of a Consul would astonish the punctilious Italians so much as curiosity that would take the form of actual inquiry. In fact, I'm forced to be "respectable"—and am to that extent miserable. However, people become habituated to anything, and I've no doubt I shall get used to "living cleanly like a gentleman." You tell me of a mild winter. Here it has been unusually cold, and to-day the weather is freezing. I just walked through the court of the Doge's palace on my way to get these photographs, at a shop on the Riva Schiavone, and I found it a mass of ice around the beautiful bronze fountains in the court. On New Year's we had snow, to the depth of several inches; but that was soon disposed of by the poor people who are paid for shoveling it up and throwing it into the canals. That couldn't be done in Jefferson, could it? However, of course the winter has been

absolutely nothing to me, Northern-born to six months'
freezing. The temperature for the most part has been that
of those first frosty days in the fall, when you begin to
make fires and think of chestnuts. In a few weeks now the
spring will open. I rather dread the coming of summer,
for I have been so well, up to this time, and in such good
spirits, whereas the hot weather always makes me hypochondriacal. But I won't anticipate evil. I am so glad and
contented to be here, and the future is all bright. I study
Italian every day, and spend my time in reading and writing. I have already sketched a poem—a love-story, which
I call *Louis Lebeau's Conversion.* The scene is a camp-
meeting one, and I think the poem will be successful. Tell
father and mother I first thought of it that night they told
me of camp-meeting, when we sat out on the porch last
September.

I hope father will succeed in his attempt on the Ohio
Legislature, though I shouldn't think from the way he
went in on the pension people, that he could have a great
number of hopes.

To-morrow I'm going to see the Italian friends with
whom I became acquainted. I wish you could know the lady,
who is Russian by birth, and only Italian by marriage. I
called to see her husband, the other Sunday, and she was
obliged to act as interpreter, speaking German with me and
translating into French for her husband. She asked me all
about my family, and how many sisters I had, and whether
they were pretty. (I made you out *syrups,* every one.)
Then she wanted to know whether I intended to marry in
Italy, or had some beloved in America, and many other
droll questions, concluding by asking me whether I was of
a cheerful temperament, or not. She also promised to make
me acquainted with Italians, and bade me come often to her
house.

Tuesday. On Saturday night, I fell in with my Russian
friend at the caffè, and we went to the opera together. The

opera was *I Puritani,* and it was beautifully sung. When it
was about finished, there was a slight commotion in the
crowd, and then a general clapping of hands, and the people rose to greet the Emperor who appeared in his box.
He is a rather handsome young soldier, and looked much
more like royalty than the old King of Württemberg, whom
I saw at Stuttgart. After bowing slightly to the audience,
he sat down, stroking his blond beard, and presently took
his opera glass and engaged in the somewhat dispiriting
occupation of contemplating the hard-favored German
ladies who were present. On Sunday, I went to see Signor
Borrozzi again, and had a very pleasant little half-hour's
visit. I send you this card, on which is his coat of arms,
for his family is noble and their name was written in the
Golden Book of the Republic. The weather has taken a
new and unfavorable turn, and after blowing cold has
compromised by snowing again. But after January, we
shall have no more cold weather, until the last of October.
Have any of you heard from Mrs. Carter since I've been
gone?

You see, I'm rather straining myself to make out this
letter. It's got cold, somehow, and at any rate, I must reserve part of my strength for a letter to Joe. When you
write next, specify some things you'd like to know about,
and don't, dear, leave me the hopeless task of telling about
everything. *You* must write to me always, Vic. And now
give my dearest love to all, and so good-bye.

Your affectionate brother,
WILL.

The "Mr. Tortorini" in the next letter, who proved himself a friend indeed, had lived several years in England and
had a passion for the English tongue and for reading
Webster's Unabridged Dictionary. His friendship began
through his desire to practise his English on the new Amer-

ican consul, who writes of him in *An Old Venetian Friend:*

"We met first in the office of my predecessor, who was holding my place and enjoying my pay, for no fault of his, during the pleasure of the Austrian government while I waited three months for its permission to act as American consul at Venice. I had received my *exequatur,* but was one day counting up my resources and wondering whether they would last till I could draw my first quarter's salary, when Pastorelli [Tortorini] mastered the situation from his imperfect English and then shouted with a sort of generous indignation, 'I will give you all the money you want!' He meant would lend me the money, but he would not let me explain the difference.

"It was well that Pastorelli was staying on in town, for with the summer heat I fell into a low fever of some sort, as he discovered one day when he came to see me at my rooms, perhaps because he missed me at our caffès. I suggested a doctor, but he said, 'If a doctor finds out you are a consul he will keep you in bed six months,' and from his skill as a pharmacist in the past he prescribed for me himself and brought me the medicine at once from the apothecary in the *campo* where I lived."

In the "little short letter" to his mother Howells told of his illness and of his friend Tortorini's kindness:

"It must be a very short letter I write now, because I have been sick for the last ten days, and am yet too weak and dull to do more than scribble a note. Your dear kind letters shall be answered in full, a few days hence, and you must not believe but that I'm convalescent, and doing admirably. I've fallen into the hands of good friends (thank God, I seem to find good friends everywhere,) and have been well cared for in my little sickness. The excellent old Genoese in whose house I'm lodged has rivaled his German wife in attentions, and Mr. Tortorini, my dear old Venetion friend, has sacrificed himself, and his favorite habits, to a frightful extent. He has prescribed for me, and kept me from death and the doctors, who have a holy alliance in Italy, and are as much distrusted as the priests. The other morning I took my medicine with such sweet resignation that the dear old fellow stooped down and kissed me, stabbing my forehead severely with his stiff moustache."

Hamilton was Hamilton, Ohio, the scene of *A Boy's Town.*

To William Cooper Howells

Venice, March 7, 1862.

DEAR FATHER:

I wrote a little short letter to mother the other day, telling her that I had been sick. I have to tell you now that I am quite well again, with good spirits and good appetite, though I was down for nearly a week with fever—bilious, I suppose it was. The people with whom I lodge were very kind and attentive to me, and I did not lack for anything during my sickness. For anything? O, surely, for home, and home, and home! For voices, for steps, for touches, for tenderness that made sickness an empire, when I was with you. We are so eager to fly away from the nest, (God forgive us,) when we get our wings fledged, and when we cannot fly back again with our poor broken plumes—that is the sad time. Do you know, I thought all through this fever, of a fever that I had in Hamilton when I was a very little child, and used to doze upon the old settee, and mother would come and kiss me, and ask me if I had slept. But I never could tell her; and I could not answer myself now if I had slept, after the dreamful intervals of not-awaking. I remember that I had been all day ranging with the boys up and down the hydraulic in the cold winter sun and wind, and came home chilled and dizzy; and mother did not know I was sick at first, nor I either, till the print of my book swam under my heavy eyes. So the other Saturday, I walked all day in the damp weather, and sat late over a German translation of Euripides that I had found at a book stall. I rose at last with aching shoulders, dull brain, and a cold shuddering from the heart out. There was no one to ask me if I were sick; but I stated the fact very clearly to myself, and had confirmation of it by ten days' illness. I think it was only my determination to not give up that saved me from a very long illness—my determination, and my old friend, Tortorini, and these good people of the house here.

You ask me how I live in Venice? Until now, in this way: I had a room at ten florins a month, and then I took my *meal* (for they only eat dinner at Venice) at a restaurant, and coffee, three or four times a day, at different caffès. In spite of my utmost economy, my living (with lodging) alone cost me two florins (exactly $1) a day. When anybody speaks to you again of cheap living in Europe, shrug your shoulders, and show the palms of your hands. If that isn't enough, wag the forefinger of your right hand back and forth, and at last scrape the bottom of your chin with the back of your hand outwards, and tell him, "Lies, lies, lies!" You can live cheaper in America than anywhere else, and better, far better,—for no American would diet himself in the manner to which the beggarly bellies of Europe are accustomed. I don't speak of the poorer people—they live upon a kind of food for cattle,— coarse fish, mush, and a tough, filthy-looking decoction formed of old boots in slices, I should think. But even well-to-do people know nothing of abundance—a dish of soup, a plate of cauliflower, boiled beef, figs,—this is dinner, and, remember, the only meal of the day. The rest is coffee and expectation. Meat is dear, vegetables are dear, rents are high. I'm talking of Italy—the cheapest place in

Europe. A friend who had been spending the winter in Hanover, because he expected to find Germany very cheap, paid $11 a week for board that we could get for $3.50 in Columbus. I'm mad when I think of the monstrous lies I used to swallow about cheap living in Europe. The folks with whom I lodge have taken me in *pension,* or boarding, for a week, and if we can agree upon terms, and I like it, we shall come to some arrangement, and I can live cheaper at least than I have been living so far. While I think of it, have you followed the Congressional proceedings attentively enough to know whether my appointment has been confirmed in the Senate? I suppose it has; but if it hasn't, won't you please write to Wade, or to Mr. Sumner (who is head of the foreign affairs committee) not to let it be overlooked. It's possible such a thing might be neglected through oversight, you know.

You asked me sometime since to tell you of country-life in Italy, and I replied that I knew nothing of it. In June, I'm to go to Mr. Tortorini's "Cawntree" as he calls his country-seat, Monselice, near the old city of Padua. Then I shall have an opportunity of telling you all that you wish to know, and will probably write something for the *Sentinel* about it. I quit writing for the *State Journal,* because I found I couldn't avoid politics, and them I'm forbidden to touch. I'm very sorry you made so pointed an allusion to the anti-Anglican feeling of my letter—such a thing might cause my removal from office, if properly worked up by a judicious enemy. It was a poor, flippant letter, and it wasn't necessary to parade my consular dignity in connection with the authorship. One of these days I'm going into the printing-offices here, and I'll write you some account of them. They do beautiful printing in Venice, and I fancy they must have well arranged offices. I don't know whether I've ever sent you my card. I enclose two—one done at Vienna, and the other (the smaller) here. As for newspapers, there are no Italian journals worth sending, except those printed in the kingdom of Italy, and they are not permitted to come to Venice. But I'll send you a copy of the *Gazetta di Venezia,* a high-toned, conservative sheet, edited by the police, the calm and judicious tenor of whose articles would delight the soul of Mr. Cooke.

I wish, father, if you have any trade, by which you could get a first-quality gold pen, you'd send me one. Let it be rather soft, but not *too* soft. I want to make a present of it to my old friend Tortorini, who never saw a gold pen till he saw mine, for they are not in Italy, nor elsewhere in Europe, except perhaps England. You can send the pen in a letter, well enveloped in soft paper.

Did you get the poem I sent you for the *Atlantic?* Did you like it? I write a good deal, here, and after the first confusion of ideas, consequent upon the novelty, begin to think somewhat—which is better than writing. I take it that if I do nothing in literature publicly until the war is over, it will be just as well. Very glad to hear the news of those three victories, and everybody here has been congratulating me. There's no doubt about the current of Italian sympathy. If you ever write to Reed, please tell him how glad I was to see the "good old *Gazette,*" and to observe that that gunboat controversy with the *Commercial* was raging as furiously as ever. Your article on the abolition of the franking privilege was excellent. I'm anxious this letter should go at once, and as I don't think of anything more to write at the moment, here's good-bye, with dearest love to all.

> Your affectionate son,
> WILL.

Of the social dullness caused by the "political discontents" mentioned in the next letter, Howells says in *Venetian Life:*

"Venice has always hated her masters with an exasperation deepened by each remove from the hope of independence, and now she detests them with a rancor which no concession short of absolute relinquishment of dominion would appease.

"The Venetians are now, therefore, a nation in mourning, and have, as I have said, disused all their former pleasures and merry-makings.

"As for the carnival, which once lasted six months of the year, charming hither all the idlers of the world by its peculiar splendor and variety of pleasure, it does not any longer exist. All other social amusements have shared in greater or less degree the fate of the carnival. At some houses conversazioni are still held, and it is impossible that balls and parties should not now and then be given. But the greater number of nobles and the richer of the professional classes lead for the most part a life of listless seclusion, and attempts to lighten the general gloom and heaviness in any way are not looked upon with favor.

"It is in the Piazza that the tacit demonstration of hatred and discontent chiefly takes place. Here, thrice a week, in winter and summer, the military band plays that music for which the Austrians are famous. The selections are usually from Italian operas, and the attraction is the hardest of all others for the music-loving Italian to resist. But he does resist it. There are some noble ladies who have not entered the Piazza while the band was playing there, since the fall of the Republic of 1849; and none of good standing for patriotism has attended the concerts since the treaty of Villafranca in '59."

To Miss Victoria M. Howells

Venice, April 26, 1862.

MY DEAR SISTER VIC:

You don't know how sorely you tempted me by saying— come home. I thought just one minute of the joy of meeting you, and of being in America again, and then I stopped resolutely, and put the thought away. It isn't for me, now, sweet and dear as it is; for nothing is further from my purpose than to return now. I shall not accomplish here just what I expected to do; but I shall accomplish some things. I shall save a little money to begin life on when I get back, and I shall have time here to go on with studies that I interrupted five or six years ago, by a too impatient plunge into the world. My health is perfectly restored, and though I am often lonesome, I'm not homesick, nor low-spirited. I am studying Italian quite earnestly, and I am going to take up French, and read the Latin and Greek classics, either in the original, or in German translations. I have commenced another poem, and keep a journal from which I hope to make a book about Venice. I hope the *Atlantic* will accept my poem, for the reason that I don't want the *Atlantic* public to forget me, but I shall not let its rejection discourage me. With a new access of earnestness, I have won new self-respect, and look forward to all the chances of literary success or failure with reasonable calm. I hope, dear Vic, that if father was hurt by anything I said to him of the correction of my poem, which he so kindly and so sincerely undertook, that you excused me all you could. Father knows nothing of the principles of the verse in which the poem is written, and I'm afraid his correction has been the death of it. But give him my dear love. I would rather lose the poem twenty times over, than cause him pain. I dreamed of being in America last night, as I have done so many, many times since I have been here; and in my dream I said to myself—looking round on the low houses nestling in the beloved trees on either side of the wide streets— "Well, this at last, is no dream, and I'm at home and awake." But a pang of regret for Venice went through my heart, for I thought I had left it too soon, and before I knew perfectly all the glorious and beautiful things that are in it. So comfort mother, dear, and beg her to spare me a little while longer. If the salary of this consulate has not been permanently increased, and is only fixed at $1500 during the war, I'll resign directly the war is over; for it won't pay to stay here for $750. If, however, mother should be sick, or her health become so feeble as to alarm you, you must write to me at once, Vic, and let me come home without delay.

The weather is inexpressibly delightful here, now, and it is spring without being summer—a thing we can't quite understand in the American climate. All day long, the little *campo* where I live rings with the music of the canaries and finches hung in their cages at the balconies of an old *palazzo* opposite.

I presume I shall be quite as much alone throughout my whole stay in Venice, as I am now. Society is so entirely different in its constitution here from what it is in America that, much as I want to study Italian life, it is difficult for me to do so. What with their political discontents, and the natural effect of their mode of education, the Venetians are eminently unsocial. There are no parties, nor anything of that kind. The ladies have a certain day in the week on which they receive company—that is, people who call from five to fifteen minutes. The men meet and talk in the caffè. As for seeking women's society for intellectual pleasure, as I used in Columbus, it is a thing so far from their knowledge, that they could not understand it. Young ladies *never* receive calls, and a young lady cannot go upon the street unless accompanied by her mother or brother. If she went alone she would lose her character. Where they happen to be in company, they are startled and stupefied if you talk directly to them, and not through the medium of the mamma. The natural consequence of which is that the young men are beasts, and the women what you might expect them. O Vic, Vic! prize America all you can. Try not to think of the Americans' faults—they are a people so much purer and nobler and truer than any other, that I think they will be pardoned the wrong they do. I'm getting disgusted with this stupid Europe, and am growing to hate it. What I have told you of society here in Italy, is true of society throughout the continent. Germany is socially rotten—and the Germans have a filthy frankness in their vice, which is unspeakably hideous and abominable to me. The less we know of Europe, the better for our civilization; and the fewer German customs that take root among us, the better for our decency. You will read the lies of many people who say that life in Europe is more cheerful and social than ours. Lies, I say—or stupidities, which are almost as bad. There is no life in the whole world so cheerful, so social, so beautiful as the American. You see people talking and laughing, here at the caffè; but do you know that this is their only social amusement? The pleasure which we have innocently in America, from our unrestrained and unconventional social intercourse, is guilty in Europe— brilliant men and women know something of it; but they are also guilty men and women. Are you getting tired of my lecture, dear? I think these things over a great deal, with sorrow for errors into which I fell regarding my country; and the most earnest, earnest prayer that my heart can conceive that America may grow more and more unlike Europe every day. I think when I return home I will go to Oregon—and live as far as possible from the influence of European civilization. While I write on this theme, I scarcely can have patience with my former impertinent and stupid ideas.

I'm not going to make you a very long letter this time, my dear sister; but there's no reason why you should shorten your reply.

Give my dear love to mother and father, and all the rest. Before I mail this letter, I will find out what Joe wants to know of envelopes, but it's useless to think of buying them here.

Your affectionate brother,
WILL.

The letter from Brattleboro must have been from Elinor Gertrude Mead, to whom Howells had become engaged, and his engagement was the "subject very interesting to me" on which he hoped to hear from his mother.

To William Cooper Howells

Venice, Aug. 22, 1862.

DEAR FATHER:

Your letter of July 31 came yesterday, and also the *Sentinel* containing extract from my letter to Vic. It was miraculously well printed—only one error of any consequence occurring. If you'll recollect that *Venice* is the name of the city and *Venetia* the name of the province, the error won't occur again. I'll write again for the paper soon, but I don't know exactly when, now. In the meantime I send the sketch for the *Atlantic,* which I didn't send last time. Will you post it to the address of H. M. Ticknor, Boston, with an explanatory note? I'm glad that the letters can go by the way of Bremen for 15 cents, and I'll pay the postages in a lump afterwards.

I've been dreadfully discouraged about the war. Two other letters which came with yours yesterday—one from Brattleboro, and the other from Columbus—breathed the same desolation that yours did. People seem so utterly disheartened, and that's the worst feature. We *can't* treat with the South on the basis of our defeats, unless we mean to yield everything. We must conquer before we can think of peace. When we have gained two or three battles, I suppose we'd better stop and let the South go. I'm satisfied that the people of the North care more about slavery than about the Union, and so what's the use of keeping up the bloody farce any longer? If we only had met secession with entire leave to secede when this first began, we should to-day have been a stronger and freer and better people than ever we were before. I see by last night's paper there's been a fight in Cedar Mountains, Va., and that the rebels retired. I believe none of our reports, the lying has been so persistent and systematic. The Garibaldian project upon Rome has fallen through. I much doubt if Garibaldi ever meant anything but a demonstration. As it was he scared all the tyrants in Europe. If he only lifts his finger, they're frightened. I wish we had some man so brave and true, and noble as he to lead our armies—that is, if we should have any armies by the time he could reach America. But it is of no use to talk in this way.

I shall await mother's letter very anxiously, for I suppose she will have something to say on a subject very interesting to me. I'm glad to hear that grandmother bears up so well, and I earnestly hope she may live to see me again.

On Monday, here, we had a celebration of the emperor's birthday—that is, the Austrian party did. I attended the divine office in the Cathedral with the other consuls, and afterwards called with them upon the Lieutenant Governor. In the evening there was a gondola procession on the Grand Canal, which was indescribably fine. The gondolas were adorned with thousands of Chinese lanterns.

I'm very well now, except for the *scirocco,* to-day. That always makes me feel unpleasant. Good-bye for the present. Dear love to all.

Your affectionate son,
WILL.

As Howells was not able to leave his consular post long enough to return to America, Elinor Gertrude Mead came to England with her brother, Larkin G. Mead, Jr., to be married, but when they found that would involve a seven days' residence there, they went on directly to Paris, where they were married at the American Legation by Dr. Mc-Clintock of the American Chapel. Mr. Dayton, the American Minister, Mr. Pennington, the secretary of Legation, and Larkin G. Mead, Jr., were the only wedding guests, and the bridal party went at once to see the Louvre. Family tradition says that the bride, in the agitation of the moment, left her muff at the Legation, and was sternly reproached by her sculptor brother for the time lost in going back for it.

Ann Flannigan was the Irish maid who had been for years with the Mead family.

To Larkin G. Mead, Sr.

Paris, Hôtel du Louvre, Dec. 24, 1862.

Two young persons, after a great deal of preliminary tribulation, were married to-day at the American legation in the presence of Mr. Dayton, his secretary of legation, and Larkin Mead (who especially desires to have his conduct on the occasion recommended). It was found that a seven days' residence in England was necessary to matrimony, and so, after the most distressing failure to procure a special license, they—that is Elinor and I—pushed on to Paris, where the affair was arranged as already stated, the ceremony performed by Rev. McClintock, and took place at 3 o'clock P. M. After which the happy couple and the adjacent brother went to see some churches and things, all looking remarkably like Elinor. This is the story in brief. To-morrow we leave for Italy at 10 A. M. and expect to be in Venice Saturday night. The writer has a vague impression that he's rather glad he's married and Elinor seems to be satisfied with her husband, although she doesn't consider him at all comparable in excellence or elegance to the table d'hôte dinner to-night at the Louvre. I remember myself to everybody and view myself in the light of an universal brother and son-in-law.

W. D. HOWELLS.

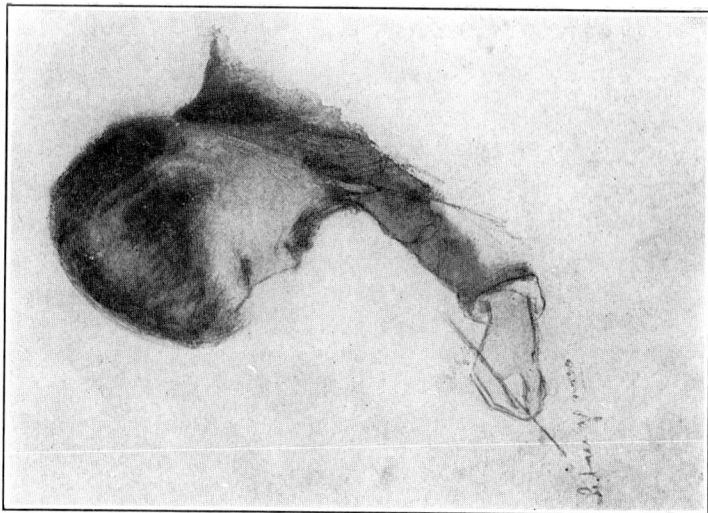

A sketch of Howells made by his wife in Venice during the first year of their marriage, 1863

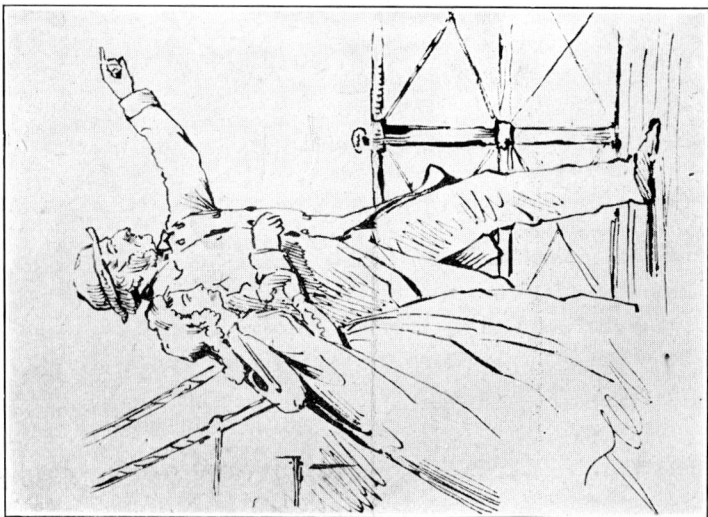

Elinor Gertrude Mead and the captain of the boat on which, in 1862, she went to Europe to be married, sketched on board by her brother, Larkin G. Mead

To Mrs. Larkin G. Mead, Sr.

DEAR MOTHER:

Since Mr. Howells wrote the foregoing we have learned that the only through train to Venice leaves at 8 o'clock P. M. and as it is too late to start to-night, we'll be under the painful necessity of spending to-morrow (until eight o'clock) here visiting the Louvre and whiling away the time as best we can in this dull city. To tell you the truth, I'm in love with—Paris and don't object at all to the Hôtel du Louvre. The wedding was a charming little affair altogether. 'Twas in Mr. Dayton's library and only six of us in all there. Though I was obliged to be married in the Episcopal form (with a ring, etc.) it was a Methodist minister who did it. It was rather trying to go rushing about so long trying to get someone to perform the ceremony without any success but it is all over now and we were married on the 24th in Paris, assisted by the Legation. Mr. Dayton said, "You are one of the legation now, Mrs. Howells." The Parliament House in London, the Church of Notre Dame, the squares, the fountains and the Louvre of Paris have quite turned my head. And a French dinner is beyond anything I ever ate. The English waiters look like clergymen and patronize you so as to make you feel very awkward. Lark behaves splendidly—is *wild* over the Louvre, talks most remarkable French aided by frantic gestures and enjoys himself hugely. I shall write all the particulars from Venice. With a great deal of love to my mother and father (how kind they've been to me!) and all the Meads, Ann Flannigan and neighbors, I am

Your affectionate daughter,

ELINOR.

IV

1863

Life and work in Venice.

To William Cooper Howells

Venice, March 15, 1863.

DEAR FATHER:
From a primary motive of laziness and further to avoid all future cause of complaint regarding my handwriting, I have adopted Elinor as an amanuensis. As I always have a great deal to say without much disposition to say it, and as Elinor never has anything to say with the greatest possible desire to talk continually, I think you will be perfectly satisfied with the result of our arrangement. You will have no fault to find with the shortness of her letters and you will find the literary merit of the joint composition improved through my furnishing the ideas and she their expression. Elinor is so well pleased with my way of saying things that she is quite willing to write herself down anything I want, and I have continually to regret that the general public which I have an equal desire to entertain and abuse, is not as complaisant. Your letter came this morning. I met the post-man with it as I was going out for some medicine of my own prescription for Elinor. (I think it is well to begin taking medicine in the family at once, and as I don't like it myself, Elinor is obliged to carry out the principle.) The post-man had two letters for me; one from you and the other from Geneva acknowledging the receipt of my draft in payment for a gold watch which I have just bought there, out of the proceeds of the trans-

lation so continually dinned into all our correspondence.

The usual monotony of our Venetian Sundays was broken
to-day by the event of English service at one of the hotels.
Even my limited experience has known livelier sermons, and
I do not think there was ever so stern a conflict between my
patriotism and my piety as when I was obliged to pray for
Queen Victoria and the English Cabinet generally.

As for the rest, we spend most of our time now in reading up the history of art. I had no idea that I could come to
feel so great an interest in the matter as I have done. But
in Venice the influences of art pervade the whole atmosphere and it is hard not to inhale something of them. The
intellectual life of the place is dead. All that remains are
the triumphs of past genius, but these are everywhere. So
our talk is a jargon, more unintelligible on my part and less
so on Elinor's, of Titians and Tintorettos, of paintings and
sculptures and mosaics, of schools and of manners, and our
reading naturally takes that direction, too. I do not think
the time lost, either, that I spend in this way. I don't know
how it is with others, but some part of every study that I
have pursued with honesty has been of use to me at one
time or other; and I don't feel my intellectual muscle so
fully developed, that I could travel on it just yet without a
little more exercise. This is a general view of the usefulness
of looking at art a little. A particular purpose is to make
some biographical sketches of the Venetian schools, for the
book-seller here, who wants me to do it, and who only
hesitates about the price I want him to pay me for the work.
Besides these books on art I have got one of the most
fascinating autobiographies that I ever read. It is that of
Goldoni, the Venetian dramatist. While on this subject I
may as well tell you that I have revived the notion that I
once mentioned to you of fitting myself for something in the
nature of a professor of modern languages, in case I should
find on my return to America the intellectual life of the

country yearning more decidedly for professors of modern languages than for journalists or even poets.

We went rowing to-day, Elinor and I, making a tour of part of the Grand Canal which she, like most of the Venetians, has never seen as a whole. The boating has rather given place, of late, to walking, but I find it so pleasant that I think I shall take to it actively again.

I have bought Elinor a sketch-book and she proposes to unite sketching with boating. Yesterday she made her first sketch in public, presenting a birdseye view from one of the bridges of "A fisherman mending his coat." The subject was quite unconscious and sat still for a long time, in spite of the eager and applausive multitude scuffling about the elbows of the artist for the best view of her creation. At last the fisherman changed his position, to get his knife, and the artist suspended her labors amid the ill-disguised disgust of the multitude. The crowd, in fact, is the only drawback on these occasions, and I hope that it will not prove too great a one. But I find that it is quite impossible for a short man like myself to stare starers out of countenance, when he can only bring his eyes to the level with their shirt bosom, and I must confess that the crowd is a sore trial to my spirit. However, the privileges of the forestiere are almost unlimited in Venice, and if people, bearing any marks of Anglo-Saxon descent were to swarm up the pillars of the Piazzetta in order to sketch the Ducal Palace from the back of St. Mark's Lion, the eccentricity would be readily forgiven by the Venetians as a perhaps vain, but by no means impossible, form of the *spleen*.

That little poem of mine which you saw in the *Commonwealth* was first printed in Mr. Conway's *Dial*, some two years ago. I have got out of the well sometime since, and have so little prospect of unhappiness before me that I think I shall probably give up seeing the stars by day in the forlorn manner indicated by the poem.

We have dined at home for a long time now, and have

consequently translated our housekeeping into English. I
hope the girls will be able to understand it better.

Mother must consider a letter like this written as much
to her as to you, but the girls are only directly addressed
when they have found time to write to their exiled relations
in foreign parts.

I suppose that we shall get the papers you sent eventu-
ally, but they haven't come yet. From emotions of disgust
as deep as your own I do not say anything about politics
either. Elinor and I unite in love to all, and I am,

Affectionately your son,
WILL.

I notice in looking over this letter, that it has a curiously
stilted effect—as if I had been posturing for print, rather
than writing at ease to you, father. But as I get used to
dictating, I can do better perhaps. Write me something of
grandmother in every letter, and always give her my love.

"The business" was a plan of W. C. Howells's for ex-
porting Jefferson-made oars to Venice.

"Our good old Giovanna" was the maid furnished with
their apartments in the Casa Falier, where they began their
housekeeping. She seemed at first the flower of serving
women, but she had a large and encroaching family that
she finally added one by one to the household, and Howells
says in *Venetian Life*:

"We trusted her implicitly, and I hardly know how or
when it was that we began to waver in our confidence. It is
certain that with the lapse of time we came gradually to
have breakfast at twelve o'clock, instead of nine, as we
had originally appointed it, and the Giovanna grew to con-
sume the greater part of the day in making our small pur-
chases, and to give us our belated dinners at seven o'clock.
We protested, and temporary reforms ensued, only to be

succeeded by more hopeless lapses. But the question was, How to get rid of a poor woman and a civil, and the mother of a family dependent in a great part on her labor? At last we hit upon an artifice by which we could dispense with Giovanna, and keep an easy conscience. We had long ceased to dine at home, in despair; and now we resolved to take another house, in which there were other servants."

So on May 1, 1864, they moved across the Grand Canal to the Palazzo Giustinian, leaving Giovanna behind.

To Mrs. William Cooper Howells

Venice, April 18, 1863.

DEAR MOTHER:

Your part of the last family letter was, as it always is, the welcomest and shortest. But it was full of fears about my health which you need not have felt. I never was better, nor so well in my life, and have almost forgotten that I ever was unwell or down hearted. Try and think of me as widening out in every direction—as having actual dimples in the fatness of my cheeks, and as growing a magnificent double chin.

I want to get through with the business first, and to tell father that the oar project cannot be made to go here: good oars can be bought in Venice for 75 cents apiece, and even if oars were not so cheap, the sort made in Jeff. could not be used, for the Venetian oar is to be pushed, not pulled, and is therefore very heavy in the blade, and very light and slender in the handle. This is no place where ship's oars could be sold to advantage, for there is scarcely any shipping. Such is the report of the growing ship-broker to whom I referred the matter.

When it comes to telling you news of our life, here, I find myself as much at fault as you do when you write from home. Like everything happy, it hasn't much event in it, and we go on from day to day, with nothing to mark them, but letters written or letters received. Between us, I think we get four a week; but never enough come from home. For the past week or two Elinor has been not very well. The warm weather coming on makes her feel the change of climate, and I think the sea air doesn't perfectly agree with her. We intend trying a change next month, for seven or eight days, and making a jaunt to Florence. This week we made an excursion to Torcello—five miles away in the lagoon, where four hundred years ago there was a prosperous city, and where now there are some broken walls, and a few scattered cottages, and vineyards and gardens. We went partly to see the old Cathedral (built A. D. 600), but principally to do our good old Giovanna a pleasure. She is fifty years old, and has never been out of Venice— never "out of these stones," as she says. We took her and her two little children, Beppi and Nina, who fairly went wild to see grass and flowers growing. In all their lives they have never set foot on anything but stone, and they ran riot over the island clutching up weeds and blossoms, and making bouquets, with the pretty instinct of the Italians. Of course the little girl fell into the water, and broke dishes, and of course poor Beppi fell asleep in the bottom of the gondola, coming back, and lost all pleasure of the return trip—for all the world like me, coming back from Cincinnati in the buggy in old Hamilton days.

We send a photograph in this letter for grandmother. Elinor would write something, but is really too unwell, and I would make this longer, but I expect a letter every day from home, and then I'll answer that. Elinor with me sends love to all.

Your affectionate son,
WILL.

The poem that Howells writes of to Stedman as about to be published, must have been *No Love Lost,* which did not actually appear till 1869, when it was printed by G. P. Putnam & Sons.

Conway was his "Ohio-time friend," Moncure D. Conway.

To Edmund Clarence Stedman

Venice, August 16, 1863.

MY DEAR STEDMAN:

It is so long that I have neglected to write to you, I have almost forgiven myself that sin of omission. But I cannot wholly forget the pleasure of our brief acquaintance in Washington, and I have yet to thank you for the letter which you gave me to your mother. Despairing of my early opportunity to present it, I sent it with the copy of your poems I brought with me, to Florence, soon after I came to Venice, and your mother replied in a way to make me feel still more my loss in not seeing her and her family. I understand that they are now returned to America, and before this you will have realized the hope you expressed to me in being near your mother. I have failed of her acquaintance, but will you let me believe myself her friend, and remember me to her?

Of all that we talked of in Washington, how little has been done! I am as much ashamed and discouraged when I think of it, as if these last two years had been different from any other two years of my past, or as if I intended to reform and work harder in the future. But out of your own experience, you must be too wise either to blame me or believe me. The Novel is not written; the Great Poem is hardly dreamed of; I think Dante "somewhat grimly smiles" when he regards (if he ever suspends the contemplation of the Beatific Vision so long,) my halting progress through his Divine Comedy. Nothing written, nothing read. And yet I'm about to publish, as you may have seen in some of the papers, a poem, which an impartial critic (my wife) thinks will make me rich and famous. Perhaps Follett, Foster & Co. will send you a copy of the book, and then I think I may trust your friendship to read it. I have a portfolio full of ms. sketches of life in Venice, and a little something commenced, which is called *A Story of the Potential Mood.* There is another poem "nearly ready," and if the public were half so eager as I am, how much would I not give them! You see, indeed, that I *have* been working, after all, but not printing. It is a sign of greatness, not to print, I think? During the past two years I have had absolute inspiration not to print, and no publisher, until now, has tempted me to disregard it. But, now, the man who first issued me in brown and gold, in the mortal company of another, has set up publishing in New York. I fear he is too good for a publisher; he has at least, a wild and touching confidence in my talent, for which I hope heaven will reward him according to his desert and not mine. He is to get out my poem very soon, and if the iron should become heated, we intend to strike it again before it cools.

And you, what of you and all the literary youth of New York? I take it that you, also, are *indrio,* as the Venetians say, at writing the Novel and the Poem. We all are, always; otherwise, I suppose we should do nothing. I have never seen Stoddard's *King's Bell,* beyond some meagre extracts in the *Post,* and of you, and Aldrich, and the rest, no public rumor has reached me. Aldrich, indeed, sent kind messages to me by my publisher, the other day, and Stoddard wrote to me last fall. The latter replied to a letter of mine written in the spring of '62, and was so evidently a bad correspondent, that I, who am prompt in these matters, dropped him at once. Piatt told me about you in one of his letters, and I know that you are out of newspaper life, and in some office at Washington. I hear that *Vanity Fair* is dead and alive again, but I have never seen it since I left home. Bayard Taylor is returned, by this time, I suppose.

Jas. Lorrimer Graham, Jr., of New York, told me that they two were to spend the Fourth of July in Switzerland together. Conway of the Conway and Mason correspondence, spent two weeks with us, this summer—a sadder and a wiser man for his essay in diplomacy. I suffered with him, for we were friends in America, and his error seemed more calamitous than it has turned out to be. He is now in England, where he is going to reside for a year.

Since we talked together, I have married—most happily, need I say? Witness, content that I never knew before! In every way the union seems perfect—certainly it is so esthetically, for my wife is an artist, in all but the profession of art. She is making some sketches which are to illustrate my poem. Imagine the life we lead in Venice! Some happy day, I hope our wives may meet, in America, when we will read them all the forlorn and desperate verses of our bachelorhood.

When I say it is frightfully hot, I doubt if I give you more than the vaguest idea of this heat—it so far passes expression.

I just left Henry Ward Beecher in the Academy of Fine Arts, one limp and helpless mass of enthusiasm and perspiration. He leaves Venice day after to-morrow, but will stay long enough to see the grand fresco, or procession of lantern-lighted gondolas on the Grand Canal, to-morrow night.

I hope you will forgive me and write to me, and believe I always have been

Yours faithfully,
W. D. HOWELLS.

This note shows how anxious Howells was that his youngest brother should have the education that he had been denied. Howells had taught himself Spanish, German, and some Greek and Latin, and a neighboring farmer had offered to help send him to Harvard, but his work could not have been spared from the printing office, and the plan came to nothing.

Perhaps it was as a result of the following note that John Butler Howells was sent to a military school in Cleveland.

To Joseph A. Howells

SUGGESTED TO JOE:

Why not send Johnny to College, and let one Howells have the stamp of the schools? I remember how I longed to go, and I lost much by not going. You couldn't afford it when I was seventeen. You can now when Johnny is the same age.

To John Butler Howells

Venice, Sept. 2, 1863.

MY DEAR JOHNNY:

I was very glad to hear from Vic that you are to go to school in Cleveland; and while I don't doubt, my dear brother, that you appreciate and will improve the great opportunity offered you, I want to tell you how I envy you —retrospectively. Joe will remember how, when I was seventeen, I longed for a far poorer chance than you now have. I thought in those days that if I could only have a year at Austinburg, it would be the greatest and finest possible thing. Well, I think so, yet—but then father could neither afford to pay my schooling nor to lose my work from the office. Will you recollect this, my dear Johnny, and do a little studying on my account, as well as on your own?

At a military school you will naturally have exercise enough. It must be your care, therefore, not to neglect any study. Few persons are hurt by overwork, but a great many by overplay.

I suppose in Cleveland you'll have some temptations and trials you've never met in Jefferson. Don't be taken with the shallow folly that anything which your conscience tells you is bad can be brave or fine. You'll find a great many brilliant fellows in this world who are also vicious. You must not believe that it is their vice gives them brilliancy.— And that's about all I think of to say to you, in addition to the advice that father and mother will give you.—My dear brother, I remember you as such a kind-hearted, earnest, good boy. I hope I shall find you, when I return, just the same old Johnny enlarged and improved. Do you remember what a good cry we had together that night I left home, when I came upstairs and kissed you, in bed?

Johnny, I want you to write me from your school, and tell me all about it, and who your friends are, and what you study. You owe me one letter now, you know. I wish you would write to Cousin Martha at Hamilton, and tell her that I'm going to answer her letter, soon. Father's fotografs were first-rate,—looked wonderfully like him. I will send him some for Griswold, one of these days.

This morning I went out to buy you a pair of white gloves, for occasions, but Elinor told me you military men used a kind of thread gloves, and so I didn't buy the kids. If there is any little thing like that, which I can send you in a letter, tell me.

Tell little Willie that I'm going to send him a perfect model of a gondola, about a foot long, and that he will get it about the middle of October, I hope. Send my love to grandmother, and give it to all the family.

Your affectionate brother,
WILL.

"Elinor's sister Mary" Mead was then a beautiful girl of eighteen, who added a sweet and joyous spirit to the youthful household. She, and her Venetian experiences, were the inspiration for *A Fearful Responsibility.*

There is, in her sister's sketch book, a drawing of her standing upon the balcony of the Palazzo Giustinian beside a somewhat drooping young man; their backs are turned towards the artist and their figures are framed in the open window against the Grand Canal. It was afterwards discovered by the unsuspecting artist to have been the unconscious portrait of a rejected proposal, and it long served in the family as an example of the fearfulness of the responsibility.

To Miss Anne T. Howells

Venice, Sept. 17, 1863.

MY DEAR ANNIE:

I have an impression that you get a very large share of the letters from Casa Falier, but as you growled considerably in your last letter, this, in part at least, shall be addressed to you. We didn't get anything from Jefferson by the Hamburg steamer of the 29th August, and we think your letters and papers failed to hit that steamer. But in order that hereafter we may know whether we get every letter or not, let us number them, and then write over the replies, "No. — received." This is number 1, for us.

I think my last was principally devoted to gossip about our visit to Petrarch's house. We have not been out of Venice, since then, but we expect to leave again for a short jaunt into the country in a few days. We shall probably revisit Arquà, in order that Elinor may sketch it thoroughly, and then we shall go on to Passagno, the birthplace of Canova. In all this voyaging, we shall have another purpose besides that of entertaining ourselves, which will appear later or not, according as success attends it.

We have, as usual, no particular news to tell of our life here and only one little incident of its extension on the other side of the world. The editor of *Harper's Magazine* has accepted a poem of mine, with an illustration by Elinor, both of which will appear as the opening paper of *Harper's* for December. The poem is called *Saint Christopher,* and the illustration represents an old gateway and statue in Venice, not far from where we live.

I suppose that before this you will have got notice from Brattleboro that Elinor's sister Mary is coming to visit us very soon—next month, we think. I hope, also, you have received—that is, Vic and Aurelia have received—the bracelets which were forwarded from Brattleboro.

I enclose for father a poem of mine, translated and printed at Padua, on occasion of the Zeni-Foratti Nuptials. It is the custom in Italy, when people get married, to print little copies of verse and circulate among their friends. The abbè Fratini, a professor in the University of Padua, made this translation, which has been much admired in that ancient city. It was printed at the University office. The original English has never been printed.

Foster, of New York, wrote me that he had seen father at the Ashtabula depot, and found him "as good as new." My poem will be published about Christmas, Foster tells me. He has the Ms. and the illustrations all in hand, and will hurry the thing along. Foster also told me that he saw dear old Price in Perrysberg, and that he thought the "world wasn't using him right."

Of course you have written us something already about Aurelia's coming with Mary Mead. Of course, if it has been contrived that she can come, it will be splendid and delightful. But all that's been said, and now we can only wait to know the facts.

Charles Hale, to whom the following letter is written, was an editor of the Boston *Advertiser,* which his father owned, and a brother of Edward Everett Hale. He printed in the *Advertiser* the sketches that afterwards appeared as *Venetian Life*.

To Charles Hale

Venice, Oct. 25, 1863.

DEAR FRIEND:

If you have received from the editors of the *Atlantic*, the mss. I begged you to ask for, I have a proposition to make you concerning the sketches of Venice which you will have found among them. I have continued writing these sketches, and have now a mass of material ready for publication about three times as great as that sent to the *Atlantic*. This I am going to publish some time next year in book form, but I first wish to publish it in some newspaper. The subject matter is about the same as that of my letters to the *Advertiser,* which I must now discontinue because it is hard here to find occasions on which to talk dates, and I always feel that the letter-form is a pretence. I would like to publish these sketches in the *Advertiser,* because they would thereby reach just the public I wish to please, and which I happen to know my letters have pleased. Well, finally, if you think you can afford to pay me five dollars a column for these sketches, you may commence publishing them whenever you like under the title of *Life in Venice,* without introduction or preface, except such as may seem best to you to make. As I have proceeded in writing these sketches, I have grown earnester in style, and solider in matter, without losing sight of my original purpose of making them very readable, and I think they would afford a good and candid view of Italian life and character esthetically, morally and materially. I hope that in considering this matter, you will do so quite apart from the friendship I trust we shall always have, and purely in a business way. You may consider the *Atlantic's* rejection of the sketches as against them, and think me wanting in delicacy to offer them to you at second hand.

If you conclude to take my sketches, care must be exercised with the first two or three, which were written with pale ink and must now be hard to read. Hereafter they will be made plain as print.

Mrs. Howells desires to be remembered, and I, hoping to hear from you soon, am

Yours truly,

W. D. HOWELLS.

Mr. Hicks, late the money editor of the *Evening Post* (N. Y.), leaves Venice with his wife, to-morrow, for Egypt. We cut out your letters about Egypt and gave to them. They were delighted, and really I think they could take nothing along in the way of tourist literature, which would be half so useful.

Titles of sketches besides those sent to the *Atlantic:*

> Story of Basio, luganegher;
> My Priest, the Inventor;
> Giovanna and her Friends;
> Expedition to Torcello;
> A Venetian Funeral;
> The Marionette Theatre;
> Gondoliers and their Stories;
> Love-Making and Marriage in Venice;
> The Mouse that Posted with us to Ferrara;
> Our friend, the Grand Canal;
> Life of the Caffè and Restaurant.

Please send me three copies of my present letter.

John Grant Mitchell was said to be the youngest general in the Union army during the Civil War, and his gallant record is well known. He married Laura Platt, the cousin of Elinor Mead, and the cousinly friendship was shared by both husbands.

To General John Grant Mitchell and Mrs. Mitchell

Venice, Dec. 13, 1863.

MY DEAR MITCHELL:

We got Laura's letter this morning, and I start the compendious reply we intend to make, by writing to you. Your wife enclosed fotografs of yourself and her, and a certain other of a sun-umbrella scene, which you doubtless remember. But I long ago made Elinor carry her own sun-umbrella, and was only to be amused by the remembrance of my former abject state. There was something else in Laura's letter which I was quite as glad to find as the fotografs,— I mean your brave likeness in the newspaper, as you rode along the front at Chickamauga under the bullets. I do not think a certain *reluctance* (I am loth to call it a harder name) in my blood at all unfits me for appreciating heroism, in others, and I assure you that I heartily exulted and triumphed in yours. I am so glad to know with absolute, irreversible certainty, that there are at least two officers in our service who have won all they have got by their own merit. Hereafter, when I grow heavy with doubt for the future, I shall leaven my hopes by saying, Mitchell and Comly! And it is a very good sign for you when the weak, irresolute faith of a man like me lays a confiding hold upon you. The multitude are not more fickle, and much blinder. God bless you! When you are President, I will be your Secretary of State.

But after all, this is not saying what I wanted to say. I do cordially rejoice in you, and I'm glad you happen to be Laura's husband, otherwise I might think success would make you forget to be our friend.

I have something to ask of you already. A younger brother of mine, S. D. Howells, has recently entered the army, as a volunteer, and I think as private. He is in Grant's army, to which I understand you belong. If he should happen to be in your brigade,—or if you ever should meet him—any kindness you can do him not inconsistent with your duty as an officer will be most gratefully appreciated by me. I am aware that you could make no occasion of service to him—but if one offers, you won't forget? A friendly word from one in your position to one in his is a good deal. Poor fellow—there may be little use in asking anything for him by the time my letter reaches you, and yet I cannot help asking.

Dec. 17, 1863.

ᵢDEAR LAURA:

You see I've been getting off some feebleness to John; but a little occurrence has taken place which prevents me from finishing this letter to him, though you can send it to him all the same.

We have,—unless I dreamed all last night—a little daughter, whom we call Winifred. I write at 10 A. M., and I compute her age at exactly nine hours. As yet, her features have that somewhat blurred effect visible in young ladies of her age; but she is understood to be the image of her father—as he might appear on a fotograf for which he sat, and wouldn't "hold still" during the sitting. Elinor has pronounced that she "isn't an intellectual-looking child," and I don't know that she is, for she has only had a very short time for mental development. However, we both love the baby dearly, and though we did ourselves disparage it a little, we were both entirely prepared to tear Mary Mead in small pieces when she said it might not be the most beautiful child in the world.

Elinor is very well, and will "soon be up and about," I hope; and then we'll really and truly and upon our word and honor answer your long, delightful letter. But we feel an early and direct announcement of this event to be your due, and so I write now, though I almost go to sleep between the i and the dot. Elinor and Mary send love, and I am, dear Mrs. Laura,

Ever affectionately,
Yours and John's,
W. D. H.

V

1864, 1865

Articles in Boston Advertiser. *Last days in Venice. English publisher for* Venetian Life. *Meets American publisher on voyage home. Looks for position in New York.*

THE letter mentioned from Howells's father told of the death of his son John, who died "with the first song of the birds" on Wednesday morning, April 27, 1864. Howells's "Elegy on John Butler Howells" was written about a month later.

To Miss Aurelia H. Howells

Venice, 1864.

DEAR AURELIA:

I enclose a letter to Sam—but I can't begin to reply to yours now, for I've been sick, and am so nervous that it's torture to write. I've just finished a long, long article on Italian Comedy, and I think perhaps I've overworked myself on that. I'm so glad to hear that you enjoyed your visit to Columbus, and especially that you liked the Platts. I think Laura one of the most charming women I ever knew. I was sure you would like her.

We're going to Rome in November, and soon after that we think of going home. So, this is your chance to visit Europe, and it is dwindling. I've written often to them about it at home, but it is rather provoking to get one letter saying we must expect you, and then never a word more about it. We should like dearly to have you come.

Tell father that if, when he hears of any paper noticing

my book, he will write to the editor and get a copy of it, I'll send his friend some more photographs.

With love to all,

Your affectionate brother,

WILL.

I'll write to you next time and a long letter.

MY DEAR SISTER:

This is a letter I wrote to you the day before Elinor got father's sad letter. It lay sealed upon my table, and I would not send it, then. But now, partly to show I have not forgotten the letter you wrote me, and partly to let you know in what a happy, careless mood, that sad news found me—I send it. I'm very sorry you cannot come to us, but I do not expect any more so great a sacrifice on your part and mother's."

Affectionately,

WILL.

Howells's articles on Venice which the *Advertiser* printed, and that finally appeared in book form as *Venetian Life,* had been rejected by the *Atlantic,* and he had suffered various other literary disappointments, but he says:

"Before I left Venice, however, there came a turn in my literary luck, and from the hand I could most have wished to reverse the adverse wheel of fortune. I had labored out with great pains a paper on recent Italian comedy—which I sent to Lowell, then with his friend Professor Norton jointly editor of the *North American Review;* and he took it and wrote me one of his loveliest letters about it, consoling me in an instant for all the defeat I had undergone, and making it sweet and worthy to have lived through that misery."

The next letter is his answer to Mr. Lowell.

To James Russell Lowell

Venice, August 21, 1864.

MY DEAR SIR:

If you are so frank to praise me, why may I not tell you just as freely how glad and proud I am of your praise? I was particularly delighted to learn that you liked my studies of Venetian life in the Boston *Advertiser,* because while I wrote those things I pleased myself with thinking that you and another dear friend (as I hope I may call Dr. Holmes) would see them and read them. I had never forgotten—how could I?—the cordial and flattering reception you both gave a certain raw youngster who visited you in Boston five years ago—you old ones who *might* have put me off with a little chilly patronage. And so I thought that though you might have forgotten the dinner at Parker's (I can tell you everything you ever said there) you still remembered having in a general way been kind to me, and would be glad to see in what I did evidence that your encouragement was not mistakenly bestowed. I wrote the Venetian studies laboriously enough, adding and altering, re-writing and throwing away as my wont is, and now when I come to put them together for a book, I find my account in all that work, for I shall have to change the printed matter very little. I shall, however, add several chapters of new matter—one on Venetian painting (treating chiefly of the pre-Titianic painters,) and several chapters on Venetian national character, as I have developed it from observation, and study of the old Venetian customs. Of course, in my book, I shall have something to say of the political situation here and the attitude of the Venetians since '59—an attitude which has influenced their character for good and evil in many ways, and which I cannot help thinking a kind of historic phenomenon, like the flight of the Crim-Tartars, and other movements arising from the universal impulse of a people. There is a great deal of work in all this—but how light-heartedly I shall do it now! The truth is, I have worked under great discouragement since I've been in Venice. The first year—after writing *Louis Lebeau*, I idled away in a kind of homesick despair. Then when I did set to work, my literary luck seemed to go against me. I sent the first of my Venetian sketches to the *Atlantic*, and the editors refused them as they refused everything else in prose and verse I sent them—refused them with a perseverance and consistency worthy of a better cause. I think it a weakness to charge failures of this kind upon want of judgment in editors, and so I chiefly blamed myself, and tried to find out the fault and mend it—though I confess I *thought* the Venetian sketches good. I offered them to my friend Hale of the *Advertiser*, thinking it right at the same time to tell him that the *Atlantic* had declined them, and to my surprise they were accepted. During their publication, breaths of applause have reached me—but no such gale as you—God bless you!—have given me. I shall first offer the book to a London publisher (for a first appearance in England will brighten my prospects in America,) and perhaps with your leave I will show your letter. I'm anxious to succeed with this book, for I've got to that point in life where I cannot afford to fail any more. Besides, I'm going to resign my office and go home, (either at Christmas or next March,) and as I have no prospect of place or employment in the States, I must try to make this book a pecuniary success. I go home in this imprudent way, because at the end of three years, I find myself almost expatriated, and I have seen enough of uncountryed Americans in Europe to disgust me with voluntary exile, and its effects upon character. Moreover, though I have by no means fulfilled all the high objects for which I came hither, I have at least so arranged my line of study that I can continue it at home; but with what unspeakable regret shall I leave Italy! You see, that's the trouble—I am too fond of Italy already, and in a year or two more of lotus-eating, I shouldn't want to go home at all.—But before I quit Venice, I shall prepare notes on some Italian subjects, to write up for you, though you need not be afraid that I shall *rush* anything upon you, and I don't think you are, for in your kind letter there was no holding back with the Wegg-like prudence that I have noticed in editors who did not like to cheapen their concessions.— And I have not got Heine out of me yet? I hoped I had. He did me evil both in my heart and my literature, but I trusted that I had overcome him in both. Well—*pazienza!* I shall try again.—I wish you could see a longish ballad of mine now awaiting refusal at the *Atlantic* office, called *The Faithful of the Gonzaga.* The subject is from Mantuan history; and I have notes enough on Mantua—travel notes of a visit paid that dear old city, and notes of researches made afterward in the Library St. Mark—to make you an article on Mantua, if I only could find the title of some recent book to hang the review on.

Forgive me for writing you so long a letter—but I have wanted to write you ever since I came to Italy, and you have given me no chance till now. My wife desires that I remember her to you very cordially; and I have no doubt our daughter (whom the whole palazzo unites, without distinction of nation, in calling *La Bebi,*) would join us if she were capable of forming the easiest Venetian compliment. But she isn't—being merely mistress as yet of a little Italian pantomime with the right hand signifying *serva sua,* which the whole North would perish before it could imitate.

Remember me to Dr. Holmes, and believe me very gratefully and cordially yours,

W. D. HOWELLS.

P.S. I know *now* why you told me to study Dante. What a God's mercy (as the Irish say) it was to me, that I was sent to Italy, instead of to Germany whither I wished to go.

I will be very glad if you will send the "honorarium" to L. G. Mead, Esq., Brattleboro, Vermont.

"Joe's possible absence from home," meant the chance of his being drafted for service in the Union army, in which his younger brother, Samuel Dean Howells, had already enlisted.

Howells could never have fully followed Lowell's advice that he should sweat the Heine out of him, as men do mercury, for he wrote later, "In a poet of alien race and language and religion I found a greater sympathy than I have experienced with any other. . . . The tenderness I still feel for him is not a reasoned love, I must own; but, as I am always asking, when was love ever reasoned?" When he stopped a day at Hamburg on his way to Carlsbad in 1897, Howells spent most of it in a vain search for Heine's house there, which resulted again and again in his being taken to Klopstock's. His only consolation in his failure was the thought of how much it would have amused Heine. On Howells's return from Carlsbad he made a pilgrimage to Düsseldorf to see Heine's birthplace.

To William Cooper Howells

Venice, August 25, 1864.

MY DEAR FATHER:

Your letter of July 31 came just now, more than a month after I had last heard from home. You may imagine it was welcome, but the news in it was extremely distressing,— Sam's sickness and Joe's possible absence from home—I can't think of anything worse for you. Rest assured that if Joe is taken from you, I will fill his place as well as I can; though I really doubt my competency to carry on a business of any kind, much less a business so extensive as yours seems to have grown. Your wish must be law with me in such a case, and I cannot think of anything more un-

worthy than my shrinking from a duty of the kind. But I
hope you will not let a desire to have me at home with you
blind you to my inefficiency in matters of business. I could
certainly edit the paper, and carry on that part of the
schooner, but I confess that the thought of subscription, advertising and stationery fills me with dismay. I know no
reason, however, why I should not try what I am good for
in that way, for I have no prospect of any certain place
before me.—*See Postscript,* for the *unless.*

Let us now understand each other clearly about the time
of my return, and to this end let me copy you a letter which
I received the other day from the poet Lowell, now editor
of the *North American Review,* to which I sent an article
some months ago, on *Recent Italian Comedies.* He says:

> Your article is in print, and I was very glad to get it. Pray instruct
> me to whom I shall pay your *honorarium.*—Write us another article
> on modern Italian Literature, or anything you like. I don't forget
> my good opinion of you, and my interest in your genius. Therefore
> I may be frank. You have enough in you to do honor to our litera-
> ture. Keep on cultivating yourself. You know what I thought. You
> must sweat the Heine out of you as men do mercury. You are as good
> as Heine—remember that. I have been charmed with your Venetian
> letters in the *Advertiser.* They are admirable, and fill a gap. They
> make the most carefully and picturesque *study* I have ever seen on any
> part of Italy. *They are the thing itself.*

Now setting aside the complimentary part of this letter
—and I don't think the writer could have gone *much*
further—this certainly opens up a prospect for me and gives
me standing. If I had only got the letter a year ago! How
I could have worked! But that is spilt milk. I hope yet to
save something of the precious fluid. So before I go home I
shall make notes on all sorts of subjects for articles—I think
of a dozen at least—(a good deal like the man that shot
one coon and cut sticks to stretch 365 coonskins during the
coming year, isn't it?) but my great object before I leave

Venice is to finish my book on Venice, which is chiefly composed of the *Advertiser* letters. This I earnestly hope will be done by the end of November, but it may run a little later. I confidently hope to get a publisher in London, as I go home—that will take a week, at least. Then, if it is necessary that I should go out to Jefferson to stay 3 or 4 months, you must allow me time to arrange for publication also in Boston or New York before I go out. I suggest, therefore, that some of you come to meet us at B. or N. Y., on our return; but this can be arranged in another letter. I confess freely that if Joe were not likely to leave you, I should have asked you for leave of continued absence till March, so profitably does it seem to me I could put in the time, here. But I do not think of that now, and shall not, till I hear that it is definitely concluded that Joe remains at home. And you must think of me coming cheerfully and gladly to your assistance. I'm sure I can't lose much in doing my duty as a son. At the same time, I do not conceal from you that I have not yet in the three years shaken off my old morbid horror of going back to live in a place where I have been so wretched. If you did not live in J. and my dear Johnny did not lie buried there, I never should enter the town again. It cannot change so much but I shall always hate it.—Of course, long before you get this letter, you will have written me further and more fully about this business.

I am very sorry to hear of dear Sam's sickness, but if it will only procure him his discharge, I hope he will be able to stand it. I should think that if his continued sickness should be represented, the matter might be managed. I was very glad to get his brief note, and I hope that in the next letter from home, he will write me more at length, and announcing his discharge.

The girls have indeed sent me a precious memorial. Alas! who could have dreamed that the clover would be growing over the eternal stillness of what was so much life, one little half year ago! It is hard to bear—I think of it very often.

Only Sunday night I walked down to the grassy field that forms the shore of the western lagoon, and saw the sunset on the solemn Alps; and as I walked there, my heart was wrung with the thought that the noble soul I should have loved to tell of all the beautiful things I have seen could never commune with mine on earth. A thousand things suggest his memory, and his "loved idea" visits me in all my bitter moments. It is too much.

Your affectionate son,
WILL.

P.S. There is this, father, to be considered on my part, relative to making so long a stay at the West when I first return to the United States. As my pursuits are of literature, and my only usefulness is in that direction, I must seek my fortune at the great literary centres. Few men live by making books, and I must look to some position as editor to assist me in my career. Well, I hoped that I should return from a three years' residence in Europe with a certain éclat, but I must profit by this éclat at once. A three months' residence in Ohio would dissipate it all, and I should have about the same standing I held before I came to Europe. This would be not altogether in other men, but great part in myself. I should be dispirited and discouraged. Many subjects that I could write up at once in New York or Boston, and thus open place for me, would pass from my mind, and the struggle for position would be twice as hard.

As to my fitness to conduct your business, I greatly doubt it. I think if you could get some one to take hold before Joe leaves (if he does at all) and learn the ropes it would be better. Our old friend Price would be just the man—he is perfectly able, true and faithful.

I speak of all this plainly, because I think it may not have occurred to you, and that you ought to know what my hopes and purposes are. Do not fear but that I should visit you long enough, or that I grudge you my help at a time you

Elinor Mead Howells, in Venice, 1864–1865

Howells in Venice, 1864–1865

need it. Finally, you know, you have but to look the ground over. If poor Joe must be taken from you, and it appears desirable to you, you have only to say come, and I come.

WILL.

To Mrs. William Cooper Howells

Venice, October 28, 1864.

DEAR MOTHER:

I will enclose a few lines in Elinor's letter, for though I have hardly time to write, I should feel guilty to let a letter go home without my hand in it.

Father speaks of my taking office for four years more. I doubt if I could manage it, and if I could, I wouldn't. When I go home, I want to go home to live, "be it ever so humbly." I am sure it will be better than the proudest life here. I only consent to remain here till spring because I think I see very great advantage in doing so; and as soon as I have notes for half a dozen papers on Italian cities I shall be off for home. Home! How my heart leaps at the thought! O mother, you mustn't think that this separation has not been as hard for me as for you. Many a time I've been so homesick I hardly knew what to do—almost as homesick as in the old childish days when it almost broke my heart to be five or ten miles away from you. (Do you remember how one Sunday morning Joe and I came riding back on the same horse from Dayton to Eureka? It was in the fall, and I can hear the hum of a spinning-wheel now, that sounded out of a log cabin door. O me—O me! I am so sorry to be no longer a child, though then I had my troubles, too!) The world isn't so wide now as it was then, and for three years I have borne to be four thousand miles away from you. Well, patience. It will not be much longer now— but O, my dear mother, we can never meet again in the old way. I am wrong to tell you, but every morning I think of someone lying so lonesomely there under the red autumn leaves, and I reproach myself for each moment's happiness, as if it were forgetfulness of him in a sad captivity.

I long to show you our little girl, who grows so good and fair. You should see how sunnily her hair is coming out of the darker color she was born with; and how sunnily her little life has issued from my gloomier nature. I hope she will he as much like her mother in character as she is like me in looks.

I'm rushing my book forward, and it's nearly done—there are but three chapters more to copy. I have very great hopes of it, as a book calculated to succeed and to do good.

Dear love to all.

Your affectionate son,

WILL.

To James Russell Lowell

Rome, Nov. 29, 1864.

DEAR MR. LOWELL:

I have to beg the favor of your intercession with the publishers of the *North American,* in order that I may have a copy of the *Review* for October sent to me at Venice. I wrote, asking this, as soon as I knew my article was to appear, it seems without effect. I hope I am not troubling you too much, for I wish to reserve your patience for trial in other ways; but I don't know how to get sight of the *Review* except through your personal kindness.

At a time when Ministers Plenipotentiary and Envoys Extraordinary are refused a few weeks' absence, I have had the streak of luck (and it couldn't have surprised me more if it had been a streak of lightning,) to get two months' leave, and so I'm at Rome—I really suppose it's Rome—instead of Venice. So far, I like feudal Italy much better than classic Italy, but I'm not prepared to say that Pompeii is not worth living for, and I dare say I shall be better friends with Rome at the end of a month than I am at the end of three days. We've been at Naples, having gone from Venice to Ferrara, Bologna, Genoa, and thence south to Naples by steamer.

To-day, as we were riding outside the city to San Paolo, the driver remarked with a casual snap of his whip in that direction, that there was the Protestant Cemetery. So we got down to go see where poor Keats lay. As we stood by the grave, the custode-boy who conducted us to it, and who stood snatching leaves and sprays from the shrubs that grew over it till I grew nervous, dreading that the dumb bush must feel the mutilation with something of the sensitive keenness of the dust below, and might next begin to run *parole e sangue*—this boy told us what I'm sure you'll be sorry to hear. There is a sister of Keats now in Rome who proposes to remove the present simple gravestone, so sufficient and pathetic, and erect an ambitious monument in its place.

But I did not mean to write a letter.

Very truly yours,
W. D. HOWELLS.

1865

Anthony Trollope, in response to the letter of introduction asked Howells to his house, but scarcely spoke to him while he was there; and he offered him none of the hoped-for help, or advice, as to English publishers, that the young American was too proud to mention. Perhaps it was the memory of this visit that made Howells in after life so gentle and long-suffering with deserving, and undeserving, young writers.

"My book" was *Venetian Life,* which Howells had sent to Trübner & Company in London.

To William Cooper Howells

Venice, June 21, 1865.

DEAR FATHER:

Elinor wrote her letter to Aurelia last night when we were still uncertain about leave of absence. To-night, thanks to your great kindness, it has come, and we are getting ready for flight the first day of July. There are a thousand things to do, and little or nothing to say, except to thank you over and over again. I think my luck wonderful in getting the leave at this time, and yours none less so in getting it extended from three to four months. I'm very greatly obliged to Mr. Cooke for his services in our behalf, and shall not forget them. It's good to hear of the old friends you mention, and to think of them as still friendly.

Our plan is to stop a week or ten days in London, where I shall still try to make my book go. I have a letter to Anthony Trollope, asking his interest in my favor, and I think he will be able to help me to a publisher. My article on *Comedy* has made me quite a reputation in Italy, amongst the Italian literati, and the English living in Italy. Curious, isn't it?—Poor Italy! shall I ever see her sunny face again?

From London, I shall write you again concerning the day and steamer that shall bring us either to N. Y. or Boston—probably the latter place.

Meantime everything is strange as a dream.

Your affectionate son,

WILL.

While Howells was in London he had made arrangements for the English publication of *Venetian Life,* for he says that before leaving Venice:

"I made my sketches into a book, which I sent on to Messrs. Trübner & Co., in London. They had consented to look at it to oblige my friend Conway, who during his sojourn with us in Venice, before his settlement in London— had been forced to listen to some of it. They answered me in due time that they would publish an edition of a thousand, at half profits, if I could get some American house to take five hundred copies."

To William Cooper Howells

Off Halifax, August 1, 1865.

DEAR FATHER:

After a very pleasant voyage, we came in sight of the new world this morning. We're all perfectly well, and tremendously delighted to think of being so near home.

Will go to Brattleboro from Boston, and then arrange for early flight to Ohio. We shall be only detained a short time in Vermont, and shall come to you as quickly as possible.

The baby has behaved magnificently, and enjoyed her voyage greatly. The weather, but for two days' fog, has been very fine, and to-day is one of the loveliest I've ever seen. The ocean is smooth as a pond, and the sky cloudless.

What a conflict of feelings there is in me, at drawing so near the old land again!

Our dearest love to all.

Your affectionate son,
W. D. HOWELLS.

When Howells first returned from Europe he planned to have his brother Joseph publish the American edition of *Venetian Life,* with Ticknor & Fields acting as agents for it. James Russell Lowell's note to Mr. Fields on the back of this letter is a proof of his faith in its author.

To James T. Fields

Jefferson, August 19, 1865.

My dear Sir:

My brother here wishes to undertake the publication in America of my book on Venice, in connection with Trübner & Co., of London. He knows, however, that your facilities for bringing it to public notice are great, and he desires that you will act as his agent in receiving the sheets of five hundred copies to come from London, and disposing of the greater part of them to the trade. The book will bear the imprint only of the London house, and will be sold as a London publication. I believe you make arrangements with authors, occasionally, to act as agent, when they bring out books at their own cost, and this is the relation we wish your house to bear toward me. My brother would be very glad to know on what terms you would undertake the sale of the book, and whether you would like to be paid a percentage on copies sold, or a certain sum for your whole trouble. He is not decided whether to have the books bound in England or America, but thinks it would be better to have them bound in London. Will you please tell us how much greater the duty on bound books is than the duty on sheets? This is a point we want solved. We also wish to know on what terms *you* would bind them in that "faultless" style of which the newspapers sometimes speak. We don't want a luxurious binding, but something decent and proper. My brother would wish to transact the whole business through your house; that is, send money by you to London, have you take the sheets (or bound volumes) out of the custom house, and dispose of the book as far as possible through your standing orders from booksellers, reserving a certain number to be sent him here. I could myself indicate certain friends in the press, east and west, to whom it should be sent, and we should expect the book to advertise itself in that way, but would also announce it by paid advertisement. All this, however, can be arranged later. Can you manage to send my manuscript, by a cheaper and safer way than I, to Trübner & Co.? I suppose you have better means of communication and will, if you wish to engage in the matter, send you the book for transmission to London from Boston.

Now, I hope you will answer all these questions as nobly and freely as they are asked; and I pray you to unite to the candor of a friend, the promptness of a business man, and let me hear from you at once.

I wish I could have run down to see you at Manchester, but I found my time too brief. I beg to be mentioned to Mrs. Fields, and am

Yours truly,
W. D. HOWELLS.

P. S. What of the stories left you? I feel rejection in my bones, but it is best to know the worst. My address is "Jefferson, Ashtabula Co., Ohio."

(Note on the letter by James Russell Lowell)

MY DEAR FIELDS,

I carried this into Boston last Saturday expecting to see you at Club. It has been in my pocket ever since! I hope you will do whatever you can, for Howells is sure to be somebody if he lives, as well as Willson. I still swear by both. I shall send you a pretty book in a day or two for your collection.

Ever yours,
J. R. L.

The plan of having Joseph Howells publish *Venetian Life* was abandoned when Melanchthon M. Hurd accepted it. Howells says in *Literary Friends and Acquaintance*, "On my way across the Atlantic I met a publisher who finally agreed to take those five hundred copies. This was Mr.

M. M. Hurd, of Hurd & Houghton, a house then newly established in New York and Boston."

Mrs. Howells had gone with her child to visit her parents at Brattleboro, Vermont.

To Mrs. W. D. Howells

New York, Sept. 14, 1865.

DEAREST:

I walked down to the *Round Table* office, this morning, and found that my engagement had taken wings overnight and flown away. The publishers could only say that for the present they couldn't give me the place: that they must wait, and see how their paper succeeded. In the meantime they begged me to write for it, and they would pay me by the column; and gave me the book (one on Dante) which they proposed to have me review. On inquiry, I find it is thought doubtful whether the *R.T.* will succeed, and as I don't care to go down with it, perhaps it is as well that my *engagement* was so brief. I shall look round for another engagement, here.

As some slight compensation for this disappointment, I may tell you that I met our friend Hurd on the street, to-day, went with him while he lunched, and proposed my book on Venice, to him. He figured the matter over, and accepted: didn't want to see the manuscript: knew it was good. I am sure father and Joe will be glad of this, for it relieves them of a slight risk which, I confess, I was always loath to put them to; and I have acted on father's advice, in trying for a publisher here. Hurd has given me a letter to Trübner & Co., and will forward the manuscript for me. I go to take tea with him to-morrow night. He made very cordial inquiries about you, and wants to look at *Disillusion,* with your illustrations. He gave me a manuscript to read and decide on, his reader being out of town. It *looks* very much as if I could get as much writing to do here, as I wanted; still I shall look for a place.

Question is: Shall I go to Washington, or not? I wish you would give me your opinion about this.

I'm rather disappointed in not hearing from home to-day, but suppose letters will come moping along before a great while. I don't know when to tell *you* to *come*. Perhaps to-morrow will decide something.

Write me full, long letters. Be good to father and mother, and all. My love to them. Poor baby! How I'd like to see her!

I hope you're well, my dear, and so good-bye.

Husband,
W. D. H.

Professor Francis J. Child became one of Howells's *Literary Friends and Acquaintance,* of whom he says:

"One of the first and truest of our Cambridge friends was that exquisite intelligence, who, in a world where so many people are grotesquely miscalled, was most fitly named; for no man ever kept here more perfectly and purely the heart of such as the kingdom of heaven is of than Francis J. Child. Children were always his friends, and they repaid with adoration the affection which he divided with them and his flowers."

The *"Thanksgiving"* verses were Howells's which Professor Child asked to include in a collection he was making.

To Professor F. J. Child

441 West 47th street, New York,
December 12, 1865.

DEAR SIR:
You are very welcome to use my *Thanksgiving* verses, I am gratified that they have pleased you, and I think I

should allow you to put my name against *Paradise Lost,* if
you asked me in such flattering terms as you have employed
concerning what really belongs to me.

I have in press (Trübner & Co., London, and Hurd &
Houghton, N. Y.) a book on Venice, chiefly made up from
my letters to the Boston *Advertiser,* but just when it will be
published I don't know. The Italian matter I am now con-
tributing to the *Nation* will also, I hope, be some day printed
in a book.

Begging again to thank you for the kind interest which
you express in my articles, and trusting to grow less unworthy your good opinion,

I am
Very respectfully yours,
W. D. HOWELLS.

To Mrs. W. D. Howells

New York, Sept. 19, 1865.

DEAR ELINOR:

I write this letter at the Colonel's office, and at his desk,
for he isn't in, just now. He returned to New York yesterday, and is not going out of town again.

The *Round Table* has taken *The Royal Portraits* for
$20, and this morning I sold *Sweet Clover* to *Harper's
Magazine* for $10. Harper's use neither *Petrarch* nor *The
Mulberries,* but I think I can work the former into the
Round Table.

Yesterday I saw John Swinton, and he thinks it not impossible that I should get a place on the *Times.* At any rate
he will see Raymond about it next week. Whether to go to
Washington, or not, in the interim, I don't know. It's dangerous, and it's expensive: perhaps it would effect something, perhaps nothing. It is said Chief-Justice Chase is in
town, and I shall try to see him.

This morning I received a letter from your father, who

said John Mitchell told him that if the Columbus people could not buy the *State Journal,* they were going to start another paper, and offer me the charge of it.

I shall write to Secretary Smith concerning the matter. It is well to keep a lookout in all directions.

My darling, you don't know how much I miss you, and our blessed little baby. I think of you at all hours in the day. It's very good and patient of you to stay where you are; but you know I'm hurrying up everything I can to bring us together again.

Your father tells me to take time, here; that I'll have found a place long before they shall get tired of you and B. at Brattleboro.

Stoddard admires greatly my Italian translations of poetry. Everybody regards me here as having *scholarship.*

Swinton has asked me to write for the *Times,* and I could get work enough here to support myself very finely this winter. Love to all.

Dearest love, your lover,
W. D. H.

"Graham" was James Lorrimer Graham, the friend of many literary men and especially of R. H. Stoddard, whose son was named for him.

"Booth" was Edwin T. Booth.

To Mrs. W. D. Howells

441 West 47th Street, New York,
Friday, October 27, 1865.

DEAREST GIRL:

Your letter hasn't come yet, to-day, though it is nearly four o'clock, but you've been so lovely in all the letters of the week, that I can forgive you, if I do not hear from you at all to-day.

We had a very charming dinner at Graham's yesterday, and I liked the company so well that I was loath to leave it and go to the theatre. Booth has one of the most beautiful faces I ever saw: it is so finely cut, so sensitive and full of character. He is not much of a talker, but very simple and unaffected in what he has to say. It was a cruel wrong to his gentleness, and yet I had to think all the time when with him of his brother. Up in Graham's library there were two plaster casts of hands lying on a shelf: one extended, and the other closed into a fist. Booth asked Graham, "Whose hand is that, Lorry?" "Tennyson's." "No, I mean the other one, the one shut." It was an inexpressible affliction to me when Graham had to answer, "Lincoln's." Booth did not speak a word of comment.

The play at Wallack's was a new one—*The Needful,* but it was extremely stupid. If you're not down here by next week I'll send you the *Nation* containing my criticism on it. To-day when I carried it to him, Mr. Godkin said, "How would you like to write exclusively for the *Nation,* and what will you take to do it?" I said fifty dollars a week, and he answered that he wanted time to think the matter over, and would let me know soon. I should prefer this sort of connection with the paper, but I don't care a great deal, for I foresee that if these journals live they will take my articles at my own prices. One thing I'm to do for the *Nation* at a fixed price, however: give it a page each week of philoso-phized foreign gossip for $15, which is $5 more than usually paid. Both the *Nation* and the *Round Table* are glad to get everything I can give them. Don't set your heart on my get-ting a regular engagement, or of course I shall not. "Just let things go on."

I *hope* you are coming down here next week. When I think of seeing you possibly on Monday, I'm almost crazy. It's getting to be near a month since we were together. I left Brattleboro the first of October. I only wish you were going to bring poor B. along with you. I must write a little on an article before leisure, and so sweet love, with kisses for B. Good-bye.

Your Husband.

VI

1866, 1867

Place on the Nation. *Becomes Assistant Editor of the* Atlantic. *Finds house in Cambridge.* Italian Journeys. *Dickens.*

HOWELLS had written his wife on December 17, 1865, "To-day Mr. Godkin engaged me to write for the *Nation* on a salary of $40 a week. This leaves me free to write for all other papers except the *Round Table;* and does not include articles on Italian subjects, and poems, which will be paid for extra."

The "something which might or might not come to good for both of us" quoted in the next letter was the offer of the assistant editorship of the *Atlantic Monthly.* Howells says in *Literary Friends and Acquaintance:*

"I reached the office and found a letter from Fields asking how I would like to come to Boston and be his assistant on the *Atlantic Monthly.* I submitted the matter at once to my chief on the *Nation,* and with his frank good-will I talked it over with Mr. Osgood of Ticknor & Fields. I had not decided to accept the place without advising with Lowell; he counselled the step, and gave me some shrewd and useful suggestions. The whole affair was conducted by Fields with his unfailing tact and kindness, but it could not be kept from me that the qualification I had as a practical printer for the work was most valued, if not the most valued, and that as a proof-reader I was expected to make it avail on the side of economy."

To James T. Fields

New York, Wednesday, Jan. 10, 1866.

MY DEAR SIR:

I have just come down to the office for the first time in four days, having been frozen up on 47th street ever since I saw you Sunday night. This fact will account for the other fact that I took no notice of your invitation, which I found here this afternoon. I regret extremely that I could not see you again. The loss of your company and of the dinner is irreparable; but cannot you write and say to me that "something which might or might not come to good for both of us"? It is a pity to lose the occasion of doing good to others, and I should particularly loathe to lose a chance of doing good to myself. Therefore, I hope to hear from you.

Pray remember me to Mrs. Fields (to whom I send a book,) and believe me,

Very truly yours,
W. D. HOWELLS.

To James T. Fields

New York, Feb. 6, 1866.

MY DEAR SIR:

I write to accept the place you have offered me, and to say that I shall be ready to assume its duties on the first of March. These duties I understand to be: examination of mss. offered to the *Atlantic;* correspondence with contributors; reading proof for the magazine after its revisal by the printers; and writing the *Reviews and Literary Notices,* for which I am to receive fifty dollars a week, while I am to be paid extra for anything I may contribute to the body of the magazine.

If you will be kind enough, in your reply, to recapitulate these conditions, I suppose our letters will form all the agreement there need be between us.

Monday's ride home was given in equal parts to hard thinking and hard freezing, and I arrived resolved and rigid.

Pray present my compliments to Mrs. Fields, and tell her that I will send her my translations from *Dall' Ongaro,* as soon as I can find time to copy them.

Hoping to hear from you,
I am very truly yours,
W. D. HOWELLS.

"Mr. Norton" of the *North American Review* was Charles Eliot Norton, and his help in house-hunting was a very real kindness, for houses were hard to find just after the Civil War. It was Mr. Norton who finally found the little house at 41 Sacramento Street, that could not be hired, but had to be bought, to secure it; and it was Mr. Norton again who persuaded his brother-in-law, W. S. Bullard, to lend most of the money with which it was purchased. These are only two instances of a constant kindness that can only be imagined from the gratitude and affection with which, as the letters to him show, it was repaid.

The friends they were "visiting delightfully" were Dr. and Mrs. Henry C. Angell, whom they had met in Venice, and these friends lasted, if not "forever," at least as long as they lived.

To Edmund Clarence Stedman

16 Beacon Street, Boston,
February 20, 1866.

MY DEAR STEDMAN:

I reached Boston yesterday evening, and have merrily spent the day in search of lodgings at Cambridge, with nothing at all for my result. However, we shall see, to-morrow, and to-morrow, and to-morrow.—And Shake-speare (it is Shakespeare?) brings one to Booth. Mr. Fields

doesn't like the notion of the long minion note, and suggests that you add the note to the article, in the body type
of the magazine. I think that so far as his own feeling is concerned, he does not care to have much biographical notice
of Booth, though he thinks with you that B.'s wishes should
be consulted. He spoke of the article on Keene (which you,
also, mentioned to me) as the sort of thing he would like to
have done.—I am not regularly in harness, yet; but Mr. F.,
knowing I would write to you, begged me to mention this
matter to you.

Mr. Norton of the *North American Review* helped me
to-day about house-hunting, and was extremely kind. We
spoke of you, and your proposed article, and I said as little
to your prejudice as I could with any degree of honesty.
On the street, we met Mr. Longfellow, whom I saw for the
first time: such a looking poet as I should like to be (and
couldn't, if I lived a thousand years) at his age: white locks,
white beard, and autumnal bloom. At T. & F.'s I had a little
chat with Aldrich, who is immensely contented with Boston.

So far, my impression has been very pleasant, except that
there seems little hope of finding shelter—and though we're
visiting delightfully, one's friends cannot last forever.

Remember me to the Taylors, Stoddards, Grahams, and
both of us to all the Stedmans.

Yours ever,
W. D. HOWELLS.

To Charles Eliot Norton

Cambridge, May 25, 1866.

DEAR MR. NORTON:
We are safely housed here in Cottage Quiet, and have
commenced the long-deferred process of feeling at home,
and of growing old. There is a fine sense of landed pro-
prietorship about the present experiment which is as novel
as it is agreeable, and which pleases me almost as much as

the security and peace in which we live. I make the most
of the sensation, for it is about the only one in the neigh-
borhood. After the life which we have hitherto led in cities,
this is singularly free from tumult. Everything is so tranquil
about us that I find the agitation of a cow in the pasture
across the street very stimulating, and am quite satisfied
with it. This morning, however, a large dog appeared at
the corner of the fence. Presently two men walked up Oxford street, and I was greatly excited. A few minutes later
a man drove by in a trotting-buggy: this appeared incredible.

Everything goes wonderfully well. The house is snugly
furnished, but for a trifle of window-curtains, which we are
not like to need, since there is no probability that the sun
will shine this summer. (The enterprise of the vegetation
is very astonishing to me: in an atmosphere as cool and
dark as that of a cellar, the grapevines are already set with
clusters; the trees are full of young pears, and the currant-
bushes are bowed down with their detestable fruit.) Our
girl Katy was born in the house of the gridiron under the
sign of the spider: she is so good a cook; and all things
about us are prosperously in keeping. We exclaim constantly
over our happiness, which I am tempted to challenge as
being of ghostly and unsubstantial event.

I meant to be at Mr. Longfellow's Wednesday evening,
for the purpose not only of enjoying myself, but of reporting the affair to you. We inadvertently let Katy go into
Boston, however, and then Elinor was afraid to stay alone
in the house, and so I failed of my wish. But another time
I shall not wrong myself, and I shall try to write you after
next Wednesday.

Mrs. Norton's very kind note comes after we had engaged to take milk of an adjacent Irishman. Elinor begs me
to thank her for mentioning Bernard, and for her trouble
taken on our account with the trades-folk. Will you oblige
me with the address of Mr. W. S. Bullard? I do not re-

member whether, according to the receipt I gave you, the interest is to be paid quarterly or monthly, and should be glad to know.

Mrs. Howells wishes to be cordially remembered with me to all of you.

Very sincerely,
W. D. HOWELLS.

Being "at Mr. Longfellow's" meant going to meetings of the Dante Club.

"Longfellow was that winter [1866–1867] revising his translation of the *Paradiso,* and the Dante Club was the circle of Italianate friends and scholars whom he invited to follow him and criticize his work from the original, while he read his version aloud. Those who were most constantly present were Lowell and Professor Norton, but from time to time others came in, and we seldom sat down at the nine o'clock supper that followed the reading of the canto in less number than ten or twelve."

To Charles Eliot Norton

Cambridge, June 8, 1866.

DEAR MR. NORTON:

I get all my letters and papers through Ticknor and Fields, and I did not think to enquire at the Cambridge office till your note had been there several days. In the meantime I was very much embittered against you, and forgot all the kindnesses you had ever done me, in the thought of the sole neglect, which, after all, you had not been guilty of. I shall be very glad to write the notice of which you speak: shall I, after writing it, send it to you, or give it directly to the printers, and let you do what you like with it in the proofs? Do not forget that you have promised me a place in the October number for my article on Italian poetry. I am working on it now and shall have it ready. I fancy it will be livelier than you would think the subject could allow: I have in the first place the character of Vincenzo Monti, one of the greatest rogues and swindlers that ever existed in life or letters.

I was at Mr. Longfellow's this week and last. There was a full session last week, but of the memorabilia I can recall only two or three things—*per esempio:* Lowell's asking Mr. Longfellow, out of his regret that the suppers were coming to an end, whether there was not an Indian epic in an hundred thousand lines which he was going to translate next. The talk was not at all general, each supperer chatting with his next neighbor, until we came to the subject of lonely walks home by night, when Lowell told of a man's jumping over a fence, and alighting directly in front of him, whereupon he tried "to look as if he had always been in the habit of having men jump down in front of him as he was walking home at night." This week Dr. Holmes was present, and he and Mr. Appleton talked spiritualism somewhat. The latter told of going to Frascati's gaming-place in Paris when he was young. "But it was horribly dull, and I shouldn't have had any amusement if it had not been for Sam Ward's borrowing a guinea of me." Mr. Dana was also present, and told traveller's stories mighty well, too. The cantos were wonderfully translated—perhaps Mr. Longfellow sends you a proof? Week before this we had the 31st canto, and the translation from

to
> *Senza risponder gli occhi su levai,*
>
> *Poi si tornò all' eterna fontana*

was incomparably good. Mr. Lowell has Cranch the painter staying with him, and last Saturday I was invited to meet him at dinner. Mr. Forceythe Willson was also invited, and I made his acquaintance. I set the trap of my poem for Mr.

Fields, and temptingly baited it with your praise and Mr. Lowell's, but Mr. Fields, after nibbling cautiously about it, refused to go in. I must say that the affair was managed beautifully on both sides, and I hardly know which to admire more: myself or Fields. I'm so well satisfied with my own skill in the matter that I can scarcely persuade myself that I failed of success.

Last night Mrs. Howells and I took tea at Professor Child's, greatly enjoying ourselves.

The deed for the house has come from Florida, and though there is an informality in it—or rather in the acknowledgment of it before the Notary, who failed to date the acknowledgment, I am advised by my lawyer to take it. To-day I expect to pay over the money. The deed will be recorded, sent to Florida for fresh acknowledgment, and then recorded again.

Mrs. Howells joins in expression of cordial regard for you all. Baby also wishes to be remembered.

Very sincerely yours,
W. D. HOWELLS.

"My book" was *Venetian Life,* and the "romance" Howells was thinking of commencing was *A Foregone Conclusion.*

Henry Israel Howells, his youngest brother, was a bright and normally developed boy of four when he was accidently hit on the forehead by the bat of a playmate. The blow must have fractured his skull, for after his death it was found to have caused an internal projection of bone, and from the time of the accident his mental development stopped and his mind remained that of a gentle and lovable child. First his sister Victoria, and then Aurelia, with the utmost patience and tenderness, devoted their lives to his care.

To Miss Victoria M. Howells

Cambridge, Mass., June 17, 1866.

DEAR SISTER:

It is a long time since I wrote to you but not since I thought of you, and you must try to let my long thoughts count for long letters. I write from six to eight letters a day —letters which I have no interest in writing, too—besides reviews and articles; and I am either making or reading manuscript all the time.

Dear Vic, I wish you could step into our quiet little home this pleasant Sunday morning, and be out of the old circle of your cares a while. We grow more and more in love with our house every day, and as the summer advances, it grows prettier and friendlier. The two pines on either side of the gate have put on a vivider green than they wore all winter long, and within a day or two the sweetbriar over our door has all burst into blossom. As to blackberries and grapes and pears, it's wonderful to see how they flourish.

Baby has the range of everything, and she's outdoors from breakfast time till dark,—Elinor and I taking her for a long walk the last thing. There's a small boy next door, who is her partner in the mud-pastry line; and except for the unhappiness that comes from over-enjoyment, I think she is perfectly contented in "papa's house."

For papa himself, he suffers also a little from the same trouble that afflicts baby. My book has been noticed in the London *Athenæum* more favorably than unfavorably—it was my fear that it would be cut up, there—and all the English critics have treated it very kindly. The other night at Mr. Longfellow's Mr. Lowell declared to the whole company, "It is the best book ever written about Italy." But that was only what he had said before in his letters to me. We've had the last of the Dante readings. On Wednesday night Mr. Longfellow finished the final canto, and we honored the close by sitting at supper till two o'clock in the morning.

I'm thinking now about commencing a romance—the scene of it to be laid in Italy, or Venice, rather—but I have ever so much work begun which I must finish first. I do no more writing for the *Atlantic* than I can help—that is, I merely write the critical notices, and try to reserve myself for more extended efforts. But my regular day's work on the magazine is by no means a light task, and it is hard for me to find time for other writing.

I hope you are well, dear Vic, and that Henry does not grow more troublesome. When I consider your task and mine, you may be sure that I do not think mine the heavier or nobler. I'm thinking constantly of my visit home in the fall, and of the pleasure of bringing mother back with me. You must not let her get the notion that she cannot come. Dear love to all. Elinor is at church, or she would join me in this message. Tell Aurelia that I miss her ever so much.

Your affectionate brother,
WILL.

The "package of books" was *Venetian Life.* "Col. J. M. Comly of the *State Journal*" was a friend of Howells's youth in Columbus.

To M. M. Hurd

Cambridge, August 13, 1866.

MY DEAR MR. HURD:

I received the package of books on Wednesday, and your letter concerning the day of publication at the same time. The latter I answered at once, accepting your suggestion of the 24th ult. Of course I shall not give away any of the copies I have, without stating when the book is to appear.

I suppose you have the list of papers which we made out

together as best deserving copies of this great work. I shall
send it to Mr. Lowell, who says he will notice it in the next
N. American Review, and to Mr. Norton, who, I think,
will review it in the Nation, though of course I cannot state
my expectation to him. I will give a copy to Rev. W. R.
Alger for the Christian Examiner, and to Mr. Justin Win-
sor, here, for the Round Table. I will also hand a copy to
the Advertiser folks. All the gentlemen named have themselves offered to notice the book, or I should not place it
in their hands for review. In fact, I'm willing—so far as
I'm concerned—that the book should appear as friendlessly
here as in England, where I have reason to be pleased with
its reception. Do you wish to make use of the English notices in advertising? Let me suggest that the notice of the
Westminster Review, for July—about half a page in the
Current Literature—puts in a nutshell all of British opinion you need use.—First and last, the book has received
a good deal of praise, but I assure you that no applause has
gratified me more than your own, for I think you have always been rather skeptical concerning it. Mr. Fields is
equally pleased with it—and if publishers really know as
much as they pretend about public taste, the favorable opinion of two publishers should give us some hopes of success
with "the general reader." As to a second edition, of which
you spoke, that is a matter quite in your own hands, and I
suppose you can determine about it very shortly after publishing this edition. I shall not begin correcting a copy till
you know, for I'm fearfully busy.—I wish you to send an
advance copy to my friend, Col. J. M. Comly, of the State
Journal, Columbus, Ohio, so that he will have it as soon as
the Eastern papers; and I don't think it would be a wise
economy to stint the press of copies anywhere.—Please
send the book, for me, as soon as published, to Bayard
Taylor, Stedman, Stoddard, and J. Lorrimer Graham, Jr.,
N. Y.

Mrs. Howells joins me in sending regards to all your family.

Very sincerely yours,
W. D. HOWELLS.

To what bookseller in Boston will you send the book?

To *William Cooper Howells*

Cambridge, Sunday, Sept. 20/66.

DEAR FATHER:

Hurd and Houghton wish to publish a second edition of *Venetian Life*—the first being all sold—and want me to prepare the copy at once. I must therefore postpone my visit till I have done this—probably till the first of next month, but I'll try to get off sooner if I can.—I know this will be a disappointment to you, but that you will at least be glad of the reason of my detention.

I should be loath, at any rate, to leave Elinor without a girl—for the one who was to come to-night is sick, and we have to wait developments. I should have a sense of neglected duty if I went to Ohio now, and I don't think you would enjoy my visit, so I wait. But I'll come the instant I can conscientiously.

Dear love to all.

Your affectionate son,
WILL.

To *Edmund Clarence Stedman*

The Atlantic Monthly, Boston,
Dec. 5, 1866.

MY DEAR STEDMAN:

I cannot write letters any more, but I can still in some sort answer them. Yours always give me delight: partly because I like to hear from you and partly because I like to be over-praised. I think it does me good to be taken for what I ought to be, and I am sure I thank you for thinking better of me than I deserve.

The proof of *Pan in Wall Street* was duly sent you, and we waited two weeks for its return. Thereafter I read the proof very carefully myself, comparing it line by line with the original, and I hope you will find it free from errors. At any rate, it is now sixty thousand *Atlantics* too late to help it, for it goes into our January number.

The small but enthusiastic admirers of Walt Whitman could not make him a poet, if they wrote all the newspapers and magazines in the world full about him. He is poetical as the other elements are, and just as satisfactory to read as earth, water, air and fire. I am tired, I confess, of the whole Whitman business.

Though you do cut us off from the hope of a visit, I am glad that you do not quite forbid us to expect seeing you. We never did quite have any talk *out,* and I think that the future owes us a chance at one another. Talking of talks: young Henry James and I had a famous one last evening, two or three hours long, in which we settled the true principles of literary art. He is a very earnest fellow, and I think extremely gifted—gifted enough to do better than any one has yet done toward making us a real American novel. We have in reserve from him a story for the *Atlantic,* which I'm sure you'll like.

With Mrs. Howells' love to Mrs. Stedman, and our joint regards to both of you, and a kiss for Stoddard,

Yours truly,

W. D. HOWELLS.

1867

The *"Paradiso"* was the third book of Longfellow's translation of the *Divine Comedy*. Evidently Howells had written a criticism of the preceding book for the *Nation.*

To Charles Eliot Norton

Cambridge, August 10, 1867.

DEAR MR. NORTON:

This has been so busy a week with me, that I have just now found time to answer your letter. We are going to Brattleboro next week, and I have, of course, had to fight my way to this possibility through myriads of infuriate manuscripts. Besides, the magazine went to press, this week, and as usual cost me unspeakable anguish at the last moment. I am not yet so far removed from the event but that I still regard my book-notices as so many elements of Ruin.

I think we shall remain at Brattleboro a month, but not longer. Our purpose is leisure and nature, but I should not be surprised if the fact proved to be literature and society. And I suppose the change of air will be the great advantage, after all.

A certain matter troubles me. I have seen no criticism of the *Paradiso* in the *Nation,* and I have begun to wonder whether you and Mr. Godkin are not depending upon me for it. My understanding was that I was to write only the second criticism, and so I have made no preparation for the third. It is now late to write it in sequence, but if it is desirable, I suppose that I can, while in Brattleboro, write something on the *Paradiso* independently of what has gone before, and regarding it in some special lights. As yet I have not had time even to read the poem.

Mr. Lowell came to see us yesterday. You know he has been at Plymouth, camping out with Mr. John Holmes and Professor Gurney; and he claims to have greatly enjoyed himself. I see the Jameses rather frequently. They are all in town. Harry James has written us another story, which I think admirable; but I do not feel sure of the public any longer, since the *Nation* could not see the merit of *Poor Richard.* It appeared to me that there was remarkable strength in the last scenes of that story; and I cannot doubt that James has every element of success in fiction. But I suspect that he must in a great degree create his audience. In the meantime I rather despise existing readers. I walked through the beautiful woods about your house, near night-fall a few days since, and though the sarcastic mosquito there hummed about my ears, I must say that I have seldom seen anything so lovely as that lookout from the trees west of the avenue towards the old mansion. The local colors were all so finely indicated in the light that also gave soft-ness to all the outlines of the trees, dropping their branches so low that they almost touched the sloping ground. I doubt if you have anything half so fine at Ashfield. All day long here on Sacramento street, we remain

> Close-latticed to the brooding heat,
> And silent in our dusty vines.

At two o'clock, John appears with the express bag from Ticknor and Fields, and an excitement like a breath of the simoon breaks over us. Then we lapse back again into merely negative existence. During the interval immediately following dinner, we read Campbell's *Life of Petrarch*— a book to the inspiring wisdom of which the proverbs of Solomon are as the babblings of folly.

With our united regards to you all,

Very truly yours,

W. D. HOWELLS.

The poem of Mr. Stedman's referred to must have been the *Feast of Harvest* which appeared in the November *Atlantic* of that year. The other poem mentioned was Walt Whitman's *Grass*.

To Edmund Clarence Stedman

The Atlantic Monthly, Boston,
August 17, 1867.

MY DEAR STEDMAN:

You will see by the postmark of my envelope that I only officially date from Boston, but really write from Brattleboro, Vt., whither I'm come for a change of air. It's not a relief in any other way, for I bring all my *Atlantic* work with me. Here I've received your letter and noted its contents, and I have begun to write you about it, without knowing in the least what I ought to say. It seems hard that a man who plays a silver-voiced pipe should refrain from a certain air because another performs it on a steam-calliope; and yet I can see a certain propriety in what you urge against yourself. I wish your poem were in season for our September number, but as it isn't—well, if it were mine, I would withhold it from present publication. This is not the first peace harvest, and next year we shall have another, and this poem of yours will always be in time—with its proper date—for a volume. There! I've got the murder out at last, and here you have your poem again.

Once, in Venice, I found a subject which promised to cure me of mortality, and I wrote thirty undying stanzas upon it. Then I went out for a walk—stopped, as my fashion was, at the first book-stall, picked up the first book, and found my story all told in it, and given to the world three years before the date of my birth. I am still mortal. But you have lost far finer work. Let me tell you how exquisite I think your idealization of the *Grass* is, and how full of delicate beauty I find many of your lines; and let me ask you, finally, not to accept my judgment in this case. I send back your poem, because I wish to deal sincerely with you, but I am not sure that I deal wisely with you, and I'd desire you to forward the verses to Mr. Fields all the same as if I'd never seen them. They will be in time any time before the 25th of August, unless he has filled out the number since Wednesday.

I suppose all your family is with you in Milford, and Mrs. Howells joins me in expression of regard for you all. My father- and mother-in-law are boarding, this summer, and have lent us their pleasant old house for a month. So we've shut up our house at Cambridge and have brought our household goods up here.

As to the treadmill, I would willingly help run one with you, for I feel the need of some income besides that I receive from my pen; but I do not see the hour of acquisition yet. Treadmills are much more costly to start and keep going than they used to be, and there are several running already. However, it is not a thing to despair of.

Hoping that I have not acted stupidly,
Yours cordially,
W. D. HOWELLS.

Como was a chapter in *Italian Journeys*.

To M. M. Hurd

Brattleboro', Sept. 8, 1867.

MY DEAR HURD:

Thanks for your cheque of $19.60 and your explanation of accounts, which I now understand clearly. I forgot to say in my last, how much I was obliged to you for the trouble you took with Trübner for my sake. Some two months ago, he sent me a statement, in which it appeared that there was a balance of fourteen pounds to be divided between us, after charging me with the cancels, but this balance was again offset by a charge of thirteen pounds *commission on sales,* and Ticknor and Fields were authorized to pay me some ten shillings, which I have not yet collected. I propose to give the sum to Mr. Trübner for the benefit of South

American and Oriental literary men, and to take my pay in glory, so far as England is concerned.—By the way, shall you send any copies of *Italian Journeys* for notice to the London press? How soon do you intend to issue the book? I should like an advance copy for the *North American*, if it is to appear before the 1st of October. I suppose if the book is liked, it will make a fresh sale for *Venetian Life*, though I never cherish hopes of anything.

I've now got all other work off my hands, and am pleasing myself with the idea of a romance, though I haven't put pen to paper, yet, and possibly never shall. But everybody writes a novel, sooner or later, and I expect it is also my destiny.

I send you a modification of the passage you object to in *Como*, and you can transmit it to Riverside for correction. In this, without changing the sentiment as to the rebellion, I remove what refers to the private troubles of Southerners, and I think this is all that can be asked. The allusion to the Southern flag is not dragged into the article, according to my thinking, but is a part of the history of the time, and ought to stand for a record of the universal feeling among loyal Americans abroad in that year.

Remember Mrs. Howells and me to Mrs. Hurd, and believe me

> Your ever,
> W. D. HOWELLS.

P. S. I have just got a letter from Mr. Houghton saying that *Italian Journeys* is ready to print, if I require no further proofs. I do not, and there will be nothing to hinder the book from going to press as soon as you have the enclosed page corrected.

"My new book" was *Italian Journeys*.

The Goodrich who was to be told about Dickens, was an Englishman who had passed from being a house painter to building organs, and though nearly three times Howells's age, had been one of his friends in Jefferson. He had a passion for Dickens. "He read a great deal, but of all he read he liked Dickens best, and was always coming back to him with affection, whenever the talk strayed."

To Mrs. William Cooper Howells

Cambridge, Nov. 25, 1867.

DEAR MOTHER:

It was very pleasant to hear from you, though you had to tell us of some sickness of your own, and of poor Henry's growing worse. All I can do is to say that I sympathize most deeply with you in the trouble. Perhaps the medicine may begin after awhile to affect him favorably. In the meantime I know how much you must all suffer on account of him. It must have come particularly hard upon you who had been away, and had not seen him gradually growing worse.

Mother, it's a great thing to us to think you enjoyed your visit so much, and it made Elinor and me both happy to have you express your enjoyment. We certainly tried to do all we could to make you welcome, and I assure you our family was very sad and lonesome after you left. The evening after your departure was indescribably dismal. It was such a great favor of you to undertake the long journey, but we fully appreciated it.

How did Vic like her book? None of you say; and I am only left to hope that it pleased her. My new book is now ready, and I'll send you a copy early in the week.

Night before last, I took supper at Mr. Longfellow's with Charles Dickens. You must tell Goodrich that he was everything in manner that his books would make you wish him to be. I had quite a little chat with him, and sat next but one to him at table. His face is very flexible, and he is very genial and easy in talk. Lowell, Darley the artist, Mr. Sam Longfellow, Fields, and Prof. Greene were the other guests; and we sat till midnight. It was a lovely time. But it was hard at the moment to remember that this man so near me was so great and had done so much to please and better the world.—Everybody here is wild about the readings, and the tickets of the second course will be sold at Auction. We have tickets for the whole first course.

With love to all,
Your affectionate son,
WILL.

The "ballad book" must have been Professor Child's collection of ballads.

To Miss Victoria M. Howells

Cambridge, Dec. 8, 1867.

DEAR VIC:

You never saw an anthracite coal fire, did you? It's jolly, malignant looking heat—a sort of merry devil; and makes the room very warm, without asking to be sawed or split or even allowed the poor boon of making everything black about it. I've just got my little open stove up, and full of blue blazing anthracite, and looking (after writing my date,) at its now familiar glow, I couldn't help being struck with the fact that you'd probably never seen it burning. We drift sadly apart in this world, and store away new associations and customs; but I suppose it will be arranged hereafter that all these shall drop away, in the process of our becoming as little children.

I'm glad you liked the ballad book. It's very carefully and sympathetically edited; and I sent it to you in remembrance of the fondness you used to have for those old things. I never forget how much we liked some books in common, as well as hated some people together.

I've heard Dickens twice since I last wrote: the first time he read the *Christmas Carol* and the trial from *Pickwick;*

the second time *Paul Dombey* and the trial again. It was the perfection of acting, and as the parts were all well played, it was better than any theatre I ever saw. It was rather sad, however, for an American, who had naturalized Dickens's characters, to find that after all they were English. But there was some compensation in the fact that abstractly, my conceptions of his characters for the most part were exactly the same as the author's. Toots was a little different, Sam Weller was not quite so sharp as I would have made him. Tony Weller was prodigious, and Mr. Winkle enough to kill. When I thought how much Goodrich would have enjoyed the *Christmas Carol* I felt guilty to be there in his place. The whole audience rose with a shout when Dickens entered; but after that he held them almost quiet. It's been a great excitement.

Meantime I've had a little excitement of my own. My new book's out, and I've seen some half dozen notices, all very favorable. I sent mother a copy, which I hope she's got by this time.

We've just got a letter from Will Dean, who wants to engage Dickens to read at St. Paul; but I think he'll hardly succeed.

As we had tickets to the whole course of readings, we invited Elinor's father and mother to go each one night with one of us, and they've been with us the past week. In fact Mrs. Mead is still here, and will probably remain a week longer. They are both very sorry they could not get here to see the senior Howellses.

Give our love to all, and believe me,
Ever your affectionate brother,
WILL.

"The novel" was *A Foregone Conclusion,* and "my Venetian poem" was *No Love Lost.* "I. Js." stands for *Italian Journeys.*

To M. M. Hurd

Cambridge, Dec. 15, 1867.

MY DEAR HURD:

I've no idea of offering my books hereafter to any one but you. I'm at work on the novel when I can get a moment, but it's slow business, and may turn out a failure. I'm very much obliged for the hint about Putnam. Should you have any objections to his publishing my Venetian poem before you book it? And do you think he'd like to? It would make nine pages of his magazine. I would not take less than $125. for it.

Mr. Norton will have a notice in the *N. A. Review* of Hassanek's admirable book if you send it to him immediately.

How does *I. Js.* sell? I'm sorry to have disappointed the *Post;* but these things can't always be helped. *Per contra*, Mr. Hillard (of *Six Months in Italy*) writes me the following letter, which I send for your private pleasure and perusal. It's a proof of a vast expanse of cheek in me to send it at all; but I'm particularly proud of it because it was not provoked by a presentation copy; besides, I show it in strict confidence to you. Please return it.

"I still think" (as you always say when you're particularly stubborn) that you'd better have sent early copies to the English journals whether the book was for sale in England or not.

Your truly,
W. D. HOWELLS.

VII

1868, 1869

Lectures at Harvard. Suburban Sketches. *First Peace Jubilee. Mrs. Stowe's Life of Lady Byron.*

IN a letter of April 26, 1868, Howells says:

"Our great sensation here has ceased with the sailing of Dickens. I dare say you'll have read of the parting scenes in New York. I saw the great man twice in society— once at the Longfellows' and once at the Fields's. He was amiable and unassuming enough, and was very far from saying anything half as good as Lowell said about him— that he was a Lion fit to lie down with Charles Lamb."

To William Cooper Howells and his family

Cambridge, March 6, 1868.

DEAR FATHER, MOTHER, AND GIRLS:

All things have conspired to celebrate my last birthday with a brilliancy known to few fourths of July. As for you at home, I hardly know which to thank most or first: mother for the watch-rack, father for his beautiful letter, or the girls for their superb present of a fruit-knife.

Life has opened fairly for me, and the years promise me new chances. I have an increase of salary ($1000) from the 1st of March [1] and I'm assured that the proof-reading will be made less and less burdensome to me, because they all feel, as Mr. Clark told me, that my value to the *Atlantic* is in my writing. Isn't this pleasant?

We've got back to our perch on Sacramento street, and have all but settled down to peace and quietness. Elinor has a new broom in the kitchen, and we are having a furnace put in, and everything comfortable. It's pretty hard to bear: for as Elinor says you can get along with discomfort or unhappiness because you're sure of it, while bliss is appalling from its insecurity. The fact that we're all very well just now increases our trepidation. If there were not a foot of snow on the ground, and our rain pipes hadn't frozen up, I don't know what we should do.

I enclose a note from Ticknor of the *Young Folks,* which will explain itself to Annie. I hope the sweet will help her to swallow the bitter. In fact, the rejection of *Jaunty* has nothing to do with its merit, and she must try again. I'll offer it to Riverside, though I don't think it would stand so good a chance as something longer and older. Yesterday I dined with Dickens at the Fields's. He was charmingly simple and unaffected, and I had a good deal of talk with him as I sat next him. One of the principal topics of discussion at table would have interested you: How far all the manuscript that Dickens has produced would reach if strung out line after line. Fields guessed 100,000 miles, Dickens 1200, Mrs. Fields 1000. By actual calculation it would only reach 40 miles.

I don't feel that this is an answer to father's letter—in fact it is merely a general acknowledgment, and I must reserve a better reply. Elinor joins me in love to all, and Crumpy sends a drawing of our new clock as seen with the pendulum (or *tick,* as she calls it) in motion.

Yours affectionately,
WILL.

[1]My salary is put up to $3500, but this pays also for articles.

The Meads were descended from Levi Mead who, as a boy of sixteen, saw the battle of Lexington and made deposition with Levi Harrison that the British had fired the first shots on the Lexington Company as it was dispersing.

He served in the Revolution, and was afterwards a captain in the Militia. There is still in the Mead family a highboy that was in the house at Lexington at the time of the battle, from the top of which the British swept the china with their bayonets: they also put a straw bed up the chimney and set fire to it and ate up the entire week's baking of the daughter of the house, Rhoda Mead, an indignant young Revolutionary housekeeper of fourteen.

To William Cooper Howells

Cambridge, May 25, 1868.

DEAR FATHER:

It must have been our expectation of Joe's visit this last week which hindered our writing to you, though there were other reasons and excuses. Mr. and Mrs. Mead were with us from Saturday night till Wednesday morning, and the leisure that I have from authoring each day was given to them instead of you. I went with the old gentleman to Lexington, where he was born, and spent a most delightful afternoon there, looking up the personally and nationally memorable places. He found a large part of his father's farmhouse built into the mansion which has succeeded it— and a fine old place it is, with deep window seats, carven window casings and mop-boards three feet high. The English made it their headquarters, planted their cannon in the door-yard, and obliged the family by setting the house on fire when they left. The neighbors saved it. The roads go by it as of old, and leave it on a lovely knoll at their intersection. In the hollow across the street is a little fish-pond, in which in the year 1800 there came near being no Elinor and Winny in the world, for there the old gentleman nearly went out of it. An elder brother saved him from drowning, and he lived to tell me the story three times within an hour, and slap my shoulders sore over it.

The Lexington battle-ground has the same shape as on

the day of the fight: many of the old buildings that witnessed the affray are yet standing, and the streets have the same direction as then. We were peeping into the windows of the Harrington house, in which Harrington, being mortally wounded at his own door, was carried to die during the battle, and an old man, his grandson, came up and took us inside. It was the quaintest place imaginable, and in the parlor had Dutch tiles round the fireplace. It is to let, rent $200 a year.—Wouldn't you like to take it?—Just think of Lexington being only twenty minutes from Cambridge, and my never going there with you and mother! It is one of the things that you must come again to New England for. I shall have Joe see it.—We are getting on well, considering, and are looking to Joe's arrival with great pleasure. I've been hard at work some time past preparing for the *Atlantic* a Thing called *Tonelli's Marriage* and an article on George William Curtis for *N. A. Review*. I think I shall do Gnadenhütten next, and then I'm going to write a short life of Lucrezia Borgia. You see I make nothing of skipping from one continent to another.—I am glad to hear of Sam's conversion, for it must be a source of happiness to him. We all join in love to you all.

Your affectionate son,
WILL.

J. M. Comly, to whom the next letter is written, was one of Howells's Columbus friends, and is described in *Years of My Youth:*

"When I knew him first, with his tall, straight figure, his features of Greek fineness, his blue eyes, and his moustache thin and ashen blonde, he was of a distinction fitting the soldier he became when the Civil War began, and he fought through the four years' struggle with such gallantry and efficiency that he came out of it with the rank of brigadier-general. He had broken with the law amid arms, and in due time he succeeded to the control of our newspaper, and made the paper an increasing power. But he had never been the vigorous strength he looked, and after certain years of overwork he accepted the appointment of minister to Hawaii. The rest and the mild climate renewed his health, and he came back to journalism under different conditions of place. But the strain was the same; he gave way under it again, and died a few years later."

"The Doctor" was Dr. S. M. Smith, Howells's old Columbus friend, whose daughter Comly had married.

To J. M. Comly

Cambridge, June 27, 1868.

DEAR FRIEND:

The sad news you tell me of your health gives me great distress, and I am heartily ashamed of having added ever so slight weight to the burdens you have. Don't suppose that I failed to enter into the spirit of your letter, or that I cared a straw about your "blowing" T. and F. But while I felt indignant that you had been subjected to annoyance by their clerk's neglect, I felt just a little hurt that you had not written a word in answer to a letter which I sent you out of an impulse of fondly remembered friendship. You are the oldest friend I have, and I couldn't bear to think you didn't care for me as much as I did for you. I had no pique, and I'm only sorry that I let my anxiety trouble you. I hope you'll let me be a more constant correspondent hereafter. I'm going to Ohio next year to see my family and you.

I found your letter awaiting my return from Newport, whither I went to-day to say good-bye to some friends about sailing for Europe: Mr. Norton (of the *North American Review*) and his family. He advanced me the money to buy the house in which I live, and has helped me with every kindness during my life in Cambridge, and of course their going away is a great loss to us. He is a man of almost ideal purity and goodness—one of those incomprehensible beings who are always looking about the world, and seeking occasion to be useful and comfortable to somebody. I shall not only miss sadly his personal friendship, but his literary sympathy which has attended me in every undertaking, here.

I saw Newport for the first time, to-day, and was enchanted with the quaint, sea-washed, decaying old place. Elinor and I dream of spending our winters there, in a few years, for the climate, by reason of the Gulf Stream's touching the coast, is of almost English mildness. But this is altogether a thing of the future. In the meantime, we don't at all like the Boston winter, which, by the way, is the only Puritanical thing in Boston.

Do you know of an old file of the *State Journal* I could get, of 1859–60–61 ? I suppose such a thing isn't to be had. Please tell me if the Doctor ever got a copy of *Italian Journeys* which I sent him? What *does* Ferguson mean by "the Judge story"? It puzzles me. Give him my love.

Now, Comly, write when you can, and in any way you please. Believe that I sympathize cordially with you in the cares that harass you, and am always your friend.

W. D. HOWELLS.

In the next letter Howells tells of the birth of his son, John Mead Howells.

"Mead" was his brother-in-law, Larkin G. Mead, Jr., who, when Howells and his wife were away on their Italian journeys, acted as his vice-consul in Venice.

While Mead was with them there, he married a beautiful Venetian, Marietta de Benvenuti, the daughter of an impoverished *nobile* family that lived above his sister in the Casa Falier. He first saw his future wife walking before her parents, after the Venetian fashion, in the Piazza, and his courtship was well advanced before she could speak English, or he Italian. Their married life was spent in Florence, where he had his studio, and he became the professor of sculpture in the school where Michelangelo once taught.

Sedgwick was Arthur G. Sedgwick, a brother-in-law of Charles Eliot Norton. He was a man of letters who fought in the Civil War; he was confined in Libby Prison, an experience from which he never fully recovered.

To Charles Eliot Norton

Cambridge, August 29, 1868.

MY DEAR MR. NORTON:

If I were not such a mere intellectual ruin, I would frame or feign some excuse for not having written to you before now; but as it is, I should bungle the best lying intention, and I won't attempt anything in exculpation. I am wrecked by too great good fortune—I am dashed to pieces on the Happy Isles. The event into which our whole life and world had so long resolved themselves, has taken place with such blissful result that it has seemed scarcely worth while for the past two weeks to do anything but idly exult. You must know before this—one continent could not contain the news —that we have a boy, born on the 14th of August, who came into this republic with as little disturbance as ever attended a citizen's advent, and whom I can't help introducing to you in this political character because of the remarkable and amusing resemblance he bears to Wm. H. Seward.

This may appear to you as all very weak and trivial in a letter; but I began by representing myself as an intellectual ruin; and I can assure you that I think nothing and say nothing wiser to any one. I think my state is partially attributable to too much female society; and what becomes of literary men in Paynim lands, where wives, nurses, and grandmothers are indefinitely multiplied in households, I couldn't in my enfeebled condition guess. I have caught quite a professional tone from the nurse, which I suppress with some difficulty here.

You will imagine that I have little to tell you of the world outside our hedge. Mr. Lowell I have seen oftener since you left than during the whole time I've been in Cambridge. The truth is I am about the only literary thing still extant here, and he comes to my house, and takes me walking with him—each time, I can see, with the vague hope that he won't bore himself, which I behold gradually give way to a settled despair as our walk draws to a close, and he finds that I have nothing in me. If the fact were not so ghastly, I think I should almost enjoy it; but it is too horrible. I look at it in quite an impersonal light, and sympathize with his disappointment as if it were my own, though I've long got done expecting any entertainment from myself. I've passed several times through your grounds of late, and found them charming. I think they are in greater beauty now than at any other time of year; and the loneliness of the house sympathizes with the first faint sentiment of autumn in the woods. What a curious little pang it gave to go, the other day, and ring your doorbell! I was there with Mead, who is at home on a few weeks' visit with his wife, and whom I wanted to have see your Tintoretto. He was greatly charmed with that and with Stillman's picture, and I moped gloomily about the rooms which have pepper enough in them to make your worst enemy weep you. This pilgrimage, and journeys into Boston, have made up the variety of my life, and I have so little courage to attempt anything grander that I gave up with a shudder an excursion down the harbor which I had meditated. It seems incredible to hear of all that you are doing, and that you and every one bear it so well. I have seen Sedgwick and Miss Dora since their return from Canada, and have enjoyed over again, in their talk, my elder travel in that province. Godkin has written two very delightful and thoughtful papers on some characteristics of society there; and generally the *Nation* continues admirable. To-day I've read an amusing review, on the whole, of *Italian Journeys,* in the London *Saturday Review* of Aug. 15. To you and me who know me, and what manner of person I am, is it not delightful to read of me as a skeptical "citizen of the world"? I am not all that the *Review* could wish, it seems—but who is? It appeared to me that the book was rather happily misconceived by the critic; but he was just enough in some strictures. I write entirely of myself this time because I know of nothing else just now; and I hope you will be as personal.

Pray give my best respects to your mother, and remember me most heartily to all your party, who are more in my thought than they are even in numbers.

Yours ever,

W. D. HOWELLS.

"The poem" that was out was *No Love Lost.*

Arthur G. Sedgwick and Henry James, Jr., had composed at about this time the following bit of nonsense to be inserted in Carlyle's *French Revolution,* by Sedgwick, as he was reading it to a small circle of Cambridge friends. They afterwards asked the elder Henry James, who was one of the circle, to explain it, which he did very carefully.

"*French Revolution*—at beginning of chapter on 'Parliament of Paris.' Cue: 'now or never'.

Word spluttering organisms in whatever place; not as now with Plutarchean comparison—apologies; nay rather without any such apologies—antiphonal, too, in the main—but born into the world to say the thought that is in them. Butchers, bakers, candlestick-makers—men, women, peasants—verily with you, too, is it now or or never."

Perhaps this success was confided to Howells during the

"several hours" Sedgwick and he spent together, as he had a copy of the joint composition.

To Charles Eliot Norton

Cambridge, Nov. 12, 1868.

DEAR MR. NORTON:

To-day I was at Mr. Lowell's when he received a letter from Miss Norton telling him of your convalescence, and greatly relieving us both of anxiety on your account; for he had just been reading me a former letter of your sister's in which she announced your illness to him. After that, you may be sure the talk was cheerfuller: we began immediately upon our enemies, who are also the enemies of good literature and mankind, and celebrated your recovery by leaving nothing of them. Mr. Lowell has been destroying our foes also in the *Atlantic,* in a paper called *The Condescension of Some Foreigners,* with a grace and ease that I am only too much afraid will delight the wretches in the midst of their misery. You, at least, who are in some sort a foreigner by virtue of being too good for this world, will certainly like it—perhaps because you're not one of the condescending ones. It appears to me one of the best things the writer has done, it is so sharp and yet so *ridente*— steel with the sun on it. There are touches in it too that make the heart ache. I grow more and more into the admiration of Lowell's power, or liking of it rather; for when I reflect that with his great gifts to persuade and to make afraid—his poetry and his wit—he has never used them once falsely or cruelly, I feel myself in the presence of a new kind of great man, in whom there is a perfect balance of law and of strength. It could not be, of course, and yet I wish that there were some means for an extension of his personal influence over young men. It is vast already, and his strength is felt throughout the whole puny body of our literature, for there is no one who would not prize his praise above that of any contemporary; but it would be well for every youngster if he could see him and hear him. Do you think I am turning into a Boswell? No, it was Johnson that made Boswell, and I am not afraid.

I imagine you laughing over the idea that I should seize the first moment of your absence from the country to plan the publication of that long-suppressed long poem of mine; but indeed, the case is not exactly so. Still, the poem is out—in *Putnam's Magazine,* and in a little volume, for which Elinor's illustrations have been in some instances engraved past all endurance. Only one notice has reached me, yet: in the New York *Evening Mail;* and as it misinterprets a chief point of the story, I should be much pleased, if it did not also praise it.

The Gurneys are quickly settled, I believe, in your house —which, however, will always stand empty, for me, till you come back to it—and we are going to see them as soon as my wife is well enough to make visits. But I suppose that even if Elinor were perfectly strong, we should not go about much this winter, for that has happened to me, which makes me insecure of the little animation and cheerfulness I could once contribute. My dear mother died on the 10th of October, after so sudden a seizure that I who had been summoned instantly had the unspeakable sorrow not to find her alive when I reached home. She had been ailing all summer, but neither she nor any of us felt uneasy at all, and it must have been paralysis that at last gave her a painless release, and to us a lifelong loss. At times, her death, and all I know of it, seems the most insubstantial dream, and at times the only fact in a world of vagaries. I need not tell you how I loved her, or how I lament her; but I beg you to accept my sad preoccupation as an excuse why I should not have answered your kindest letter long ago. I sent it and Mrs. Norton's out to mother, who read them both with the greatest interest and pleasure; and in the last letter but one that came before that dreadful telegram, she begged to be remembered to you.

Harry James has just been here (I am finishing this letter on Sunday the 15th,) and left the manuscript of a story which he read me a week ago—the best thing, as I always say, that he has done yet. He seems in firmer health than ever, and is full of works and purposes.

Nov. 23. As I have nearly every day talked about you, or heard from you through one friend or another, I feel less ashamed than I ought perhaps for not having finished this letter before now: it seems as if I had finished it, somehow. Last night I spent several hours with Sedgwick both at his room and in mine, for after I had made my call, he was tempted by a prospect of moonlight and beer to walk home with me. Mr. Rouse was calling upon Miss Ashburner, and professed—the talk giving occasion to his remark—that she was the first person he ever saw who didn't understand Welsh. This evening came Miss Grace Ashburner to borrow some easy Italian literature for Miss Theodora, it being decided that the accustomed *Prigioni* of beginners was a sentiment or two too tearful and humble.

Yesterday and to-day have been days *proprio* of Italy. You should see the dead leaves how they lie twinkling in the sun on the little slope under the trees across the way. It takes but a little to make one very happy at times, but somehow we are always trying to get allopathic doses of bliss. Yesterday, it was the last favor of fortune to walk with Harry James to the Botanical Garden, and sit in the sun on the edge of a hotbed of violets, and think of the notices still to be written. What is better than to punch one's cane into a sandy path? You must have good company, of course.

The Emerson lectures came to an end one week ago. I heard the last: how little wisdom it takes to lecture the world! On the horse car coming home was Mr. Gurney who told me a good deal of his editorial beginnings, and I am glad that the *Review* will go into such careful and able hands. He is making an effort to enlarge the circle of contributors, and I hope he will succeed; but outside of Cambridge and Godkin, it appears to me that our literary review-writing world is only one vast Tuckerman. The *Atlantic* enters the new year with an amazing show of great names, and in the January number we shall really have some good things, as we shall also throughout the year. But I am not proud. For my own work I've done an episode of American history for the magazine, and if it is liked, I have a mind to try something else in the same direction. Lucrezia Borgia would not be wooed in any Boston library, and I have relinquished my suit, not without some pain and mortification. But I hear a biography of her has just been published in England. Have you happened to see it?

Think of my having been offered a professorship in Union College the other day! They imagined that I know something about Rhetoric.

Dear friend, I hope this silly letter will find you much better, and I hope that some one of your family will remember how glad I shall be to get a few words directly about you,—when it is perfectly easy to write. Mrs. Howells joins me in love to you all.

Yours very cordially,
W. D. HOWELLS.

Mr. Lowell brought me his new volume, the other day, and I was delighted to find it dedicated to you with that exquisite *Agro Dolce*.

1869

The next letter was written to his wife in Brattleboro, where she had gone to be with her father during what proved to be his last illness.

"The lectureship" offered Howells by President Eliot was an appointment as University Lecturer, which he held for the winters of 1869–1870 and 1870–1871. These were the first two years of President Eliot's administration, and the appointment of University Lecturers to give courses of lectures outside the usual curriculum, meant for both men and women, was the beginning of the Graduate School. The subject of Howells's lectures for the first winter was *New Italian Literature,* and for the second winter, *Modern Italian Poetry and Comedy.*

To Mrs. W. D. Howells

Cambridge, June 23, 1869.

DEAR ELINOR:

Of course you must stay as long as seems desirable for your father; but I've already written you something of this kind. All I ask is that you should have a due regard for yourself, and not overdo. I suspect that your strength is nothing but nerve, and I beg you to keep the fact of your own poor health in mind, as far as you can consistently with present duty. This is a very trying time for all of us, and I fully share the anxieties of it. We get on very well here, and you need not be troubled about home affairs.

Last evening Mr. Lowell came on the part of President Eliot to urge me to a second decision about the lectureship. I ran in to see Osgood about some possible future partial freedom from proof reading, and he promised that they would give me time to prepare those lectures *anyway;* so I came home, and wrote a letter to Mr. Eliot *declining* the office again on general principles. This morning Mr. Eliot not having received my letter, came personally to urge me, and I "took it for a sign" and accepted! So I'm a professor in spite of myself. I told him what a superficial fellow I was, and warned him of his risk, but it made no difference.

Winny said *nothing* worth while to-day, but Johnny

fans himself with a palm leaf fan, and puts his feet on the table when he sits at meals. And is altogether the "wickedest man in" Cambridge, which makes his papa the happiest, of course. I hope Charley's news of your father will be more encouraging.

Your
W. D. H.

Doorstep Acquaintance and *A Pedestrian Tour* were collected in *Suburban Sketches*, where the proposed *Pleasure Excursions*, after appearing under that name in the *Atlantic*, joined them as *A Day's Pleasure*.

There were two Peace Jubilees in Boston, the first National Peace Jubilee opening on June 15, 1869, and the second on June 17, 1872. What Howells had written about the Jubilee was an article in the *Atlantic* called *Jubilee Days*. The same title was later used for the little paper issued daily by James R. Osgood, and edited by Howells and Thomas Bailey Aldrich, during the second Peace Jubilee.

To Henry James

Cambridge, June 26, 1869.

MY DEAR JAMES:

I had it in my heart to answer you as soon as I'd read your letter; but I hadn't it in my power; and so your missive has lain upon my table to reproach me, and I've endured torments from it. You see that although you had used me very ill in not writing me sooner, my resentment was all melted away by the air of homesickness in your letter, and for a day I really flattered myself that there was some reason why you should be so fond of me. But that is past now, and the Light Man himself could not address you more coldly than this husband and father. I don't know but I've got a touch of that diarist's style; I confess the idea of him fascinated me. He's one of your best worst ones; and I'm sorry we hadn't him for the *Atlantic;* though it is good policy for you to send something to the *Galaxy* now and then. I'll enclose some scraps of print, by which you'll see that *Gabrielle de Bergerac* is thought well of by those whose good opinion ought not to be of any consequence, but is. It really promises to make a greater impression than anything else you've done in the *Atlantic.*

I suppose I was right to carry your letter to your brother, and that he was wrong to show it at once to the rest of your family. Wherever the error is, it is now too late to repair it. Here we enjoyed it all; and Mrs. Howells hunted up the April *Atlantic* and read *Doorstep Acquaintance* over again. Just at present, however, we are thinking of things that make even my literature seem unimportant. Mrs. Howells's father has lain very sick for the last three weeks, and it is very uncertain yet whether he will recover. From day to day he was not expected to live; but she has been with him for nearly two weeks, at Brattleboro, whence she now writes me that there is a little change in him for the better. Add to these anxieties the horrible tumult of this Jubilee business, and the largely increased editorial business, and you have something like an excuse for my not answering you at once. I will enclose what I've written about the Jubilee, which will tell a long story in itself, and help to say also what I've been doing. The summer has passed very quietly in Cambridge, and as like twenty other summers as possible. Thanks to a slow but uninterrupted spring, and a good deal of wet weather since the foliage started, we are a thought leafier than usual; and you may guess how pleasant it is in that little grove over the way from us, and in fact in every part of the commonplace old town—which like some plain girls has a charm quite independent of beauty. Even in Cambridge, I enter quite into the spirit of your homesickness, and feel the fascination which you miss. The town has very few positive advantages; but it is a prodigious satisfaction to feel that meeting

any acquaintance upon the street, you are well-nigh sure of
meeting some person who is not common or mean in his
mind, but is full of appreciation and liberality. This appears to me the character of the whole population. I should
think there was less intellectual vulgarity here—the worst
sort, by the way—than anywhere else in the world. And yet
it's a hard place to live in, expensive, inconvenient, and at
times quite desolate. My own stay here seems often drawing to a close for these reasons, and yet I should be exceedingly unhappy anywhere else, I'm afraid. At any rate, I
don't think we shall remain much longer in this neighbor-
hood. All Ireland seems to be poured out upon it, and there
is such a clamor of Irish children about us all day, that I
suspect my "exquisite English," as I've seen it called in the
newspapers, will yet be written with a brogue.

July 18. You see I am not a ready writer—of letters at
least. Till now, I've not seen the hour when I could sit down
with a clean conscience to finish this—or if at any time my
conscience was clean my head was empty. Since I began to
write—three weeks ago—Mr. Mead has died, and I have
been to Brattleboro to see laid in the ground all that was
left of the kind, cheerful, simple old man. He was one who
felt so friendly toward the whole world that he imagined
it a good one, and led the very happiest life here. He was—

> So full of summer warmth, so glad,
> So healthy, sound, and clear and whole,
> His memory scarce can make me sad.

But after all it has been a depressing experience, and my
wife has felt it deeply. We have now Mrs. Mead with us,
and are trying what we can to keep up the illusion of mere
absence to her. For a man who never intended to recognize
death as among the possibilities, except in an abstract and
general sort of way, I have, within a year, seen enough of
it to convince me of an error in my theory of life. It can
never again seem the alien far-off thing it once did; and

yet acquaintance with it has robbed it of something of its terrors. Shall I say it has been at once realized and unsubstantialized? I had always thought to find death in the dead; but they are "but as pictures"; I feel the operation of a principle which seemed improbable formerly, but I am not frightened at its effect as I had always thought to be. I don't mean, of course, that I don't fear to die—God knows I do—but in other times, the mere imagination of death was enough to fill me with unspeakable anguish. I had hardly got back from my father-in-law's funeral, when our baby's nurse was called away to her little son, in Charlestown, who after a day's sickness died. Mrs. Howells was still at Brattleboro, and you may guess my troubles in taking care of our boy in the nurse's absence. It was sad enough, but even more absurd than sad;—a bachelor and childless man can never understand it all. Next day, to please the poor soul who had lost the whole world she lived for, in her son, I went to see him. It was a wonderful contrast to the scene I had just witnessed at Brattleboro', where ages of Puritanism had strengthened and restrained the mourners from every display of their grief. The little one lay there on a kind of couch, with candles and vases of flowers about him—an awful, beautiful vision, hallowing and honoring the shabby room, as the most triumphal aspect of life could not have done, and presently the mother cast herself upon him, and bewailed him with a wild heart-rending poetry of anguish. I could not bear it; I broke down, and cried as heartily as she did.

Well, you've had enough of all this, which has lately occupied me to the exclusion of nearly everything else; and which I hope you'll forgive my writing about; it had to be this or nothing.

I saw your family shortly before they left for Pomfret, and I've since had a little note from your father, saying that they were well and most contented with their place. I miss them a good deal—not because I saw them very often, but because it was a pleasure to be able to see them when time favored. Nearly every one is out of town, in Europe, or in the country,—Lowell alone of the "few immortal names" is left. He called at my house, yesterday, and I walked down town with him in the windy, sunny afternoon —down Oxford street; and I wish I could picture you here the beauty of those willows, which line the deserted railway track, as the breeze took them and tossed up the white of their leaves. What a lovely bit of wildness it is, along there!—though there's provokingly little of it, and it's as hollow and false as a stage scene,—absolutely nothing but a few willows, with a growth of lady-slipper hiding empty tomato cans and other rubbish about their roots.

I'm not sure that the August *Atlantic* will reach you, and so I shall tear out the installment of *Gabrielle* and *Jubilee Days* and send them in this letter. Your story is universally praised, and is accounted the best thing you've done. There seems at last to be a general waking-up to your merits; but when you've a fame as great as Hawthorne's, you won't forget who was the first, warmest and truest of your admirers, will you?

I'm writing now and have nearly finished something I call *A Pedestrian Tour,* and which is nothing but an impudent attempt to interest people in a stroll I take from Sacramento street up through the Brickyards and the Irish village of Dublin near by, and so down through North Avenue. If the public will stand this, I shall consider my fortune made; and shall go on to write out a paper on *Pleasure Excursions* to different places in and near Boston. The *Nation* hasn't pronounced yet upon *Jubilee Days*—should it be adverse perhaps I sha'n't feel encouraged to go on. Horrible, isn't it, to have only one critic for 40,000,000 of people? I don't know whether you'll have heard of the honor conferred on me by the new president of Harvard; but at any rate I'll do myself the pleasure to tell you of it. He's asked me to deliver one set of lectures in a course to post-graduates; and accordingly I'm to lecture along with Lowell, Child and Whitney. *Ci pensi!* Of course I take modern Italian literature, not knowing anything else, and feeling secure in the general ignorance concerning that. Now for an honor the new President of the United States did Winny at the Jubilee. He kissed her! She was very anxious to see him, for reasons of her own, and I led her near the sofa, where he sat, and told her to ask a certain friendly looking old gentleman who sat near Grant to show her the President. He did more: he led her up to Grant, "And the Presentdent," says Winny, "he took me in his arms, and said I was a nice little girl, and kissed me; and then the Presentdent's son kissed me, and laughed at me; and so I ran away." She was very proud for a day or two, and proposed to "save" the cheek Grant kissed as long as she lived, but really only kept it sacred for a half day. She sends her best love to you, and the enclosed tin-type, which she had taken on the Jubilee grounds about an hour after being kissed. It's uncommonly precious, on that account. The boy is not able to express the friendship he feels for you, but I make bold to send his regards. He grows strong and troublesome, which is all we could wish, I suppose.

July 24. Waiting the receipt of your address from your father, I add a few more lines to this letter, which seems not to grow better with age. We have lately amused ourselves with the simple joys of a trip down the harbor to Nantasket beach, where we had adventures dear to timid souls—such as getting softly aground in the mud off the pier. The trip was voted a great success, and we mean to take many another like it. Yesterday I got a very tame horse and drove my womenkind over to Lexington—a lovely road, full of that safe wildness which pleases me. In Lexington we added a final charm to the excursion by inquiring the price of board at the hotel, and making ourselves believe for a moment that we'd go out and spend some weeks there. It was with a kind of dismay that I learnt the pleasure was quite within my means. You'll have heard from other sources, no doubt, before this letter reaches you, that your brother Wilkie and Arthur Sedgwick have rowed in open boats from Boston to Mt. Desert. I've read the last proof of your *Gabrielle* and it's really magnificent, as Mrs. Howells, a very difficult critic, declares. Aren't you going to send us anything about your travels? Do.

Well, good-bye. Write, if you've the heart after reading this. Europe has no such gift as a letter from you to bestow. Mrs. Howells sends her regards, and I am

Ever yours,
W. D. HOWELLS.

The True Story of Lady Byron's Life, by Mrs. Stowe, was printed in the September *Atlantic,* 1869. Mr. M. A. De Wolfe Howe, in *The Atlantic Monthly and its Makers,* says that the article so outraged a large number of its readers that the circulation of the magazine suffered a generous reduction.

Lowell's "glorious poem" was *The Cathedral.*

To James T. Fields

Cambridge, Aug. 24, 1869.

DEAR MR. FIELDS:

My resolution to keep a diary concerning the editorial business, and send it to you regularly twice a month was altogether too bright, too beautiful, to last. Yet while it endured, you will own it must have had its fascinations— such a propriety in it—so amusing to me, so satisfactory to you. Well, we will check the unavailing tear: the business, though unrecorded, has been promptly done, and we are already arrived at the time when we begin to look for the return of the Autumn and of you. I am glad you liked the

August number so well: I put in the things you directed
and filled out according to my own judgment, from the
mass of material, that seems to grow like the liver of
Prometheus the more it is preyed upon. The September is
equally good, though Mrs. Stowe's sensation of course be-
numbs the public to everything else in it. So far her story
has been received with howls of rejection from almost every
side where a critical dog is kept. The *Tribune,* and one or
two Western papers alone accept it as truth; but I think the
tide will turn, especially if its publication in England elicits
anything like confirmation there.

As to stories, you know *The Foe in the Household*
ends in December. Mr. Hale brought in a curious thing, a
week or two ago, called *The Brick Moon,* which will run
from October till December inclusive; and besides this, I've
taken five or six short things, of 10 or 12 pp. each; but the
accepted Mss. have mainly been sketches and essays—a
capital essay by Sheldon, among the rest. I've taken one
poem, by and with the advice and consent of Mr. Lowell,
and another upon my own judgment from Bayard Taylor.
It's extremely fine, I think (*An August Pastoral*) and
I get it into the October. And then—shut your eyes and
open your mouth—Lowell has written for your pet January number, a glorious poem of 12 pages. He read it to
me yesterday, and I thought it magnificent—an opalescent
beauty with every sort of intellectual light and color in it,
and full of all dreamy tendernesses, too. It's ready now; and
think of my denying myself the triumph of putting it in at
once and waiting for you to get the glory later. Think, and
blush, for having put off those two lectures of —— on
me and my numbers! It's some comfort to remember that
I've told everybody you made up the magazines before you
left.

I've begun Dr. Jarvis's papers on *The Increase of
Life* in the October; Clarke closes with *Mahomet* in
November (a very successful and honorable set of papers);

Shaler ends his *Earthquakes* in Dec.; Mrs. Thaxter, though her first paper was greatly praised, has not followed it up; Goldwin Smith has sent nothing; (and small loss to us as things have fallen out,) I haven't got to Prof. Wilder's things yet—we had so much other science. Mrs. Agassiz has two charming papers on *Dredging in the Gulf* (Oct. and Nov.) ; Mr. King has not yet sent any of his sporting articles. I followed up the *Recent Travels* in the Sept. with a similar article on *A Poetical Lot,* and I'm glad that the first struck you favorably. I won't repeat what Lowell said of the second because pride is sinful. My notion was to vary the monotony of the notices by a sort of paper that would give me more elbow room. In Nov. and Dec. I'll have notices; and in Nov., also, a study of some parts of Cambridge, called *A Pedestrian Tour.* I've had such a streak of good luck in volunteer contributions that I don't lament your bad luck in England so much as I otherwise should. You won't perhaps value the suggestion any more because I offer it unasked; but I don't think it pays at all to take English stuff unless it's first chop; *Minor Shows of London* and Mrs. Lynton's paper are *not* first chop, and I hope you'll fail in the attempt to get anything more of like quality. The Morris sonnets are very pretty, and the other little poem will go into the October. I enclose a list of the articles accepted, that may possibly be interesting or useful to you, and also the contents of the November number as it has gone to the printers.

I believe I haven't got into difficulty with any one, made you enemies or changed the general policy of the magazine; so there will be no occasion to repeat the scene which took place on the return of the chief editor of the San Diego *Herald.* Concerning this last sentence Mr. K—— could have written on the margin "A *scene* cannot *take place,*" which reminds me that he is no longer reading proof at the University Press. I lament him for some reasons, but I believe on general principles that we're proof-read too much. The Parton articles are interesting, but have on the whole been received with something more than the usual misgiving. I suppose that they are more popular than otherwise. Shaler's papers have been a very fair success; and Clarke's have been liked nearly everywhere. *The Foe in the Household* has lost ground a little, I think; Harry James's story is a great gain upon all that he's done before, in the popular estimation. Dr. Holmes is a firm believer in Mrs. Stowe's article: Mr. Lowell if no longer a doubter of it, still a disliker. It seems to be pretty generally allowed it was awkwardly done. I see this, but I think the story is true and ought to have been told. People say Mrs. Stowe should have given names, dates, and places in full. You saw that she made one mistake, stating the Byrons lived two years together instead of 13 months. We'd the greatest difficulty with her in getting her to read her proof at all. Kirk and I both read it carefully, and sent it to her; and *she wouldn't return the proof!* but sent a copy which Dr. Holmes had gone over. I then read it again, and enclosed it to Dr. Holmes, who accepted all my corrections; but this was done hastily, with the printers at my back, and with a view to have everything, as nearly as possible, just as Mrs. Stowe had written it. She had misquoted wherever she could, nearly—the last conversation as she gave it between Byron and Fletcher was all wrong.

Mrs. Howells joins me in cordial regards to you and Mrs. Fields. I know you must be enjoying yourselves, and I hope you feel easy about the *Atlantic* here. Our family has been uncommonly well; but Mrs. Howells has lost her father: the kind old man died July 5. There is nothing new in Cambridge. So adieu!

W. D. HOWELLS.

The "meals from Porter's tavern" were sent to them already cooked, as their dinners had been in Venice, where they hungrily watched their slow approach by gondola up the Grand Canal.

To William Cooper Howells

Cambridge, September 22, 1869.

DEAR FATHER:

For fear I should forget it, as I have done for several times already, I'll say here at the beginning that I never saw Mrs. Stowe's article till it was in type. I think, however, I should have taken it if it had been left to me, for I don't at all agree with those who condemn her. Always supposing that she has probable evidence in support of her story, I don't see why it shouldn't have been told. The world needed to know just how base, filthy and mean Byron was, in order that all glamor should be forever removed from his literature, and the taint of it should be communicated only to those who love sensual things, and no more pure young souls should suffer from him through their sympathy with the supposed generous and noble traits in his character. The need of this was so great, that even if Mrs. Stowe had had no authority to tell the story, I should almost be ready to applaud her for doing it. Generally I don't like her way of doing things—she did this particular thing wretchedly—but I don't condemn her for having done it. I believe I'm only one of three or four in America who don't. If it should turn out that she cannot confirm her statements, then it'll be a different affair. But the editor of *Macmillan's Magazine* in London telegraphs that there is evidence to support them.

I send you a circular to show how our coöperative house-keeping progresses. In the meantime we're perfectly suited with our meals from Porter's tavern, and find the system to work as well here as in Venice. The only thing that troubles us is how to get rid of the superfluous provisions.

Please remember me to the Garfields when you write them. You must have found their visit a great pleasure.

With love to all,

Your affectionate son,

WILL.

Lowell, in *A Good Word for Winter,* says, in speaking of the snow, "It was a pretty fancy of the young Vermont sculptor to make his first essay in this evanescent material." The young Vermont sculptor was, as Howells writes, his wife's brother, Larkin G. Mead, who was born in Chesterfield, New Hampshire, and grew up in Brattleboro, Vermont. Here he modelled at the crossroads one night a colossal figure of the Recording Angel in snow, which was found by the astonished townspeople on New Year's morning.

To James Russell Lowell

Cambridge, October 16, 1869.

DEAR MR. LOWELL:

Before the chill of the theme penetrates through the charm you cast about it and cools me off, I must write to you of the pleasure I've taken in your good word for Winter. I'm no Winterist, as you know; but your art made me feel almost a tenderness for the old rogue. The essay seemed to me in manner and spirit as great as your very best talk, and for my part I don't think there can be anything better than that. "It's just as Lowell talks!" said the for-once-agreeing critics of this family; and one of them—who is an editor—thought what a sin it was you would not make up your mind to write something like it for every month's *Atlantic.* As I read I almost smelt the familiar fume of your pipe, and I'm half ready to swear that I saw you put a log on your fire, turn round (you turn round *rounder* than anybody else) and stand with your back to the blaze, your hands on your hips, and your eye taking a book on an upper shelf for a land-mark to infinity. Few ever praise this precious personal charm in the essay, but all must be conscious of its beauty. I thought the character of the seasons in the beginning of the article exquisitely sketched,—especially the Lamartinish, Heinesque sentimentality of Autumn,—and I marvelled throughout at your luck in making your own thoughts and your quotations of one piece. Mrs. H. considers you particularly delightful in your liberties with W. W. and I don't say no: only, where were you not particularly delightful? The whole was so good, that I don't think even my admiration—which I'm sensible grows a little hystericky when I try to express it— can make it appear otherwise to the author himself. With all my heart

Your truly,
W. D. HOWELLS.

P. S. The "young Vermont Sculptor" (you know?) is Mrs. Howell's brother Larkin Mead. The statue was made on the last night of the year, and he called it, poetically enough, The Recording Angel.

> Take all this, *paron
> mio caro,* if it seems the
> touch of irreverence, for
> that of affection.

James Russell Lowell to W. D. Howells

Elmwood, Under the rain.

MY DEAR BOY,
    You know very well that I would rather have you fond of me than write the best essay that ever Montaigne conceived as he paced to and fro in that bleak book-room of

his. But for all that, I am grateful for what you say, since a gray beard brings self-distrust—at least in my case, who never had any great confidence in anything but Truth. But what I write this for is only to say that to be sure I knew who the "young Vermont Sculptor" was, and pleased myself with alluding to him for your sake—for when my heart is warm toward any one I like all about him and this is why I am so bad (or so good) a critic, just as you choose to take it. If women only knew how much woman there is in me, they would forgive all my heresies on the woman-question—I mean they would if they were not women.

But then I am a good critic about some things, and I see how you have mixed *me* and my essay. Why, I was thinking only this morning that, if I could have you to lecture to, I could discourse with great good luck, for you always bring me a reinforcement of spirits. Well, whatever happens, you can't be sorry that I thought so much of you as I do. With kindest regards to Mrs. Howells,

Always affectionately yours

J. R. L.

To M. M. Hurd

13 Boylston Place, Boston,

February 4, 1869.

My dear Hurd:

I am most agreeably surprised at the amount of your very welcome cheque: my most soaring expectation did not fly higher than half of it. Is it not odd that *V. L.* leads off? *I. J.* is so much better.

I heartily wish that I had something to make a new book out of, but I don't yet clearly see my way to another volume. All my schemes for biographical and historical sketches have failed because of poverty of material. You remember I told you of Lucrezia Borgia: it was impossible to get anything in the libraries here. So with some episodes of

American history; and now unless I can write up some little papers on contemporary life like *Mrs. Johnson,* I don't see what I'm to do.—There were enough of those articles on modern Italian literature in the *North American Review* to make a volume, but I doubt if it would sell, and otherwise my writings are too heterogeneous to be booked together under any one cover. Where in the world did you see my *Life of Lincoln,* and when?

Have you ever heard Mr. Putnam say how my poem sold?—I'll do all I can to help off Piatt's book as soon as it comes out.

We partly hoped to go to New York this winter, but the addition to our family was so expensive that we couldn't afford the journey. We all join in regards to you and yours.

Very truly yours,
W. D. HOWELLS.

VIII

1870, 1871, 1872

Lowell Institute lectures. Becomes Editor of the Atlantic. *Second Peace Jubilee. Edits* Jubilee Days *with Aldrich. Builds Cambridge house.*

THE "lectures on *'New Italian Literature'* " were his Harvard lectures.

To James Russell Lowell

Cambridge, May 22, 1870.

MY DEAR MR. LOWELL:

I sent, as you suggested, and I desired, the ticket to Mrs. Lowell's sister, and I've secured thereby a most patient listener to the lectures on *New Italian Literature,* which are now making such a stir on Sacramento street. The theatrical people say that a "paper house" is always very cold and inapplausive as compared with a "pay house," but so far, my free tickets have brought me greater glory than the subscriptions have. The base-ball club seduced all the male students away from my class, but the gentlemen who come in on my passes were there, to a martyr. I have bribed the barbarian darky by the way, and now anybody comes that likes. The college Steward himself should not be shut out. I've an audience of twenty, and the quality is even more distinguished than the quantity. Up to the close of yesterday the lectures had not been received with yells of derision— Mr. Child, for example, did not hiss, once, nor Mr. Longfellow ask to have the lecturer put out—and so I'm emboldened to ask if I couldn't, quite unexpectedly to myself,

155

be invited to give the things at Cornell next year. I really think they're not so dull as they might be, nor so absolutely void of instruction; but if you don't care to suggest the matter to Mr. White, by all means, don't. If you do, I shall await the result in modest ignorance of the whole affair.

I imagine you sighing for Cambridge, in spite of Ithaca the fair; and to tell you the truth, the town is just now looking her prettiest. She seems to be dreaming of the days when she was wholly orchard, and she's all decked in apple blossoms, look what way you will, and orioles, listen when you will.

I don't think there's much news, worthy to be so called.— Harry James is come back from Europe, and Dennett has called upon me. (He went also to see you.) These are the greatest events of life for me, unless the fact that my boy learns a new word every day, is greater.

Yours always,
W. D. HOWELLS.

The Lowell Institute lectures which Howells gave were twelve in number and were given under the title of *Italian Poets of our Century*. It was Francis J. Child who suggested him for this course of lectures, and he says of this kindness in *Literary Friends and Acquaintance*:

"Of course it was only so hard worked a man who could take time and thought for another. He once took thought for me at a time when it was very important to me, and when he took the trouble to secure for me an engagement to deliver that course of Lowell lectures in Boston, which I have said Lowell had the courage to go in town to hear. I do not remember whether Professor Child was equal to so much, but he would have been if it were necessary; and I rather rejoice now in the belief that he did not seek quite that martyrdom."

To William Cooper Howells

Cambridge, Oct. 30, 1870.

DEAR FATHER:

Your last letter makes us very sad about you, and we shall be anxious till we hear again. I hope that you will be able in some way to get perfect rest for a time. It seems to be the thing you most need, for I think you have had an uncommonly trying year.

Since I wrote last, I have given two of my lectures in the Lowell Institute. At the first I was considerably un-nerved, and read too rapidly; but last night, I had the severe critical testimony of Elinor in my favor, as well as that of Mr. Lowell, who was kind enough to come in to the lecture, and who declared himself interested and con-tented with the performance. My audience is about two hundred and fifty, which is much larger than the usual audi-ence: in fact, many courses are delivered to twenty-five or thirty people.—Perhaps the girls will care to know that I appear in evening dress, and Elinor at least thinks I'm very "pretty-looking." In spite of all these encouragements, how-ever, I doubt if I should like lecturing as a profession, and I'm exceedingly glad that I withdrew from the field as a popular lecturer.

We've got our Hannah back again. She was so sorry to have left us that she refused all other places, and became sick about it. Mrs. Lowell saw her at the Intelligence Office and Hannah opened her heart, and told her that she wouldn't go to anybody but Mrs. Howells. So, as we didn't like our new cook we sent word to Hannah to come back, and here she is. I think the whole affair is a great praise to Elinor.

All send love.

Your affectionate son,
WILL.

Bret Harte to W. D. Howells

Rooms of the *Overland Monthly*
San Francisco, Nov. 5th, 1870.

MY DEAR MR. HOWELLS:

The conviction being strong upon me that I should be somewhere near Boston at this date, I withheld myself, photo-and-autographically, that I might burst upon you as an actual and joyous presence with somewhat of that "breezy freshness," all you Eastern Critics are fond of finding in the *O. M.* While thus impending I thought of many clever things to say to you extemporaneously—the wh. I have now forgotten.

My coming being postponed, I send you two sun-flattered pictures of myself. I am told by disinterested friends that they are infinitely better looking than I am—one went so far as to declare the taking of them "sinful"—but you shall give the nicest one to my fair but unknown admirer, whose acquaintance thereafter I shall prudently drop.

You are responsible for the spoiling of one photographic plate. At the supreme moment during the "sitting," while I was trying to look at the usual uninteresting speck on the wall with an interested expression, the operator turned his back upon me, and I thought of your fancy of his "hiding his tears" and laughed to the destruction of the plate. The general sadness of these pictures is the reaction.

I expect still to see you this winter. Until then I shall read you—for it might be that a closer and more intimate knowledge of your methods might spoil your work for me. Do you really go through "a day's pleasuring" grimly, with the intention of *ex post facto* reflections? These and many other impertinent questions I shall ask you, O most excellent writer of excellent English! Until then, *adios*.

BRET HARTE.

MR. HOWELLS, Cambridge.

1871

This newspaper clipping was enclosed in the following letter:

Mr. Bret Harte arrived in this city about eleven o'clock Saturday forenoon, and went immediately to the residence of Mr. W. D. Howells in Cambridge. Mr. Harte is accompanied by his family, consisting of his wife and two children.—*Advertiser*.

To William Cooper Howells

124 Tremont Street, Boston,
March 5, 1871.

DEAR FATHER:

Our friends went yesterday morning, and we have subsided again into our usual quiet. It has been a very pleasant visit to us—one of the pleasantest that we've ever had made us, but of course we're glad to be alone now, for we were all fairly worn out by the social part of it. Besides our party, the Hartes were entertained somewhere every night. I dined with him at Longfellow's, Agassiz's and Fields's, trying to beg off each time, but urged by him to go. It seems rather absurd for a host to be following his guest about in this way, but it is the usual one, and in spite of the enormous fatigue, I enjoyed it. Harte is quite unspoiled by his great popularity—which he values at its true worth—and is a thoroughly charming good-hearted fellow. He reminded me in some things—tones of voice and laughter—of Joe, and I kept wishing that Joe and he knew each other. Perhaps they will, some day, especially if Joe comes East this summer, for it is likely that the Hartes and ourselves will seek some refuge together by the seaside. Till now, Elinor and I have met no young people so congenial. It came out one day at dinner that we were all of the same age—all born in '37. Harte will probably live in New York, though he may be engaged to write emissively for Osgood & Co. Next winter he thinks of lecturing; though none of his plans are matured yet.—Elinor is tired out, of course, though buoyed up by the triumph of her party, which is generally allowed to be one of the most brilliant ever given in Cambridge. I wish the girls could have been here. I haven't had a moment yet to look at your memoir, but I'm going to give the afternoon to it. I'm quite eager and curious about it.

Love from all to all.

Your affectionate son,
WILL.

This further account of the Hartes' visit is taken from a letter of Mrs. Howells to her sisters-in-law, and gives a vivid picture of the enthusiasm for Bret Harte and of the entertainments of the time and place.

"You know how we happened to have the Hartes here? Will had a pleasant correspondence with Bret, and when he said he was coming East—last summer, sometime—invited him to visit us when he was on, knowing nothing of his family. Mr. Harte did not come then, but later wrote that he was coming to Boston with his wife and two children, and, of course, Will repeated his invitation, including the family.

"There had been a perfect furore over Bret Harte's writings among nice people here, and he was received with open arms. One day he dined at Lowell's, the next at Longfellow's, and the next they both dined at Agassiz's. One evening he went in to the Fields's, but they had to refuse invitations from every quarter—especially he, from clubs and associations.

"The visit went off splendidly—but *the party!* How shall I do justice to it? You know we've been here five years accepting civilities and never done much in return, and this gave us a grand opportunity to really give our friends a treat—for everybody was curious to see Bret Harte. Sarah Sedgwick wrote, 'I cannot write a formal reply to your thrilling invitation for Monday,' and all were pleased—and nearly everybody we asked came. Mrs. Fiske got up off a sick bed, and the high-church people all made an exception of this occasion. Wasn't it rash, though, to send out the invitations Friday morning before I really knew if they would be here? As it was, their engine broke down and they had to stay overnight on the way, instead of being here Friday night as they intended. The reason the party was a success was that we being new people could bring together different sets, making more variety than there is generally in Cambridge parties.

"The house is admirably calculated for a party, the people were beautifully dressed, and the supper was very nice. Smith the caterer provided it at a *dollar and a half a head!* The man brought linen, silver, dishes, coffee, chocolate, ice cream, salad, bread and cake. Afterwards he and another man washed up the dishes and took them off—and at twelve o'clock all was quiet."

1871

John Hay's paper must have been an instalment of *Castilian Days* which began in the *Atlantic* in January, 1871.

To John Hay

The Atlantic Monthly, Boston,
March 22, 1871.

My dear Hay:

I can't help telling you, with the lamentable want of originality which pursues me when I want to express my pleasure in a thing, what a very great pleasure this paper of yours has given me. Perhaps something in the subject peculiarly affected me, for I've loved Cervantes ever since I was ten years old, but vastly more I'm sure I owe to your beautiful, exquisite treatment of it. My blessing on you!—I shall not be disappointed if this does not make a great impression in the magazine: I shall only have a new reason for despising our readers.

Yours,
W. D. HOWELLS.

In a letter of April 16th to his father Howells had enclosed this cutting from the Boston *Advertiser:*

We are authorized to say that on the 1st of July next Mr. James T. Fields will retire from the editorship of the *Atlantic Monthly,* and the chair he vacates will be taken by Mr. W. D. Howells, for some years the assistant editor of the magazine. The withdrawal of Mr. Fields is in pursuance of his purpose to give up active business, and does not involve any change in the general aim and scope of the periodical with which his name has been so long connected. He will continue his papers entitled *Our Whispering Gallery* through the year; and the literary taste and standing of Mr. Howells furnish sufficient guarantee as to the future of the *Atlantic* under his management.

"My story" was *Their Wedding Journey,* of which Howells says in an earlier letter to his father:

"At last I am fairly launched upon the story of our last summer's travels, which I am giving the form of fiction so far as the characters are concerned. If I succeed in this—and I believe I shall—I see clear before me a path in literature which no one else has tried, and which I believe I can make most distinctly my own. I am going to take my people to Niagara, and then down the St. Lawrence, and so back to Boston."

That his path proved a success is shown by Howells in another letter to his father, of December 14th of the same year, where he writes:

"I meant to have sent you before this a copy of *Their Wedding Journey,* but I had great difficulty to get any of it, not being at the store in person, and only secured 8 copies on Friday out of the last lot of the 1st edition. The book was published Tuesday, and on Wednesday noon more than the whole 1500 were ordered from the publishers. Another 1000 will be out next Wednesday, but of course that will be too late for the holiday sales. 5000 could have been sold if the book had been printed a few weeks ago— Osgood says. Of course this is very harrowing as well as very flattering. I hope the sale will still continue. I send you one of the books to-day."

To William Cooper Howells

124 Tremont Street, Boston,
April 23, 1871.

DEAR FATHER:

I was so glad to learn from your last letter that you and the girls are all getting well. I think that the past week's fine weather must have given you another turn ahead, and I hope soon to know that you are in perfect repair again.—No doubt your sixty-odd years are some-thing to blame. I find my thirty-four not altogether guilt-less of the fact that I wake up every morning with sore bones, though I do no sort of bodily labor, and don't think of anything else to account for it. Seems to me that when I was younger, I had every morning a fresh feeling that's wanting now. But perhaps I forget. We are certainly none of us in this house so sick as to have any right to complain of our infirmities, except poor Mrs. Mead, who has had very much such an attack as yours, and recovers from it very slowly. The children are both remarkably well, and Elinor needs nothing but strength. It seems to me that hers is a curious case: no positive disorder, and yet this continued feebleness, which nothing seems to help. The only consola-tion is that she does not lose ground.

Last night we went to dine at the James's, and had a very pleasant evening. The most amusing thing was the visible constraint put upon old Mr. James by his family. Now and then he'd break out and say something that each of the others had to modify and explain away, and then he'd be clapped back into durance again. Willy James, who has been sick for such a long time, seems really to be getting well, at last.

A week ago I dined at Mr. Longfellow's and enjoyed myself greatly, as I always do there. I feel that I've not only been in contact with a great man, but a very good and humble man. Lately, he's asked me quite often to his house, and of course I never miss going. Did I tell you of a pleasant incident of the Bret Harte dinner there? After cigars and cordials, Longfellow's brother-in-law, Mr. Tom Appleton, proposed that he should show us the cellar of the old house, and so he lit a taper, and led the way. The cellar is perhaps 150 years old, and it's built with heavy vaults and arches of masonry and floored throughout with brick, and it looks very much like some old cloister. It gives one a most vivid idea of the honesty and earnestness with which people built in the beginning of the last century.

I have had no word from Cornell, and it is not likely that I shall lecture there this spring.

The editor of the *Independent* sent back your *Camp-Meeting,* because it was too long for them, and now I'm trying it with *Lippincott's Magazine,* of which I know the editor. I shall keep trying it. I don't think you ought to urge yourself to any sort of mental labor at present.—I send under another cover, the proof of the first part of my story. Some changes will be made in it before publishing. I'd like to know what you and the girls think of it.

All join in love to all.

Your affectionate son,
WILL.

1872

Howells's father and mother were Swedenborgians and he had been brought up in that faith. His father wrote two Swedenborgian tracts, *The Science of Correspondences*, and *The Freewill of Man and the Origin of Evil*, that were published as pamphlets by the New Church Press of London.

To William Cooper Howells

124 Tremont Street, Boston,
Jan. 28, 1872.

DEAR FATHER:

I hope you've got back safely, and have had a good time. I'm quite curious to know about your visit to Medina. All goes on with us here much in the old way; but for the past week we've suspended our theological readings. The fact is the subject has grown a little too exciting, and I should willingly never resume it if I did not think it a duty to do so. In Swedenborg I'm disappointed because I find that he makes a certain belief the condition of entering the kingdom of heaven. I always tho't that it was a good life he insisted upon, and I inferred from such religious training as you gave me that it made no difference what I believed about the trinity, or the divinity of Christ, if only I did right from a love of doing right. Now it appears to me from the Testament that Christ was a man directly, instead of indirectly, begotten by a divine father; and for this persuasion, which I owe to the reason given me of God, Swedenborg tells me I shall pass my eternal life in an insane asylum. This is hard, and I can't help revolting from it. I am not such a fool as to think I can do the highest good from myself, or that I am anything in myself; but I don't see why I cannot be humble and true and charitable, without believing that Christ was God. I am greatly disappointed, and somewhat distressed in this matter. At times I'm half minded never to read another word of theology; but to cling blindly to the moral teachings of the gospels. I should like extremely to talk with you.

I have no news that I can think of. We are all well, and send love.

Your affectionate son,
WILL.

Robert Dale Owen, son of Robert Owen, was an abolitionist. He helped to found the Smithsonian Museum and was also one of the foremost champions of spiritualism in the United States.

"Mr. John Holmes (a brother of the Doctor)," whose delightful letters were published in 1917, was a much appreciated friend, of whom Howells writes in *Literary Friends and Acquaintance*:

"Holmes was one of the first Cambridge men I knew. He held his native town in an idolatry that was not blind, but which was none the less devoted because he was aware of her droll points and her weak points. He always celebrated these as so many virtues, and I think it was my own passion for her that commended me to him.

To William Cooper Howells

124 Tremont Street, Boston,
Feb. 25, 1872.

DEAR FATHER:

Each past week seems very empty as I sit down to write of it on Sunday, and I don't know an emptier one of late than this just ended.—I'm discontented with it because I have failed to do any work worth mentioning. Socially, however, it was not so bad. On Wednesday, Elinor and I lunched at our next door neighbor's (Mr. Browne) with Robert Dale Owen and Mr. Tom Appleton—Longfellow's brother-in-law, who has never done anything but eat good dinners and say witty things, and who is the most ardent spiritualist in Boston. Of course the talk was of spiritualism, and I was surprised to find how very little that was astonishing either of these people had to say. I can't say that I doubted their experiences, but merely that they seemed unimportant and inconsequent. Still I think Mr. Owen a most charming old man, with a real light of peace and as of spiritual converse in his face. Appleton remarked this while Owen was absent, and said that the same expression was to be seen in portraits of Swedenborg.—By the way, what did you think of James's notice of Owen's book in the *Atlantic?* I believe that he pressed too far the idea of an impersonal immortality—which practically is no immortality at all. I suppose that I understand Swedenborg very dimly, but if I do understand him, it seems to me that man's state hereafter, whether in bale or bliss, is one of less dignity than on earth—that there is less play for his powers, and that the very union of his will and intellect deprives him of individual consciousness, and cripples him.—There are a thousand points I'd like to talk with you upon.

Thursday I dined with Lowell—that being his 54th birthday, and of course we had a most lovely time. No one else but Aldrich and Mr. John Holmes (a brother of the Doctor) was there. Aldrich and I had clubbed our resources, and presented Lowell with a drinking flask to carry to Europe with him—which was a very successful present. He goes in June, and I wish you'd be here before that time, for I want him to dine with you here.

With love from all to all,

Your affectionate son,

WILL.

"Shepard" was Augustus D. Shepard, Howells's brother-in-law, who had married Mrs. Howells's youngest sister, Joanna Elizabeth Mead.

To Miss Aurelia H. Howells

124 Tremont Street, Boston,
May 7, 1872.

DEAR AURELIA:

I hope you are still improving, and that this letter will find you well enough to sit up if not go out doors. I wish you were here to see how lovely the spring looks in Cambridge —it's never been so fine, so gradual, so like the Spring of poetry. Getting home from New York, I found it about ten days later than the spring there, and I dare say we're somewhat behind Jefferson, too, unless the lake ice has kept you back.

My visit in New York was a wonderful round of dinners and breakfasts. I was there five days, and never once dined alone. Osgood, whose guest I was, took me to the Union League Club, where they have some rooms at the disposal of members and their friends, and here I got a glimpse of such club-life as you read of in Thackeray. The place is a palace, and the men are so comfortable there, that I don't wonder they're in no hurry to marry and set up less splendidly for themselves.—Osgood gave a dinner for me at Delmonico's, at which among other people were Joseph Harper of Harper & Bros., John Hay, Bret Harte, Chas. Dudley Warner, Jr., W. De Forest, and the sculptor Quincy Ward. The dinner was of course very elegant, and we had lots of fun, giggling and making giggle; but I think the drollest thing that happened was Harper's getting Ward all mixed up with Artemus Ward, Mark Twain and Josh Billings, and complimenting him elaborately on his books! Warner is a very nice fellow, but looks like a Western Re-

serve Yank. I had breakfasted that morning at Elliot Shepard's, and lunched with Stedman; the next night I dined at
Shepard's with some of his Vanderbilt connection—his
brother and sister-in-law, whom I found very agreeable, and
the simplest, most unassuming people I almost ever saw.
Next day I had to go out to Scotch Plain to see Mrs. Mead,
who is quite feeble, and so I missed a lunch which Mr.
Harper wanted to give me. In the afternoon, I went down
with Henry Howells to his place on Long Island and spent
the night. It's lonely, but one of the most beautiful places
in a wild way I ever saw, and the sail to and fro on the
East River is delicious. I got back in time for a breakfast
with John Hay at the Knickerbocker Club—one of the most
aristocratic,—where I met a new company of artists, literary men and *dilettanti*—including Harte and Ward again.
It was if possible a little finer affair than the dinner, and it
fitly crowned the visit.—I made some calls on ladies with
Harte, and saw lots of people of all kinds. This merely an
outline of the business—to write it in full would take "volumes."

I enjoyed myself, but I like Boston best and Cambridge
best of all. New York is large and jolly, but it's too much of
a good thing.—We are all well and hoping soon to see
father. With love to all, and wishes for your health,

Your affectionate brother,

WILL.

This "peace Jubilee" was the second one held in Boston,
and during it *Jubilee Days, An Illustrated Daily Record of
the Humorous Features of the World's Peace Jubilee,* was
published by J. R. Osgood & Co.; it was a small paper
edited by Aldrich and Howells, with pictures by Augustus
Hoppin.

"The hundred anvils," were used in giving the "Anvil
Chorus."

To James Russell Lowell

July, 1872.

DEAR MR. LOWELL:

We have an article on the Isles of Shoals by Mrs. Thaxter, who has written indistinctly the name of one of the islands. Can you possibly tell me if it is Londoner's or Loudoner's, or either of these without the apostrophe?

You ought really to go to the Peace Jubilee. It is not only a big, but a grand thing,—as you shall learn further in the August *Atlantic.* I am going every day, though I don't expect to hear anything toward the last.—Somebody said in the crowd yesterday, that the ceremonies were to begin with prayer by a hundred ministers. I got in too late for this; but it is all true about the hundred anvils.

Yours ever,

W. D. HOWELLS.

The "new house" was number 37 Concord Avenue, and "Bua" was a corruption of "Boy" that Howells's son applied to himself.

"My story" was *A Chance Acquaintance.*

The "Perry" of this letter and many others, was Thomas Sergeant Perry, a boyhood's friend of Henry James and a manhood's friend of Howells, equally valued in a triangular friendship that time and distance never diminished. Howells held that Perry knew more about literature than any man living, and they walked and talked it together, sometimes in America and sometimes in Europe. They joined in compiling *The Library of Adventure by Sea and Land,* a subscription book intended to make their united fortunes; which it would have done if the public had only enjoyed reading it as much as they had enjoyed making it.

"My friend Boyesen" was Hjalmar Hjorth Boyesen, the author of *Gunnar* and many other novels.

To Henry James

The Atlantic Monthly, Boston,
September 1, 1872.

MY DEAR JAMES:

If I attempted a letter of the generous length of yours,
I should feel bound to give it up at the start, but if you'll
let me begin with four modest pages, I think you may hear
from me soon, at any rate. The days go by here very much
as usual, and with that strong family likeness to each other
which would enable one to recognize a Cambridge day anywhere, but their going has at least brought the long terrible summer to an end, and that's some merit. In the meantime, we take a very great interest in the new house which
this daring family has begun to build. The lot is part of
Mr. Parson's garden, on Concord Avenue, and not far from
the Observatory grounds. The cellar is dug, and the lumber
is partly on the ground, and every day Winny and Bua and
I visit the place, they to play on the sand and boards, and
I to watch the cellar wall a-building, and admire at myself
for giving employment to four men, two boys and two
horses. The money's all somehow to come out of me, but as
yet, the future house and the opportunity of letting the poor
earn their bread, seem to be freely bestowed upon me by
some good power outside of me. My satisfaction is marred
by nothing but occasional thoughts of my story, which I
brought to a close in July with such triumphal feelings that
I would not have exchanged my prospect of immortality
through it for the fame of Shakespeare. Now I regard
it with cold abhorrence, and work it over, shuddering.
This too must pass away: anyhow I begin printing in January, and I dare say I shall be ready to agree, and more,
with anybody who praises it. Your own story—*Guest's
Confession*—opens in the October number, and closes in
November. I think I shall put the Florentine story into

January. *Guest's Confession* reads excellently, I assure you, and I'm certain will make favor for you. On some accounts I'm sorry you couldn't have brought out a volume this fall; it would have served to assemble the liking and reputation you've won. I think yet you might make a successful book of the romantic tales.

I have seen something more than usual of Perry, lately; and I'm working hard to get him the sub-editorship of the *North American Review.* It depends upon the problematical chief, for the publishers are quite willing. I think it a pity Perry should go to New York, and be Dennettized. One Dennett's enough—and to spare. The *Nation* has regularly brought me your letters, and I've liked them, as I like everything of yours. If you asked me, I should say you tended a little too much to the metaphysical expression of travel, as opposed to the graphic; but this tendency is what I heard Lowell praise when I objected to it before. At present they have no chief on the *North American Review.* The October number was left *planted,* by both the late editors, and I'm putting it together from such material as I can get, and proof-reading it. My friend Boyesen has been here all summer, but has now gone back to Urbana. I'm to print a Norwegian story for him next year. What do you intend to do for literature in '73?—a year destined to be famous.

I send love from my wife with my own to your whole party, and I hope you'll write as promptly as I have written. I see your people rather often, now; but I have long seasons of non-intercourse with mankind when I feel too inert to transact the social pleasures, though I've always the grace to be ashamed of myself.

Yours evermore,
W. D. HOWELLS.

P. S. Of course it's all right about Miss ———'s poem. It was good enough to print; but my chief pleasure in printing it would have been the thought that it gratified the Bootts. To whom, by the way, please remember me cordially, in any communication you have with them. The weather is so fresh that I've a fire in my stove this morning; and if you were here, we might take the longest and briskest walk of the year without discomfort. Alas! how the years go by, and how little they leave behind. When I think of the walks we have taken, we seem less substantial in the past than the shadows of the clouds that drifted over the same autumnal paths. Sometimes the whole intolerable mystery of the thing comes over me suffocatingly—and I don't feel as if a first-class notice in the *Nation* were worth striving for. But this of course is disease. I hope you are happy, and that you are putting by for the public a store of the honey you find on those Swiss mountain sides. But I don't envy you those acclivities, but O my lagoons of Venice, and the seaweedy smell of the shallows!—those I do begrudge. *Ricorditi di me*—when you lie there in your boat, and at least say, Poor Howells, he liked Venice, though perhaps he didn't understand her.

IX

1873, 1874

A Chance Acquaintance. Atlantic *sold to Hurd & Houghton.*
Poems. *Editorial experiences on the* Atlantic. *Translates d'Aste's*
Sansone. A Foregone Conclusion.

"MY STORY" was *A Chance Acquaintance,* and the
"new story" was *A Foregone Conclusion.* "Your
Madonna" was Henry James's *Madonna of the Future,*
printed in the March *Atlantic* of that year. "Your Roman
romance" was *The Last of the Valerii,* and "the Delphic
Dennett," the critic of the New York *Nation.*

To Henry James

Cambridge, March 10, 1873.

MY DEAR JAMES:

I hope you'll be properly affected by the size of this sheet:
its extent is an emblem of my friendship for you, for I'm
reducing the size of my notepaper generally.

First let me thank you with all my heart for your criticism
on my story—rather, on my heroine. It came too late for
the magazine; but I have been able to check the young
person a little before handing her down to the latest posterity in book form. Her pertness was but another proof of the
contrariness of her sex. I meant her to be everything that
was lovely, and went on protesting that she was so, but she
preferred being saucy to the young man, especially in that
second number. Afterwards I think she is at least all I pro-
fess for her. I like her because she seems to me a character;
the man, I own is a simulacrum. Well- or ill-advisedly I
conceived the notion of confronting two extreme American

types: the conventional and the unconventional. These always disgust each other, but I amused myself with the notion of their falling in love, which would not be impossible, if they were both young and good looking. Now conventionality is, in our condition of things, in itself a caricature; and I did my best for the young man, but his nature was against him, and he is the stick you see. Of course the girl must be attracted by what is elegant and fine in him, and provoked to any sort of reprisal by his necessary, cool assumption of superiority. She cannot very well help "sassing" him, though she feels that this puts her at a disadvantage, and makes her seem the aggressor. I have tried to let this explain itself to the reader as much as I can; but it is a kind of thing that scarcely admits of dramatic demonstration, and I feel that the whole thing is weighed down with comment. However, I've learnt a great deal in writing the story, and if it does not destroy my public, I shall be weaponed better than ever for the field of romance. And I am already thirty pages advanced on a new story, in which, blessed be heaven, there is no problem but the sweet old one of how they shall get married. In this case I'm sorry to say they don't solve it, for the hero is a Venetian priest in love with an American girl. There's richness! And now peace to me and my work. I've been burning to tell you how much I like your "Madonna," and to report the undissenting voice of acclaim with which it has been hailed. Ever so many people have spoken of it, the Delphic Dennett alone remaining mum. Truly it has been a success, and justly, for it is a bravely solid and excellent piece of work. All like the well-managed pathos of it, the dissertations on pictures, the tragic, most poetical central fact, and I hope that many feel with me its unity and completeness. Every figure in it is a real character, and has some business there. The sole blemish on it to my mind is the insistence on the cats and monkeys philosophy. I don't think you ought to have let that *artista* appear a second time, and, I confess, to have the cats and monkeys for a refrain at the close, marred the fine harmony of what went before, till I managed to forget them. I have your Roman romance, and I shall print it very soon. I like it, but I shall tell you more about it when I get it in print. I'm glad that we're to hear from you every month, and I rejoice that you think of doing a serial for next year. Whether you'll find Venice a good working climate, I'm not sure. I'd rather do my loafing there. But it's delicious in early summer, and with sea-baths, I don't see why you shouldn't get on.

All the family at Casa Howells are well; but they have had their colds and other woes this winter. My wife in particular has been very delicate, though with a little promise of spring she's at least gaining courage if not health again. She agrees with you about Kitty's pertness, and is otherwise my terriblest critic, as always. The children are all that a fond papa could desire. The two oldest, you know, but little maid Mildred is the jolliest and prettiest of all. She is really a little beauty, and as amiable as the day is long.

The house gets on as well as could be expected in a winter which has forbidden plastering. It's all finished outside, and we're to be in it—if we put our faith in carpenters—by the first of June. You divine truly that I have seen no one this winter. The other night I went to one of the Rev. Peabody receptions, and to-morrow we're invited to the Golden Wedding of Dr. and Mrs. Palfrey. About once in three weeks Mr. Longfellow has regularly taken pity on me, and had me to dinner. This is the whole story. I don't know whether anything's been going on or not, but I love all my fellow men here as heartily as if I had met the whole human family once a week. I thank you for not telling me too much about Rome. Such things are hard to bear. I hate the American in Europe,—because I am not he. At times the longing is almost intolerable with me, and if I could see any way of keeping the bird in the hand while I clutched at those in the bush, I should go. I have a scheme for work some day in Italy which I hope to carry out. It would take me there just about the time the children should be studying French and music and keep me there five years. *M'aspetti! Intanto le reverisco!* Mrs. Howells and the children join me in love.

Yours ever,
W. D. HOWELLS.

P. S. I'm glad Osgood is to get out a volume for you. Imagine getting up this morning and finding a heavy snow-storm in full blast. It was almost heart-breaking. We've now had three months of snow and sleighing.

"Our house" progressed steadily, and on July 20th Howells wrote to his father:

"This is the first letter I write in my beautiful new library, which is more charming than I could make you understand by the longest description. The ceiling is richly frescoed; below the cornice, and running down to the chair-board the room is a soft buff paper and then dark red to the floor. The book-casing, drawers and closet are heavy chestnut; the hearth is of tiles, and the chimney-piece rises in three broad shelves almost to the cornice. This is the glory of the room and is splendidly carved, and set with picture-tiles and mirrors; on either jamb of the mantel is my monogram, carved, and painted by Elinor, who modified and improved the carpenter's design of the whole affair. This splendor was all a present to me from the builder, and was kept a secret until Friday afternoon when I was allowed to behold it for the first time. The work on the other rooms is nearly finished, now, and nothing remains but the papering of our parlor."

To William Cooper Howells

124 Tremont Street, Boston,
April 6, 1873.

DEAR FATHER:

Bua has been in doubt lately whether he should be a soldier, a sailor, or an artist; but this morning he came swaggering into the library and said he was not going to be either of those: "I'm to be *just a common man,*—like you, papa!" This rather stung my vanity, and I made him understand, as well as I could, that to be an author was not to be a common man, at all. So he is going to be an author, he says. But I really think his destiny is art in some form. He has the quickest and most correct eye, and he is always observing lines and shapes. He goes about with two pencils in his pocket, and is always drawing something.

Have any of you at home been reading *Middlemarch?* We are now reading it aloud, with ever growing amazement at its greatness. I think it's very badly executed, as a piece of literary art, but as an intellectual achievement, it is wonderful. It's richly worth reading.

I see by the last *Sentinel* that you've been having trouble over Garfield's vote on the salaries. It looks like quackery on the part of those who assail him; but it's a pity that he had not at once refused to take his back salary. But I don't agree with you that the salaries were sufficient before. As things go, they were not living salaries, and must have continually tempted members to large and small stealings. But the trouble is far back of all that. I'm afraid that the people themselves have corrupt and loose ideas and principles.— Luxury has undermined everything. That sort of race redemption for which old James hopes is not at hand yet; perhaps we're just now being "let into our evils" as a preliminary to it.

Our house has the first coat of plastering on it at last,

and it begins to look like a house in earnest. It's very pretty, and I wish you could see it.

With united love to all,
Your aff'te son,
WILL.

John Hay had written Howells of his engagement to Miss Stone.

To John Hay

The Atlantic Monthly, Boston,
Aug. 31, 1873.

MY DEAR HAY:

While I lament my own loss, I rejoice that you are so much more profitably employed than you could be in writing for the *Atlantic*. Love-letters are the true belles-lettres, and it is a privilege and an honor to devote one's self to them, not permitted to every man of genius. Rumor has already blabbed your news to me, and I only waited your sign to offer you the congratulations which I now do with all my heart. If I'm so unlucky as to come to New York too late to see Miss Stone's fotograf, I shall make bold to ask an introduction to Mrs. Hay.

My wife joins me in regards.

Yours ever,
W. D. HOWELLS.

P. S. I've been struggling to believe that I have had an indirect acquaintance with Miss Stone. But I give up. I find that I've only heard of her through Miss Huntington of Cincinnati, who told my sister-in-law, Mrs. Shepard of New York, about her. What I heard I should have thought rather extravagant praise for a saint in Paradise, but I know that it would appear mere derogation to you; so I don't write it.

W. D. H.

"The Mercato Tom-Brewero" was an Italian version of

the shop where most of literary Cambridge did its market-
ing. There is a story that once when John Fiske paid an
installment on a long-outstanding bill there, he said to the
astonished proprietor, "And now, Mr. Brewer, we will let
bygones be bygones." Mrs. Howells was much given to
memoranda, and a friend who had exchanged his overcoat
for her husband's first discovered his mistake by finding in
the pocket a slip of paper saying briefly, "Blow Brewer."

In an earlier letter of August 26th to James, Howells
says of *A Chance Acquaintance:*

"Directly after I got your last letter I sent you my
book, which I hope you received. You would be amused at
the letters I get—some forty, now—from people unknown
to me—begging for a sequel. The trouble is that they are of
such various minds as to what the end ought to be. Miss
Lane writes us from Quebec that half a dozen gentlemen have called, to see the rooms in which Kitty lived. This,
I take it, is being a novelist in dead earnest, and I am push-
ing forward my Venetian priest's story all I can; but I
shall hardly begin printing it before next summer."

"My poetry" was his *Poems,* just published in 1873, and
the "new story" was *A Foregone Conclusion.*

"Dr. Holland" was Josiah Gilbert Holland, who, with
Roswell Smith, and in connection with the Charles Scribner
Company, founded *Scribner's Magazine.*

The *Atlantic* had been sold to Hurd and Houghton.

To Henry James

The Atlantic Monthly, Boston,
Dec. 5, 1873.

MY DEAR JAMES:

To-day, I met your mother on the Corso, in the vicinity
of the Mercato Tom-Brewero, and she gave me your news,
as you Italians say. Part of these was that you had been
writing a notice of my poetry for the *North American,* but

that you had been anticipated by another "party"—and the review was at home, in manuscript, and I might read it before it was sent off to seek its fortune. This I did with great consolation and thankfulness, for the leaf that has been commonly bestowed upon my poetical works by the critics of this continent has not been the laurel leaf—rather rue, or cypress. You have indeed treated my poor little book with a gracious kindness which I shall not forget; and I hope it isn't immodest to add with the first real discernment that has been shown by its critics. Thanks; and whilst I am in the way of it let me thank you also for what you say in your last letter both in praise and in blame of *A Chance Acquaintance*. Your strictures are fairly made, and I know that I ran along the edge of a knife-blade to reach that dénouement. Sometimes it seems to me all clumsily wrong; and again I have the motive as clearly before me, as I had at first, and feel that nothing could drive me from that conclusion. But much is to be said against it, and you have said it very justly. As to the new story, it draws near the end, with, I hope, a gathering intensity. I long to get it all once fairly on paper, so that I can view it as a whole, and begin to clean it up a bit. The effects are still so much in the rough, so much at lose ends, that I have a certain *brivido* in touching it, and I should like to jump the rest down at once. I have to work at it so interruptedly, too, that the pleasure of working at it is greatly marred. Excuse, as Artemus Ward says, the apparent egotism. I have your *Last of the Valerii* in the January number, and I like it very much. It did not strike me so favorably in manuscript as it does in print; but now I think it excellent. By the way, I hope you won't send any of your stories to *Scribner's*. We have of course no claim upon you, but we have hitherto been able to print all the stories you have sent, and so it shall be hereafter. Scribner is trying to lure away all our contributors, with the siren song of Doctor Holland, and my professional pride is touched. Your *Chain of Cities* goes into the February, and your *Siena,* which is charming, into the March number. And what do you think of our dear old *Atlantic's* being sold! But it changes nothing but the publisher's imprint; even the editor remains the same. Aldrich and I had a Black Thursday when we heard our periodicals were in a state of barter, and scarcely knew whether we were to be sold with them or not. But we were both made over. I am sorry to part with Osgood, who was a good master; but Hurd and Houghton promise me fair, and you know they were my first publishers. The printing will hereafter be done at the Riverside Press; and if you were again in Cambridge, I hope we should have many a stretch across the flats together. In one's own company it is not a merry walk, especially in winter. But I console myself with thinking that it is business and not pleasure, anyway. The social season in Cambridge opens with some sprightliness. I was at your brother Wilkie's Infare, which was full of enjoyment for me, and apparently for everybody else. I seem to be dining out a good deal, too; even to-night I am going to Col. Dodge's on Quincy street. Dinner at 7—what do you think of that for our simple Cambridge? I haven't fairly got used yet to the Nortons being at home, and I haven't seen Charles more than twice. He is better in health, but he comes home with a dreadfully high standard for us all. We may attain it as blessed spirits a thousand years hence. The fall-and-winter Englishman is beginning to appear. I have met him twice—at your house and at the Gurneys'; a very peaceful Briton, indeed, and disposed to inform himself. To this end he has bought my "works," as I'm given to know. There is also a Russian amongst us, studying bugs with Agassiz—one Baron Ooten—something, whom I want to be calling Gregory Ivanovitch, out of Turgénief.

Our babes are all well, and Mrs. Howells sends you her warmest regards. No more at present.

Affectionately yours,

W. D. HOWELLS.

1874

Of Keeler, in *Literary Friends and Acquaintance,* Howells says:

"Ralph Keeler wrote the *Vagabond Adventures* which he had lived. He had been, as he claimed, 'a cruel uncle's ward' in his early orphanhood, and while yet a child he had run away from home, to fulfil his heart's desire of becoming a clog-dancer in a troupe of Negro minstrels. But it was first his fate to be cabin-boy and boot-black on a lake steamboat. When he did become a dancer (and even a danseuse) of the type he aspired to be, the fruition of his hopes was so little what he imagined that he was very willing to leave the Floating Palace on the Mississippi in which his troupe voyaged and exhibited, and enter the college of the Jesuit Fathers at Cape Girardeau in Missouri. From college Keeler went to Europe, and then to California, whence he wrote me that he was coming on to Boston with the manuscript of a novel which he wished me to read for the magazine. I reported against it to my chief, but nothing could shake Keeler's faith in it, until he had printed it at his own cost, and known it to fail instantly and decisively. He had come to Cambridge to see it through the press, and he remained there four or five years. Then, during the Cuban insurrection of the early seventies, he accepted the invitation of a New York newspaper to go to Cuba as its correspondent. He went and he did not come back. He was not indeed garroted as his friends had promised, but he was probably assassinated on the steamer by which he sailed from Santiago, for he never arrived in Havana, and was never heard of again."

To M. M. Hurd

The Atlantic Monthly, Jan. 9, 1874.

DEAR HURD:

I'm glad that Stedman's going to send me something, and

I hope that Stoddard will do so by and by. He never has sent more than one poem during the eight years I've been here: that I declined not for literary reasons, but because it was calculated to trouble our religious readers. Harper could have printed it with impunity; but the *Atlantic*, with its repute for scepticism, could not. As for putting him on the same footing with Emerson and Longfellow, I should do that willingly if he were as great.

I'm glad you like the February number. I hope to make that for March still better; and in fact I've got good material for the whole year.—I'm afraid that the *Polaris* is now rather past as a sensation; though without doubt if some survivor of it could tell his story it would be intensely interesting. I don't think a series would do: the Arctic business has been exploited a great deal, already.

I've not yet seen Aldrich's paper on Keeler, though I know what it is. Poor fellow! It does seem too sad to lose him in that way. He was a man who had ever so much kindness in him, and his death is a real tragedy. You know he left with me his narrative of Owen Brown's escape from Harper's Ferry, dictated to him by O. B. himself—one of the most intensely interesting things I've ever read. I hope to print it in March or April. It's entirely non-partizan.

In March we shall have a poem from Emerson—the first contribution for four or five years.

I wish you'd write me each month what you think of the magazine, and any very pertinent comment, for or against, that you hear.—I have always been a faithful reader of all notices of the mag., and I'm anxious to know as much of public opinion as I can; though I don't rely greatly upon it —it's fickle.

Mrs. Howells joins me in regards to you and yours.

Very sincerely,

W. D. HOWELLS.

Howells, in explaining the circumstances of this letter in *Literary Friends and Acquaintance,* says of Emerson:

"He had given me upon much entreaty a poem which was one of his greatest and best, but a proof-reader found a nominative at odds with its verb. We had some trouble in reconciling them, and some other delays, and meanwhile Doctor Holmes offered me a poem for the same number. I now doubted whether I should get Emerson's poem back in time for it, but unluckily the proof did come back in time, and then I had to choose between my poets, or acquaint them with the state of the case, and let them choose what I should do. I really felt that Doctor Holmes had the right of precedence, since Emerson had withheld his proof so long that I could not count upon it; but I wrote to Emerson, and asked (as nearly as I can remember) whether he would consent to let me put his poem over to the next number, or would prefer to have it appear in the same number with Doctor Holmes's; the subjects were cognate, and I had my misgivings. He wrote me back to 'return the proofs and break up the forms.' I could not go to this iconoclastic extreme with the electrotypes of the magazine, but I could return the proofs. I did so, feeling that I had done my possible, and silently grieving that there could be such ire in heavenly minds."

To Ralph Waldo Emerson

The Atlantic Monthly, Cambridge, Mass.,
January 22, 1874.

MY DEAR SIR:

On looking at the enclosed proof I hope you may still find it possible to let me have your poem for publication in the March *Atlantic*. It seems to me that its interest depends only in the very slightest degree upon the occasion to which it refers. Of course this is a matter for you to decide: but I venture to say that none of your readers would attach more or less value to *any* poem of yours because it was printed a month earlier or later. I shall be very sorry indeed if I lose your poem, but I should regret infinitely more the appearance of having been at all wanting in consideration. Let me explain, therefore, that three or four days elapsed before you even conditionally consented to let me have the poem. A week or more passed then, and when I wrote for your final decision, you did not answer me. Finally, on the 5th of January you sent the poem, when the last forms of the February number were ready for casting, and when, if I had thought it well to put it in near Dr. Holmes's poem, the proof-reading would have delayed the publication of the number several days. I now see that the better course for me would have been to return the poem to you, and ask your consent anew for its publication in the March number. However, you can suppress now, if you will, and the same end will be reached as if I *had* returned it. With me the mortification of losing it will be sufficient penance for my over-anxiety to keep it.

Very respectfully yours,
W. D. HOWELLS.

MR. EMERSON.

Comly was the "Clive Newcome" of Columbus days, who had become the editor of the Columbus *Ohio State Journal*.

"The doctor" was Dr. S. M. Smith, who had insisted upon lending Howells money when he was going to Venice and whose daughter Comly had married.

To J. M. Comly

Cambridge, March 21, 1874.

MY DEAR COMLY:

Many thanks for your news of the doctor and your family. It's all so sad that it's hard to realize now how much better it is than it has been. You say very little of yourself, my dear old fellow: I hope that your health endures the tremendous strain on it. I send back the dispatch, thinking you'd perhaps like to keep it.

Did I speak in my last of the charming visit I'd had with Warner and Mark Twain at Hartford? It seems to me quite an ideal life. They live very near each other, in a sort of suburban grove, and their neighbors are the Stowes and Hookers, and a great many delightful people. They go in and out of each other's houses without ringing, and nobody gets more than the first syllable of his first name—they call their minister *Joe* Twichell. I staid with Warner, but of course I saw a good deal of Twain, and he's a thoroughly great fellow. His wife is a delicate little beauty, the very flower and perfume of *ladylikeness,* who simply adores him —but this leaves no word to describe his love for her. As for Warner and his wife, they are all that you could desire them. I hope you'll be able to come on here some day, and see all the nice people I'm saving up for you!

With our united love to your wife,

· Yours ever,

W. D. H.

Lowell's poem was his *Agassiz,* printed in the May *Atlantic,* 1874.

Larkin Mead's studio was in Florence.

To James Russell Lowell

Cambridge, March 29, 1874.

DEAR MR. LOWELL:

I'm immensely glad to get your poem, (which is now in type for the May no.,) not only as editor, but as a lover of great verse. I hear you speak it from the print—it is so like you; it has a sanguine complexion and a mellow voice; it is thought through and through as no one but Lowell could have thought it, and it embodies Agassiz perfectly. Everywhere are lines in it that give me high delight, but I believe I like it best from

> Now forth into the darkness

on to the end. The mood seems to me even finer than that of *The Cathedral,* and the poem has a greater simplicity or singleness of motive. You seem to me unique for the sort of warm-colored thinking I find in such poems as this and the *Commemoration Ode.* I could only compare you with the famousest, and then I should not find your like save in greatness.—The phrase is priceless, but I hated to have you say "Land of Broken Promise." I don't believe you believe it.

It was very good of you, and very like you to visit Larkin Mead's studio. Mrs. Howells and I are both grateful to you.—We write our regards to Mrs. Lowell.—I long to have you home again.

Affectionately yours,
W. D. HOWELLS.

To James Russell Lowell

The Riverside Press, Cambridge, Mass.,
May 25, 1874.

DEAR MR. LOWELL:

It made me very happy to get a letter from you to-night. It came just in time to be read aloud at tea to Mrs. Howells; and we said, with that disposition to kiss your hand which we have whenever we think of it, that this letter looked exactly like that letter you wrote me at Venice accepting my *Recent Italian Comedy:* I got it from the *postiere* in Campiello dei Squellini, and we both went up to heaven at once. But that letter had a blue envelope and this a white one.—My wife and all the children join me in love to you and Mrs. Lowell.

I've sent your message to Aldrich whom I haven't the least idea you've offended in any way. We've often talked of you, and he simply seemed loth to trouble you with letters. But I've no doubt he'll write now.—It was by pure accident that your name was left out of the list of contributors, and we all gnashed our teeth over the omission. As for the new proprietors, they were only too proud and happy to get your poem, and will be glad of anything more you can give us. I wish we might have a contribution from you every month. Mr. Houghton is wise enough to think there is no one like you. The *Agassiz* got us repeated orders from the news-companies.

I have written to Osgood, and as soon as I learn that the poem is in the printer's hands, I'll make the corrections you give me.

We go to Jaffrey, N. H., for the summer, but I shall run down to see you, when you come. I'm immensely glad you've set the time for returning, though I don't wonder you hate on some accounts to turn your back on the Mother-World. But America is worth a thousand of her, after all, in spite of the cynical utterances of a certain poet who shall be nameless, and I would not on any account go back—for less than a two years' stay. You see what it is to be a true patriot. In fact it comes very natural at this time of year in Cambridge to love one's country. The apple-blossoms are worth all that past of which Mr. Norton sighs to find us disinherited. There is one apple-tree in Miss Wyman's back yard worth the whole of the middle-ages. And only imagine the orioles tilting the cups of blooms, and draining the honeyed heel-taps everywhere.

A rivederci presto!

W. D. HOWELLS.

"The play" was a translation of Ippolito d'Aste's play of *Sansone* which was acted by Tommaso Salvini on his

American tours. The translation was acted by Pope under the title of *Samson*.

To S. L. Clemens

The Atlantic Monthly, Boston,
July 11, 1874.

MY DEAR CLEMENS:

Your letter and telegram came to our mosquitory bower whilst I was away in Canada, and I failed to see Mr. Pope here. But Thursday I ran down to Boston to call on him, and I've arranged to translate the play for him. As it is owing to your kindness that I'm thus placed in relation with the stage—a long-coveted opportunity—I may tell you the terms on which I make the version. He pays me $400 outright on acceptance of my version, and $100 additional when the play has run fifty nights; and $1 a night thereafter as long as it runs. When my translation is done, I'm to tell him, and he will send his check for $400 to you, and I'll submit my MS. to him. If he likes it, you send me the check; if he doesn't, you return it to him.

You perceive this isn't hard on Mr. Pope. The terms were my own—he would have given me $500 down, but I didn't think he ought to buy a pig in a poke, and I felt that I ought to take some risk of a failure. I liked Mr. Pope very much, and I should be glad of his acquaintance, even if there were no money in it. As it is, imagine my gratitude to you!

My regards to all your family.

Yours ever,
W. D. HOWELLS.

The "fable" which Howells could not take was *A Fable for Good Old Boys and Girls*.

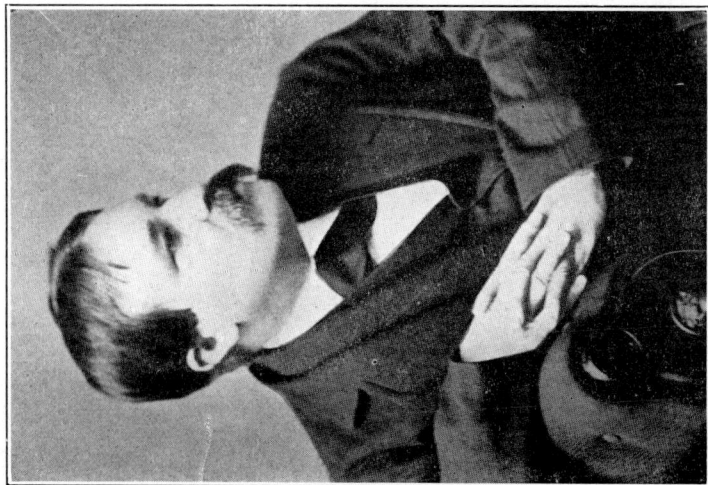

Howells in about 1874, when editor of the *Atlantic*

Howells in 1888, when he wrote *A Hazard of New Fortunes*

To S. L. Clemens

The Atlantic Monthly, September 8, 1874.

MY DEAR CLEMENS:

I'm going to settle *your* opinion of the next installment of *A Foregone Conclusion* by sending back one of your contributions. Not, let me hasten to say, that I don't think they're both very good. But the *Atlantic,* as regards matters of religion, is just in that Good Lord, Good Devil condition when a little fable like yours wouldn't leave it a single Presbyterian, Baptist, Unitarian, Episcopalian, Methodist or Millerite *paying* subscriber—all the dead-heads would stick to it, and abuse it in the denominational newspapers. Send your fable to some truly pious concern like Scribner or Harper, and they'll extract it into all the hymn-books. But it would ruin *us.*

I've kept the *True Story* which I think extremely good and touching, with the best and reallest kind of black talk in it. Perhaps it couldn't be better than it is; but if you feel like giving it a little more circumstantiation (you didn't know there was such a word as that, did you?) on getting the proof, why, don't mind making the printers some over-running.

The fotografs were most welcome, and I'm sorry that I can't send back anything but thanks. I admire the attitude and the asthma, and the whole landscape, and I've put them all three up on the mantelpiece where I can look at them whenever so disposed.

There are parts of the *Fable* that I think wonderfully good even for you—that touch about Sisyphus and Atlas being ancestors of the tumble-bug, did tickle me.

Pope writes back and pretends to be overjoyed with the version of *Samson.*

My best regards to Mrs. Clemens, for whose speedy recovery I devoutly wish.

Yours ever,
W. D. HOWELLS.

"Brunetta" was Eugenio Brunetta, of whom Howells says in *A Young Venetian Friend:*

"We lived in greater and greater ease with one another; he became a house friend of such inclusiveness that after a year or so, when we went a journey to Rome and Naples and left our little one in charge of her uncle the sculptor, who came from Florence to be my vice-consul, Biondini [Brunetta] joined him in the care of the baby and the consulate."

Howells and this Venetian friend had taught each other their respective tongues, and when he returned to Italy in 1882 Brunetta was living in Verona, where they renewed their friendship.

"Padre Giacomo" was Padre Giacome Issaverdanz, a brother in the Armenian Convent of San Lazzaro at Venice. He was a friend of Howells and served as the suggestion for Don Ippolito in *A Foregone Conclusion,* though the story itself had no connection with him. He often breakfasted with the Howellses in Venice and in *Venetian Life* Howells says:

"Our breakfast-table talk wrought to friendship the acquaintance made some time before, and the next morning we received the photograph of Padre Giacomo, and the compliments of the Orient, in a heaped basket of ripe and luscious figs from the garden of the Convent San Lazzaro. When, in turn, we went to visit him at the convent we had experience of a more curious oriental hospitality. Refreshments were offered to us as friends, and we lunched fairly upon little dishes of rose leaves, delicately preserved, with all their fragrance, in a 'lucent sirup.' It seemed this was a common conserve in the East; but we could hardly divest ourselves of the notion of sacrilege, as we fed upon the very most luxurious sweetness and perfume of the soul of the soul of summer."

When Howells returned to Venice in 1883 the preserved rose leaves had changed to Turkish Paste, Crumbs of Comfort much appreciated by the children of the family, but the old friendship was unchanged, and remained so until Padre Giacomo's death in the monastery he had retired to in Armenia.

To Charles Dudley Warner

The Atlantic Monthly, Cambridge, Mass.,
Sept. 28, 1874.

MY DEAR WARNER:

(What makes you address me as *Mr.* Howells? I'm always afraid you're mad at something.) Your letter renewed the pang of parting, and at the same time was most welcome, for it had already come to seem a long time since we had passed a word with you.

Sept. 30. And still longer, now, after my letting the foregoing sentiments ripen a couple of days. I'm so glad you stopped for the Saturday Club dinner. Yesterday Dr. Holmes was here, and spoke of his pleasure in meeting you. But who doesn't do that? Mrs. Warner and you have made our little lunch-party an admired success; and as for the visit, how could it help being nice when there were such materials of triumph in the visitors? There! How do you feel *now?*—It would have been better, wouldn't it, to let the Houghtons come an hour earlier with the carriage? The delay is the only thing I have against you, and Mrs. Howells says (from the force of habit) that even that was all my fault.

To-morrow we go to a private reading in Mr. Long-fellow's parlor, where a young Readress is to make her first appearance.—There's no other news, I'm afraid. I send you a pair of introductions. Brunetta is my dear friend, whom I saw every day in Venice, and who taught me that poor small Italian I know. Padre Giacomo you've met already. I'll send other letters before you get to Venice.

We *do* love you both. Come back safe, and don't you dare enjoy a single thing without saying, "How the Howellses would like this!"—I should like a mummy if you can get one cheap.—The Grays gave a garden-party for you yesterday afternoon.—Elinor will answer Mrs. Warner, to whom she now sends love with me.

Affectionately yours ever,
W. D. HOWELLS.

Mark Twain's "little story" was *A True Story,* which appeared in the *Atlantic* for November of that year.

To M. M. Hurd

The Atlantic Monthly, Nov. 7, 1874.

MY DEAR HURD:

I'm shocked to find that I've let your last, very kind letter go so long unanswered, the more so that I ought to have replied to your question about the book publication of *A Foregone Conclusion.* The arrangement for that was made with Osgood before the transfer of the magazine, and referring your query to Mr. Scudder I found that he had this understanding of the matter.

Our Bret Harte negotiation *did* fall through, but I've more than made good the loss by securing Mark Twain for a series of sketches next year. I'm glad you liked his little story, for I thought it wonderfully good—one of the most artistic things in its way that I'd ever seen.

If our contributors all keep their promises, we shall have
a great year in 1875, and I do hope the subscription list
will sympathize. I should work with so much better heart if
I felt that I was on a mounting wave. Not but that I think
I've done pretty well *in quantity* this year, for besides editing, etc., I've written a *hundred and forty pages* of the
magazine. You won't be surprised if I don't do so much
next year, I hope.

I'm sorry to return Mrs. ——'s poem which I should
keep if it were good enough. Of course you know there is
no *Atlantic* "ring," and I commonly find that people who
pretend to believe in such a thing are those who want to
influence editors by something besides the merit of their
work.

Yours ever,
W. D. HOWELLS.

In January we shall have Longfellow, Holmes, Mark
Twain, Aldrich, Stoddard [R. H.], Miss Phelps, Owen,
etc.

"The letter from Limerick" was addressed to Mrs. Clemens and supposed to be written in the year 1835, but it was
really intended for Howells, Twichell, and Aldrich, who
figure in it as the Lord High Admiral, the Archbishop of
Dublin, and the Marquis of Ponkapog.

"The piece about the Mississippi" was one of the *Old
Times on the Mississippi* papers which appeared monthly
in the *Atlantic* from January until July, in 1875.

To S. L. Clemens

The Atlantic Monthly, November 23, 1874.

DEAR CLEMENS:

The deliberation with which I respond to your letters of
Friday is but a faint token of the delight that their coming

gave me. I hope you're going to let me keep the letter from Limerick: at any rate I'm going to keep it till I've showed it round—especially to Aldrich and Osgood. I quite agree with Twichell about its deliciousness. You not like Lamb! When the L. in your name stands for Lamb, and you know very well that you were christened Charles, and afterwards changed it to Samuel, for a joke. Mrs. Howells is simply absurd about it, and thinks it better than the most tragical mirth in *A Foreg. Conc.*

The piece about the Mississippi is capital—it almost made the water in our ice-pitcher muddy as I read it, and I hope to send you a proof directly. I don't think I shall meddle much with it even in the way of suggestion. The sketch of the low-lived little town was so good, that I could have wished ever so much more of it; and perhaps the tearful watchman's story might have beeen abridged—tho this may seem different in print. I want the sketches, if you can make them, *every month.*

Don't say another word about being late at lunch. I hope we know how to forgive a deadly injury,—especially when we know what is going to happen to the person when he dies.

Mrs. Howells thanks you ever so much for the fotografs. We both admire the babies, who seem to have behaved uncommonly well under fire of the fotografer, and to have come out seriously charming. We think they and the house the prettiest in the world. Give our best regards to Mrs. Clemens and the Twichells.

Your visit was an inexpressible pleasure. We hope for that great day when you shall bring your wife.

Yours ever,
W. D. Howells.

"My book" was *A Chance Acquaintance.* "The Doctor" was Doctor J. G. Holland.

To Edmund Clarence Stedman

The Atlantic Monthly, Dec. 8, 1874.

DEAR STEDMAN:

You won't think it in immediate return for your kind words that I send you my book, for I had it in my mind to to so ever since it came out. But I *am* glad of your praise, and I thank you for offering to review me in *Scribner's*. I'm rather amused than otherwise by the attitude of the Doctor. If he would only do me the favor to write a good poem, I should exult to commend it in the *Atlantic*, though he had just been making an attempt on my life. In fact, I've tried several people of taste with "The M. of the M.," and nobody would promise to praise it or even to spare it, so I tho't it best to let it go unvexed. I knew very well that they wouldn't print anything friendly about me or anything *by* me from my experience with the Aldrich biography, which I offered to do out of pure good will to him, and which the Doctor denied me the high privilege of doing under threats to his publishers of resignation. I suppose he can say now with a good conscience that I'm angry because *Scribner's* rejected one of my articles. As a matter of advantage or disadvantage, I really care very little about reviews anywhere, unless they can come from men who like yourself have felt artistically; I'm in a perfect maze of doubt as to what the effect of criticism on a book may be. *Arthur Bonnicastle*, ignored by all the critical *authorities*, sells 25,000; Turguénief's *Liza*, 1000, with the acclaim of all people of taste. *Come si fa?*

Thanks for your insight into my processes. No man ever felt his way more anxiously, doubtfully, self-distrustfully than I to the work I'm now doing.

Yu shal hav the Wūster spelling uf cours, if yu lik. For my ōn part, I so detest al idl and unecesary leters in riting, that I wŭd willingly banish them from print, and I think that by going over the various English spellings uf the past, one cŭd realy arive at somthing lĭk a sens of uniformity strugling with the pedantry uf the lexicographer, and cŭd construct a tru orthografy from the authors uf the midle period. But it is the *Atlantic* publishers ho have introduced the Webster spelling, not I. I wil kēp the stanza yu spōk uf; no doubt, yu'r rīt.

Yurs ever,
W. D. Howels.

"The story" was *A Foregone Conclusion.*

To Charles Eliot Norton

Cambridge, Mass., Dec. 12, 1874.

Dear Mr. Norton:

Your note made me very happy indeed, and I thank you for it most cordially.

If I had been perfectly my own master—it's a little droll, but true, that even in such a matter one isn't—the story would have ended with Don Ippolito's rejection. But I suppose that it is well to work for others in some measure, and I feel pretty sure that I deepened the shadows by going on, and achieved a completer verity, also.

I'm very glad that you perceived how entirely I left, or desired to leave, the interpretation of everything to the reader.

Yours very gratefully and truly,
W. D. Howells.

William Cooper Howells had been sent as American consul to Quebec in the spring of 1874.

"My book" was still *A Chance Acquaintance.*

To William Cooper Howells

The Atlantic Monthly, Dec 20, 1874.

DEAR FATHER:

Our *Atlantic* dinner on Tuesday was very successful and happy. There were about thirty contributors present, and we had speeches from nearly all. I was prepared with a written speech, which I read. Mark Twain spoke twice, and so did several others. I sat at one end of the table with him and Aldrich near me, and we had a particularly jolly time. After the dinner, Aldrich and I staid all night with Clemens at the Parker House, and sat up talking it over till two o'clock in the morning. The only drawback was the absence of some of the older contributors, who were, all but Doctor Holmes, detained by one fatality or other.—From your printed and written accounts of it, I should think the sort of weather you're having in Quebec was perfection. I'm really astonished at the capabilities of your hall stove. We little thought in bargaining for it last summer, what an engine it was.—Perhaps you think now, with the older Quebeckers, that winter is their best season.—You perceive that I haven't a word of news. I'm glad you like the Parkman so well. My book has sold 3000, already, and is still in lively demand. It hasn't had one adverse notice, yet.

All join me in love to all of you.

Your affectionate son,

WILL.

X

1875, 1876

Hires house at Shirley from the Shakers. Private Theatricals.
The Parlor Car. *Writes campaign Life of Hayes in three weeks.*
Out of the Question.

HYWEL is the Welsh for Howells and the "royal
blood" was supposed to come from Hywel Dda,
the Welsh king of Alfred the Great's time, who codified the
laws of Wales.

To William Cooper Howells

The Atlantic Monthly, Cambridge,
Jan. 3, 1875.

DEAR FATHER:

I enclose two letters from brother Taffys, which I tho't
wd interest you. By this time the girls must be getting up
some sort of pedigree, and will be glad to know that we have
royal blood in our veins—I always knew there was something curious about my blood, but I didn't like to let on
about it. But now I feel like throwing off all concealment. It
simply boils in my veins to think that low blackguard Guelph
is going to occupy the throne of my ancestors. Mr. Lewis,
you see, merely wants to connect us with a famous scholar:
this is rather beggarly; but since he was kind enough to
write, I've made bold to promise him that you would answer his letter more fully than I could, and I hope you will
do so. I couldn't tell him very much about our Rhys ancestors.

We have less news than usual this past week, and I really don't know what to write, except our united love. All well—I no worse.

Your affectionate son,
WILL.

To William Cooper Howells

The Atlantic Monthly, Jan'y 31, 1875.

DEAR FATHER:

Elinor wants me to say to Annie that she inquired the other night of a whole dressing-room full of ladies, and none of them had a place for Marie. I will ask at James's to-day, and they may know of some place. You had better send us Marie's address, and if we hear of anything, we can let her know. She could easily get a place by advertising, and we should be most glad to take her ourselves if we were not already so well provided for. I thought she was an extremely nice girl.—It was at the house of Mr. Houghton of the Riverside that Elinor met all those ladies. We had gone to hear old Mr. James read his locally famous paper on Carlyle, whom he loathes. It was a bitterly personal reminiscence. One of the stories he told was of Carlyle and Tennyson. Carlyle was wishing Duke William (as he called Wm the Conqueror) back again, and Tennyson said, "Yes, have back your Duke William, to cut off eleven hundred Cambridgeshire gentlemen's legs, to keep them from bearing arms against him!" "Ah! that was a vera sad thing for Duke William to do. But apparently he thought he had a right to do it, and upon the whole I think he had." "Well! If your Duke William comes back again, he'd better keep out of my way, I can tell you, or he'll find my knife in his guts." The only consoling thing, says James, that he heard said that evening.

You don't tell me whether Henry approves or not of the long "snug" winter you're having. Does he go out every day? Bua and Winny were talking of him at breakfast, this morning, and lamenting that it was so long since they had seen him.

Last week we were without water, except as we carried it from the neighbors', from Sunday morning till Thursday evening, the pipes being frozen in the street, at a depth of nearly five feet. How deep do they lay them in Quebec? Do they ever freeze there?

We all unite in love.

Your aff'te son
WILL.

"Haskins" was an actor who had a plot for a play that he wished to have written for him, and Clemens had suggested his getting Howells to write it.

"Twichell" was the Rev. Joseph H. Twichell, Clemens's friend and clergyman, who had come on alone from Hartford and successfully attended the Concord centennial, seeing everything, and riding on the tops of trains when he couldn't get inside them. Howells and Clemens had failed in their joint effort to reach the Concord centennial, and in *My Mark Twain* Howells gives a full account of their failure:

"We both had special invitations, including passage from Boston; but I said, Why bother to go into Boston when we could just as well take the train for Concord at the Cambridge station? When the train stopped, we found it packed inside and out, and we left it to go its way without the slightest effort to board it. We remounted the fame-worn steps of Porter's Station, and began exploring North Cambridge for some means of transportation overland to Concord. The liverymen to whom we appealed received us, some with compassion, some with derision, but in either mood convinced us that we could not have hired a cat to attempt our conveyance, much less a horse, or vehicle of any description. A swift procession of coaches, carriages, and buggies, all going to Concord, passed us, inert and helpless, on the sidewalk in the peculiarly cold mud of North Cambridge. We began to wonder if we might not stop one of them and bribe it to take us, but we had not the courage to try.

"We hung about, unavailingly, in the bitter wind a while longer, and then slowly, very slowly, made our way home. We wished to pass as much time as possible, in order to give probability to the deceit we intended to practise for we could not bear to own ourselves baffled in our boasted wisdom of taking the train at Porter's Station, and had agreed to say that we had been to Concord and got back. With all these precautions we failed, for when our statement was imparted to the proposed victim she instantly pronounced it unreliable, and we were left with it on our hands intact."

The proposed, but too astute, victim was, of course, Mrs. Howells.

To S. L. Clemens

The Atlantic Monthly,
April 27, 1875.

MY DEAR CLEMENS:

As soon as I get fairly launched in my story again, I shall be glad to come to Hartford, but I must start before I can stop. Mrs. Howells was pleased to be included by you and Mrs. Clemens in the arrangement I had made for myself alone when I planned those little informal Saturday runs to Hartford, but she says she can't join me on the first three or four.

I don't wonder you found that bed hard; we got all the sleep out of it, and left it a mere husk or skeleton of the luxurious couch it had been. We shall not ask for anything better when we come again.

Thank you for thinking of me for Mr. Haskins's play. I should certainly like to talk with him, for I believe I could write a play in that way—by having an actor give me his notion.

Now, Clemens, it really hurts me, since you seemed to wish me so much to go with you to New Orleans, to say I can't. It would be the ruin of my summer's work, and though I think something literary might come out of it for me, I haven't the courage to borrow any more of the future, when I'm already in debt to it. You are very good, and I'm touched and flattered that you want my company so much as to be willing to pay vastly more for it than it's worth.

We did both of us have a glorious time when you were here, and we long for another visit. There seems to be a slight disparity of statement between Mrs. Clemens and yourself as to her coming with you soon, but we hope you won't mind each other, but come.

It was like Twichell to have the sort of Centennial he had. It shows what can be done by drifting with the current, instead of opposing it with energy and genius, as we did. Mrs. Howells was charmed with your account of Twichell's performance, and Mrs. Clemens' report of your own attempted mystification. I hope you did not betray the fact of my pitiable terror in returning uncentennialed to the bosom of my family?

Yours ever,
W. D. HOWELLS.

Howells had asked Mrs. Kemble to write her recollections for the *Atlantic*, where they appeared under the title of *Old Woman's Gossip*. The first instalment was printed in the August number of 1875, so Mrs. Kemble's undated letter must have been written early in that year.

Mrs. Fanny Kemble to W. D. Howells

York Farm
Branchtown, Philadelphia
Monday 20th

DEAR MR. HOWELLS:

Here is my *Mess* (you said I might call it what I liked) will you do me the kindness to tell me how many of the *printed* sheets I send you will make up the accustomed quantity that you expect from me. I have taken to printing entirely and hope the Devils (perhaps in America printing is not a diabolical operation) will think me an angel in consequence—but I do not at all know how many printed sheets I ought to send.

The print of Longfellow came quite safely and I thank you for your kind agency in that matter—the friend for whom I sent for it *told* me she subscribed for the Magazine —I solemnly hope she spoke the truth—and rather believe she did.

Your Mrs. Farrell is terrific—do for pity's sake give her the Small Pox—she deserves it—I admire my daughter's Roman sketch very much—I hope you do. Why don't you come on and make acquaintance with her—if you will put up with me I will put up with you.

Yours very truly
FANNY KEMBLE

Clemens had traded his typewriter, one of the earliest ones, to his publisher Mr. Bliss, for a saddle; instead of giving it to Howells as he had promised to do. He wrote:

"The saddle hangs on Tara's walls down below in the stable, and the machine is at Bliss's grimly pursuing its appointed mission, slowly and implacably rotting away another man's chances for salvation.

"I have sent Bliss word *not* to donate it to a charity (though it is a pity to fool away a chance to do a charity an ill turn) but to let me know when he has got his dose, because I've got another candidate for damnation. You just wait a couple of weeks and if you don't see the type-writer come tilting along towards Cambridge with an unsatisfied appetite in its eye, I lose my guess."

"That story" was *Tom Sawyer.*

To S. L. Clemens

The Atlantic Monthly,
July 3, 1875.

Dear Clemens:

I care nothing about that type-writer personally, but I'm sorry for you, because I had about made up my mind to let you give it me. You may never have another opportunity to do me a charity.

Sorry to hear that Mrs. Clemens is poorly. I hope she is better by this time.

Mr. Boott, who wrote that *No More Music,* says he is much pleased at your notion of giving it to Miss Kellogg to sing. He would like to know, I suppose, how she likes it.

You must be thinking well of the notion of giving us that story. I really feel very much interested in your making that your chief work; you won't have such another chance; don't waste it on a *boy,* and don't hurry the writing for the sake of making a book. Take your time, and deliberately advertise it by *Atlantic* publication. Mr. Houghton has his back up, and says he would like to catch any newspaper copying it.

Yours ever,
W. D. Howells.

I have seen Haskins. His *plot* was a series of *stage-situations*, which no mortal ingenuity could harness together. But I think I shall write him a play. He offers me $50 a night for 50 nights; then $3000 down; then $50 a night, on.

On July 5th, Clemens had written that he wished Howells would promise to read the MS. of *Tom Sawyer*, saying: "I don't know of any other person whose judgment I could venture to take fully and entirely," to which the following letter was the prompt reply.

To S. L. Clemens

The Atlantic Monthly
July 6, 1875.

DEAR CLEMENS:

Send on your MS. when it's ready. You've no idea what I may ask you to do for *me* some day. I'm sorry that you can't do it for the *Atlantic,* but I succumb. Perhaps you'll do Boy No. 2 for us.

Here's some more music from Mr. Boott which he thought might suit Miss Kellogg better than "No More."

I count it a pleasure and privilege to read your story. There!

I'm very glad Mrs. Clemens is better, and very sorry for poor little Susy.

Yours ever,
W. D. HOWELLS.

Clemens had proposed that Howells should dramatize *Tom Sawyer* and take half of the first $6000 he received for it in payment.

"My story," which was coming into the daylight, was *A Foregone Conclusion,* and at "Shirley" Howells had taken a house of the Shakers for the summer.

"My friend Colonel Waring" was George Edwin Waring, Jr., who raised the Frémont Hussars during the Civil War, and became Commissioner of Street Cleaning in New York in 1894. In *My Mark Twain,* Howells gives a glimpse of him with Clemens:

"Once, when Osgood could think of no other occasion for a dinner, he gave himself a birthday dinner, and asked his friends and authors. The beautiful and trooper-like Waring was there, and I recall how in a long rambling speech in which Clemens went around the table hitting every head at it, and especially visiting Osgood with thanks for his ingenious pretext for our entertainment, he congratulated Waring upon his engineering genius and his hypnotic control of municipal governments. He said that if there were a plan for draining a city at a cost of a million, by seeking the level of the water in the down-hill course of the sewers, Waring would come with a plan to drain that town up-hill at twice the cost and carry it through the Common Council without opposition."

To S. L. Clemens

The Atlantic Monthly,
July 19, 1875.

MY DEAR CLEMENS:

It's very pleasant to have you propose my working in any sort of concert with you; and if the $3000 were no temptation, it *is* a temptation to think of trying to do you a favor. But I couldn't do it, and if I could, it wouldn't be a favor to dramatize your story. In fact I don't see how anybody can do that but yourself. I could never find the time, for one thing. My story is coming into the daylight, but when I get it done—say Sept. 14,—I'm going off to Quebec on a two weeks' *rest,* and then I'm going to tackle a play of my own, which is asking to be written. Besides all this, I

couldn't enter into the spirit of another man's work sufficiently to do the thing you propose.

I'm going up to Shirley to-morrow to see if the last
touches have been put to the preparation of our quarters
there, and my wife will probably follow on Thursday. Her
health has been most wretched all summer, and we earnestly
hope for benefit from this change. We are both very sorry
to hear your half-hearted report of Mrs. Clemens. Newport, I should think, would do her good. You'll find my
friend Col. Waring a capital fellow, and most usefully
learned in everything a stranger wants to ask about Newport.

Yours ever,
W. D. HOWELLS.

Private Theatricals was published in book form as
Mrs. Farrell.

To Charles Dudley Warner

Shirley Village, Mass., Sept. 4, 1875.

MY DEAR WARNER:

Thanks to your kindness the two volumes of Carducci
came promptly to hand: they were just what I wanted, and
if the debt cannot be decently forgotten, why I suppose I
must some day pay you for them.—I directed the River-
siders to send you all the *Atlantics* for this year, and I hope
that you have got them by this time. I supposed of course
you were getting them, all along.—We are here, in the
country, where we have been for the past six weeks, near
the Shakers, with whom we are on intimate terms of friendship, and about whose strange life I'm going to make a
little paper for the magazine. They present great temptations to the fictionist, and as Mrs. Howells has charged me
not to think of writing a story with them in it, I don't see

how I can help it.—The new prematurity is called *Private Theatricals,* and is, as you conjecture, a six-monthser.—I gulped all your flattering fault-finding with the innocence which authorship is never rid of. I understand that you want me to try a large canvas with many people in it. Perhaps, some time. But isn't the real dramatic encounter always between two persons only? Or three or four at most? If the effects are in *me,* I can get them into six numbers of the *Atlantic,* and if they aren't, I couldn't get 'em into twenty. Besides, I can only forgive myself for writing novels at all on the ground that the poor girl urged in extenuation of her unlegalized addition to the census: it was such a 'very *little* baby!—I've got your first chapter (*manners*—to make you wait all this time, while I was gabbing about myself!) which appears in the Nov. *Atlantic* under the gifted title of *Orienting.* When I return about the first of next month, I'll get all you've sent him, and try to run you into every number.—By the way, I heard you were going to write a story for *Scrib.* If it's true, it's a mean shame, and you will suffer for it.—Lee and Shephard have failed—*badly.* It hits Osgood, but it won't break him.—I was down at Cambridge yesterday, but saw nobody except Lathrop, who is doing well on the magazine.—Mrs. Howells sends love to Mrs. Warner. She is a little better. We go on Monday to Chesterfield, N. H., and then to Quebec. My devotion to Venice.

Yours ever,
W. D. H.

Orienting is delightful!

"This notice" was of *Sketches New and Old,* by Clemens, and the petition which he wished to have signed by Longfellow and Lowell was to ask the United States to enact laws against the piracy of foreign books, as a step towards international copyright.

To S. L. Clemens

The Atlantic Monthly, Oct. 19, 1875.

MY DEAR CLEMENS:

The poor fellow who wrote this notice thinks I had better show it to you before I put it in type. He says he's afraid it's awful rot; but he hopes you may look mercifully on it. Please return it to me (with objections) at once. You can imagine the difficulty of noticing a book of short sketches; it's like noticing a library.

I spoke to Longfellow about the international copyright petition. He will gladly sign it—if it doesn't entail any cares upon him. I'll see Lowell soon.

How much will Bliss take for your type-writer *now?*

Yours ever,

W. D. H.

To S. L. Clemens

The Atlantic Monthly, Boston,
Nov. 5, 1875.

MY DEAR CLEMENS:

The typewriter came Wednesday night, and is already beginning to have its effect on me. Of course it doesn't work: if I can persuade some of the letters to get up against the ribbon they won't get down again without digital assistance. The treadle refuses to have any part or parcel in the performance; and *I* don't know how to get the roller to turn with the paper. Nevertheless, I have begun several letters to *My d ar lemans,* as it prefers to spell your respected name, and I don't despair yet of sending you something in its beautiful hand writing—after I've had a man out from the agent's to put it in order. It's fascinating, in the meantime, and it wastes my time like an old friend.

Don't vex yourself to provide a companion piece for the *Literary Nightmare,* though if you've anything ready, send it along. But it will do magnificently as it is. I've been reading it over, with joy.

I hope to get at the story on Sunday.

Yours ever,
W. D. HOWELLS.

To S. L. Clemens

The Atlantic Monthly, Nov. 21, 1875.

DEAR CLEMENS:

Here is the *Literary Nightmare* which I'm going to put into the January, and want back by the return mail. I couldn't give it up.

I finished reading *Tom Sawyer* a week ago, sitting up till one A. M., to get to the end, simply because it was impossible to leave off. It's altogether the best boy's story I ever read. It will be an immense success. But I think you ought to treat it explicitly *as* a boy's story. Grown-ups will enjoy it just as much if you do; and if you should put it forth as a study of boy character from the grown-up point of view, you'd give the wrong key to it. I have made some corrections and suggestions in faltering pencil, which you'll have to look for. They're almost all in the first third. When you fairly swing off, you had better be let alone. The adventures are enchanting. I wish *I* had been on that island. The treasure-hunting, the loss in the cave, it's all exciting and splendid. I shouldn't think of publishing this story serially. Give me a hint when it's to be out, and I'll start the sheep to jumping in the right places.

I don't seem to think I like the last chapter. I believe I would cut that.

Mrs. H. has Mrs. C.'s letter to answer. In the meantime she sends love, and I will send the MS. of my notice some time this week,—it's at the printer's. How shall I return the book MS.?

Yours ever,
W. D. HOWELLS

Took down *Roughing It* last night, and made a fool of myself over it, as usual.

To William Cooper Howells

Cambridge, Nov. 27, 1875.

DEAR FATHER:

I don't know whether Elinor has told the girls of my having a typewriter, but here you have evidence of the fact. It belonged to Mark Twain, who got so tired of it that he was glad to trade it off for an old saddle; the man who owned the saddle preferred to give it up while still sane enough to have legal authority for such an act of surrender, and so Clemens sent it on to me. The principal trouble with it seems to be that the keys have to be struck so hard as to make your fingers sore; but this difficulty might be got over, I should think, by having some sort of strength-gaining leverage for the key-board. Or perhraps a softer cylinder to strike the types against would serve the purpose. One becomes sufficiently unconscious of the mechanism with a little practice, to be able to use it with comfort, and great speed is certainly possible. I wonder whether Mr. Ross is still as much enamored of his machine as at first?

On Friday evening I dined at Henry Adams's with Lord Houghton, whom I found a very agreeable man, with plenty of delightful talk about people that I wanted to hear of. He had known Heine, and spoke of him a good deal. Also of other Jews he had known—Disraeli amongst the rest. He said D. had always been perfectly consistent in two things: He had always been a stedfast Jew and a stedfast Republican. Wasn't that news about the Queen's Prime Minister?

Houghton looks somewhat like the portraits of Washington, chiefly on account of the bulge given to his lips by a very badly made set of false teeth, which dropped down from time to time, and had to be put back with the tongue or finger. He is an elderly man, and quite bald. This was the third time I had been asked to meet him.

With our joint love to all,

Your aff'te son,

WILL.

"Mr. Astor" was William Waldorf Astor, and "David Gray" was the poet, and editor of the Buffalo *Courier,* whom John Hay called "The loveliest of his sex."

"My present story in the *Atlantic*" was *Private Theatricals.*

To John Hay

The Atlantic Monthly, Cambridge, Mass.,

Dec. 18, 1875.

MY DEAR HAY:

You need not fear but I shall be kind to Mr. Astor in spite of his millions; I once believed that rich men were to be blamed for their wealth, but now I think they are to be pitied and I shall be very compassionate to your friend, who, by the way, I think called on me with his mother for my consular verification of their signatures, in Venice. At any rate I shall accuse him of having done so and try to found some claim upon his beneficence through that service.

It's well that you can plead a suffering family at Warsaw, for on hearing that you had visited Boston without letting me know, I renounced you with the self-devotion that we feel in giving up unworthy friends, and thought very poorly of you for a long time. But this rigid mood melts before your excuse; only don't do it again. If ever I come to Ashtabula county, single or doubly, you may depend upon seeing us both in Cleveland. We have a great desire to see Mrs. Hay, of whose willingness to see us it gives us ever so much pleasure to know. Until I got your letter, I was not quite certain whether you had left New York or not: I heard conflicting rumors about the fact. I don't know whether or not you're glad to be out of the turmoil of newspaper life; if you're not I'll take leave to be glad for you; you owe a debt to literature which you've made everybody believe you can pay handsomely, and I wish you would begin to reimburse the needy muse through the *Atlantic*. (I knew the editor couldn't be kept out much longer—forgive his vulgar insistence!) Why shouldn't you be able to send me something now, at last? Many a year have I tried to get you to do it.

I try to imagine your occupations and associations, but fail to do so through ignorance of Cleveland. I suppose you see David Gray of Buffalo, now and then. I think him a lovely fellow, and I was so sorry to hear from Mark Twain that he was not prospering in a worldly way. Clemens I see four or five times a year. Harry James is gone abroad again not to return, I fancy, even for visits. Aldrich has got home and is living quietly at Ponkapog—which sounds like a joke, but isn't. He and his wife paid us a visit last week.

I'm greatly pleased that you liked my *F. Conclusion*. The present story in the *Atlantic* is a much slighter affair, and lacks a strong motive such as that had.

Mrs. Howells joins me in regard to Mrs. Hay, the *Töchterlein* and yourself.

Yours cordially,
W. D. HOWELLS.

1876

"Our holy-land contributor" was Charles Dudley Warner. Clemens's *Jumping Frog* was in his volume of *Sketches New and Old*. "Your boy-book" was *Tom Sawyer*.

To S. L. Clemens

The Atlantic Monthly,
Jan. 4, 1876.

Yes, my dear old fellow, on *Scrofulous Humor* or any other comic subject, except Theology which I'm now reserving for our holy-land contributor C. D. W. I would be mighty glad, as you know well enough, to have something from you every month.

We were both—Mrs. Howells and I—getting up a bad state of feeling towards you both, because you hadn't made any sign of existence for so long, when your *jumping-frog* came luridly hopping along, and looking as if he had just got out of a pond of H. fire. Now we are all right again, and we join in best wishes for your continued health and prosperity. How does the novel? The more I think back over your boy-book the more I like it.

Is it true that you're going to Europe in the spring?

Yours ever,
W. D. HOWELLS.

To William Cooper Howells

Cambridge, Jan. 23, 1876.

DEAR FATHER:

Aurelia's long and satisfactory letter to Elinor came the other day, and enlightened us as to your present life; and the diary is, according to Elinor, a very lively record of the past. But Aurelia must consider that it is so much manuscript to me, and excuse me if I haven't read it yet. I hope to do so before long. Vic's play I sent off on Thursday, I think, and I suppose it will have reached you before this does.

I'm sorry whenever I fail to write you on Sunday, but

you must know from your own experience what a desperate affair it sometimes looks like, when you sit down and try to conjure up some sort of general intelligence. I am ashamed to repeat the silly gossip of our social life, and there is very little else to tell. We have both gone out a great deal more this winter than ever before, and though it is all very pleasant, it is distinctly unprofitable. For a social animal it is amusing to observe how little man can see of his fellows without becoming demoralized by it. To us a great deal of society comes now-a-days in the way of invitations which we can't, for one reason or other, refuse. Elinor attributes them all to my growing reputation, and when she doesn't feel like going, "takes it out of" me for being so famous. The worst of it all is for the children, who have a right to more evenings than we spend with them, and who all complain grievously when they find us dressing to go to a dinner or a party. Bua says he does hate to hear the front door close after me when I'm going out; but they are all very good and patient, and it's only a brief outburst of disapproval. Still we both feel the disadvantages of our present uncontrollable way of living so much that we talk very seriously of going into the country for two or three years, now when it w'd do the children so much good, and w'd give us the sort of repose and retirement that we both need. If we c'd get the right kind of tenant for our house, I think we sh'd make up our minds in a day. We c'd of course go abroad for the same money that we sh'd spend here in the country, and merely to live in Europe now w'd be education for the children. But one at my time of life loses a vast deal of indefinable, essential something, by living out of one's own country, and I'm afraid to risk it. If we leave Cambridge at all, we shall probably go to some such place as Ponkapog, where Aldrich lives, within ten or fifteen miles of Boston. Where we were last summer is rather too far away.

The winter has lagged along towards the end of January, and we have not yet had snow enough to cover the ground. Except for two or three cold snaps the mercury has stood at about an average of fifty degrees. Your talk of sleighing is almost unintelligible. The other day I met an Irishman carrying a willow twig all covered with catkins. Here and there in the yard we find new green leaves of clover. I suppose we're to pay for it somehow, but how it doesn't yet appear. I'm delighted that the *Galaxy* people have paid Annie something on her story. If she gets three hundred dollars for the whole it will be doing very well. But I advise her to take whatever they send without remonstrance. It's fortunate for her to get a thing published now-a-days when all the magazines are so full.

I hope she is writing something else. She ought to give up society and coffee, and devote herself to literature and oatmeal. I c'd give equally good advice to all of you, but I don't suppose you'd take it, and besides I've still got my own case on my hands. So I send our united love instead.

Your aff'te son,
WILL.

Enough of the bricks from Aldrich's chimneys had blown down to make a joke for him and his brother-authors. He wrote Howells:

"I cannot at this moment put my finger on the line that connects the publishers in America with the falling of my chimneys in Charles street, but I feel very keenly that somebody in the trade has got to suffer presently, and *will* not regard the thing as a joke. The sight of a brick lying in the road turns my stomach."

To Thomas Bailey Aldrich

The Atlantic Monthly,
March 21, 1876.

MY DEAR ALDRICH:

I've just sent Mr. Garrison a note asking him to pay you that $150, and I suppose you'll get it at once.

Your tumbling chimneys have made me the reputation of a subtle humorist. I have but to say, "Aldrich's chimneys have blown down, and he has been ordered by the city to rebuild 'em," in order to raise a first-class laugh. I spent Sunday before last with Clemens, and I never saw a man enjoy a joke so much. He was more appreciative even than Fields.

I should like very much to have your *Q. of Sheba* and still better to read you my play, but I'm afraid to come to Ponkapog; or rather a just sense of self-respect forbids me. As long as Mrs. Aldrich considers me a double-dyed Iago, instead of an innocent with a Jack of Hearts on his sleeve, I can't come. But why don't you come here, and pass the night? *Everyone* respects *you* in *my* house, and whatever we think of you, we shall say nothing to wound your feelings. Do come, and bring the ballad and the two chapters.

Yours ever,
W. D. HOWELLS.

I've got a lovely letter from Stoddard [R. H.] to show you.

To William Cooper Howells

Cambridge, April 9, 1876.

DEAR FATHER:

We have been through another brief winter since I last wrote, and have come out into spring again. The season is almost as backward as it was three weeks ago, and I don't think we shall soon have warm weather. Mr. Storer, who called last Sunday night, told me of the enormous snowdrifts in Quebec, which your photographs afterwards showed. If you're continued in office I must sometime see

Quebec in winter. Winny, as she wrote you, is delighted with her hat, which is certainly beautiful. I didn't suppose the *sauvage* was at all capable of such work. Winny will wear the hat this summer with due pride in it, though probably she'll never say so. I can now begin to realize in her silence how unsatisfactory you must have found me on that journey up the Ohio when the most you could get out of me in regard to anything was "Yes, indeed." I suppose we all grow more demonstrative as we grow older.

This week, I have been twice to see *Uncle Tom's Cabin* as played by the Howards, who brought it out in 1852. Howard has long been an acquaintance of mine—he lives in Cambridge—and Wednesday afternoon he took me behind the scenes and introduced me to his wife, Topsy. She had her black paint on, and as she was going to play again in the evening, she said it was no use to wash up. Her two little boys came into the dressing-room, and she put her arms round them, and it was a very pretty, domestic effect. She was very sensible, well-mannered and lady-like. I went again yesterday, and took John and Winny and Winny's little friend, Lilly Guild. They were delighted, of course, though Winny still prefers *Romeo and Juliet*. One thing struck me: how, slavery being gone, the life had gone out of the tragedies it produced. The sorrows of people 2000 years ago, would have affected me more than those of people so lately slaves.

When we got home in the evening, I found waiting me a copy of *Voreilige Schlüsse,* a German translation of *A Foregone Conclusion,* which Auerbach, the novelist's son, has just published in Stuttgart.

With love to all,
Your affectionate son,
WILL.

Mr. Storer spoke with great cordiality of you, and the kindness you had shown his family.

"This poem" was *How the Old Horse Won the Bet,* which appeared in the *Atlantic* for July, 1876, and "Mark Twain's last" must have been *Facts Concerning the Recent Carnival of Crime in Connecticut,* that was printed in the June *Atlantic* of that year.

To Oliver Wendell Holmes

The Atlantic Monthly,
May 13, 1876.

DEAR DR. HOLMES:

I think this poem most delightful, and I shall be very glad indeed to have it. If you give it me at once—as I hope you will—please send it to Mr. Garrison at the Riverside Press, marked "copy for July *Atlantic.*" I'm going to Philadelphia for a week.

What will you think of my taste, I wonder, when I tell you that I think Mark Twain's last, one of his very best? In spite of certain inequalities, I think it in some points his very best; it seems to me to go deeper than anything else he has written, and it strongly moved me from its serious side.

I felt obliged by my conscience to so much candor, but if what I say impeaches my judgment of your poem, pray believe me joking: I want that poem at any cost.

Yours sincerely,
W. D. HOWELLS.

"My small play" was *The Parlor Car.*

To S. L. Clemens

The Atlantic Monthly,
June 8, 1876.

MY DEAR CLEMENS:

Your last letter came just as I was hurrying off to Philadelphia, and I hadn't time to do it half justice. One thing was your kind offer to go down to New York with me to see my small play. It has not yet been given and I have not heard from Daly anything about it. I have heard from others, however, that he promises rashly; and I dare say it's quite likely that on second thought he doesn't find the play desirable. Small blame to him, in any case. I shall quietly pass it down to posterity in the September *Atlantic*.

I have written a mighty long account of the Centennial in the July number, and I shall now hammer away at my comedy. We go into the country for the summer, next week, and I'm to run up to the farm this morning to see that everything's in order.

I have sent Sage's paper back to him. Everything you say of it is true; and yet it somehow fell too far below the other paper in freshness and character. I hope he won't be discouraged about sending me other things.

Let us hear from each other now and then during the summer, and drop me a line to say just when you're going to Elmira.

Mrs. Howells salutes Mrs. Clemens from the habitual sick-bed.

Yours ever,
W. D. HOWELLS.

"We Smiths" referred to the President's grandmother, who was born Chloe Smith. She had much artistic talent which she expressed in embroidering flowers from nature, and to get the exact colors for them she sometime unravelled old carpets: she had also a firm religious character, which she showed by rolling up her work on Friday and putting it away under the far side of her four-posted bed, because if she worked on her embroidery Saturday, she might think of it on Sunday.

President Rutherford B. Hayes to W. D. Howells

Columbus, O.   27 June 1876.

MY DEAR H.:

I am glad the family affections have a boost. We Smiths are so proud of our family, that I know unfortunate outside people like you and Lucy must feel at a disadvantage in being so mated. But in these times of swelling fortunes we try to be considerate. Then you don't know how fond we are of managing to let folks know in a casual way that the editor of the *Atlantic,* the author of etc., etc. is our cousin. Blessings on our vanities. How happy they make us. I am now realizing what Mr. Monroe said to Mrs. Adams when she had condoled with him on his weary welcomes and receptions, "Ah, madam," said he, "a little flattery enables one to bear a great deal of fatigue."

Well, our love to Elinor and you, and the young folks, and think of me in your prayers.

Sincerely,
R. B. Hayes.

Warner had written that he was bringing Howells a scarabæus from Egypt, and that Mrs. Warner had an Arab scarf for Mrs. Howells. Howells had the scarabæus that Warner gave him set as a scarf pin, and it was one of the few pieces of jewellery he ever wore. When he was summoned to meet the Crown Princess Frederick of Prussia in Venice, Mrs. Howells, in the excitement of the moment, cleaned the scarabæus so thoroughly that it looked like a piece of green soap, but the son of the family hastily restored it to antiquity with a burnt match.

To Charles Dudley Warner

Townsend Harbor, Mass.,
Aug. 1, 1876.

My DEAR WARNER:

You may think from the cool indifference with which we've apparently treated the matter that we have friends going about all over the country with scarabæuses and other little testimonials in their pockets, but this is not the case. We read of your own and Mrs. Warner's kind thought of us with real affection—without a pang like those which the gift-bearing Greek usually brings with him. It is very good indeed of you to have remembered us, and we thank you both cordially. Sometime soon I hope we shall meet. I was so sorry not to go down on Osgood's second invitation to see you, but it was terribly hot (as it was I was overcome by the heat a few days afterwards at Shirley) and we were in the midst of a most squalid and harassing quarrel with the people with whom we were boarding, and who stood to us in the curious relation of both hosts and tenants, for I had hired the house and they the farm of the Shakers. It ended by our packing our trunks like the Arabs a week ago, and coming to this place where we find ourselves in incredible luxury and peace.—I am going to use your 4th chapter, *Jerusalem Neighborhoods,* in October, and one of those you left with Osgood in November. I don't sufficiently know the scope of your book to make a name for it, and I've been trying vainly in the dark. I'm sorry it's to be out so soon, for it cuts me off from the material. What shall I put you down for in the programme for 1877?

Yours ever,
W. D. HOWELLS.

To S. L. Clemens

Cambridge, Aug. 5, 1876.

MY DEAR CLEMENS:

I wrote you a long and affectionate letter just before you left Hartford, and you replied with a postal card; on which, instantly forgetting all the past kindnesses between us, I dropped you. You may not have known it but I did. Now I find I can't very well get on without hearing from you, and I wish you would give me your news—what you are doing, thinking, saying.

We went first to our Shaker place in Shirley Village, but that proved a wonderful failure, and ten days ago we came away to this place—Townsend Harbor, Mass.—where we find ourselves in the utmost clover, and where we propose to stay till November.

I've just finished my comedy, *Out of the Question,* with a fair degree of satisfaction, and now I'm about to begin a campaign life of Hayes, which Mr. Houghton wants to publish. (You know I wrote the life of Lincoln which elected him.) I expect that it will sell; at any rate I like the man, and shall like doing it. Gen. Hayes is Mrs. Howells's cousin, and *she* thinks that anyone who votes for Tilden will go to the Bad Place.

What are you doing with your double-barrel novel? Now that books are so dreadfully dead, why don't you think of selling it to the *Atlantic* for next year? Mr. Houghton wants me to ask you to name a price, and he promises to prosecute anybody who copies it.

My wife joins me in cordial regards to Mrs. Clemens.

Yours ever,

W. D. HOWELLS.

"The P. C." was *The Parlor Car,* which had just appeared in the September *Atlantic.*

To Charles Dudley Warner

Townsend Harbor, August 23, 1876.

MY DEAR WARNER:

I *do* want you after October. Osgood told me that he wanted to publish at a date that cut me off from the use of you in November. So I gave you up. But I think you're right to delay; and send on the Cyprus chapter, please.

I am actually writing the Hayes book in three weeks— reading the immense mass of material, making copy, and correcting proof all at once. It'll probably come out Sept. 7. The man fascinates me, and the work interests me intensely, but all the same I'm almost dead.

Glad you liked the "P. C." The fact is *I* was the serpent who tempted Eve. In that way I learnt so much about women—started early.

Yours ever,
W. D. HOWELLS.

"A long story in dramatic form" must have been *Out of the Question.*

To Charles Eliot Norton

Townsend Harbor, Mass., Sept. 24, 1876.

DEAR FRIEND:

I'm exceedingly glad you have read my book with a good opinion of Hayes, who merited a better book than I could make in three weeks. My work does not at all represent the richness and beauty of the material put into my hands; but if I'd had six months for it, I could have given it the color I wanted. However, if you've got from it the notion of a very brave, single-hearted, firm-willed, humorous, un-pretentiously self-reliant man, I haven't quite failed. As I studied the material I had to check myself in the claims I wished to make for him; I had to remind myself that if I

praised him so much, I should inflict a real discomfort upon
the man personally, which I had no right to do. Some lines
of Lowell's from the Elm-Tree ode—

> Soldier and Statesman, rarest unison,
> High-poised example of great duties done
> Simply as breathing—

embodied my conception of him better than anything I could
have said (of course!), but I took them out of my title-page
where I had them, because I felt that it was better to under-
state than to overstate such a man.

The summer indeed has gone, and we are going after it
to-morrow, when we all set out for Cambridge. It has been
a most voluminous season, and the odd experiences are
almost a match for those of last summer. But I'm getting
tired of odd experiences, and long for a little respectable
commonplace. In addition to the Hayes book, I've written
a long story in dramatic form (an invention of my own)
and have begun that *New Medea* I once told you of.

With our best regards to all the ladies,

Yours ever,
W. D. HOWELLS.

"The *Blindfold Novelettes*" refers to a plan Clemens
and Howells had invented which was for twelve authors to
write stories, each using the same plot without knowing
what the others had done with it, but this plan was never
carried out.

To S. L. Clemens

The Atlantic Monthly, Oct. 8, 1876.

MY DEAR CLEMENS:

I think with you that the notion of the *Blindfold Novelettes* oughtn't to be dropped. The difficulty is to get people
to write them. You would do it and so would I, but Al-

drich is doubtful. Do you think Warner would do one? If I could scrape up four or five authors, I'd be all right. If you'll simplify the skeleton of the story, and send me your new plot, I'll try again. I know the thing would be a good card for the magazine, and the owners are crazy over it.

I wrote you that I would leg like a centipede for C. W. Stoddard, whose virtue-ward leaning frailties I love and admire. But it would be well to get David Gray to make interest with Tilden, wouldn't it? Nobody knows what is going to happen. The only certainty is that the *Life of Hayes* hasn't sold 2000 copies. There's success for you. It makes *me* despair of the Republic, I can tell you. And the bills continue to come in with unabated fierceness.

Mrs. Howells and I in our own political eclipse, still rejoice in your effulgence. Your speech was civil service reform in a nutshell. You are the only Republican orator quoted without distinction of party by all the newspapers, and I wish you could have gone largely into the canvass. Lowell was delighted with your hit at plumbers.

In a few days I'll send you the proof of your too-small contribution for December. Couldn't you let me have something for January?

Yours ever,
W. D. HOWELLS.

The Contributors' Club of the *Atlantic* had just been invented by Howells.

To S. L. Clemens

The Atlantic Monthly, Oct. 10, 1876.

MY DEAR CLEMENS:

We begin our Contributors' Club in January. Do send me at least a ¶, spitting your spite at somebody or something. Write it as if it were a passage from a private letter.

Yours ever,
W. D. HOWELLS.

"Millet" was Francis Davis Millet, the artist; and where he seemed "bound to go" was to the Russo-Turkish War. He served there as war correspondent for the New York *Herald* and the London Daily *News* during 1877–1878, and was attached to General Skoubolloff's staff.

To S. L. Clemens

The Atlantic Monthly, Nov. 30, 1876.

MY DEAR CLEMENS:

Here is Millet's letter, received to-day. His terms are reasonable, certainly; but he seems bound to go. I don't know when he means to come back. Perhaps you may think worth while to write him.

There are two pictures for sale by that painter—Eugene Benson—who did the oriental scene over Appleton's mantelpiece. I'll see them, and write you of them.

You ought to write something better than that about *Helen's Babies*. You use expressions there that would lose us all our book-club circulation. Do attack the folly systematically and analytically—write what you said at dinner the other day about it.

I am still looking up the spot-ivy business. I'm going to see Dr. Gray about it, and get a bit of true spot to send you. I doubt *both* the present specimens.

Your visit was a perfect ovation for us: we *never* enjoy anything so much as those visits of yours. The smoke and the Scotch and the late hours almost kill us; but we look each other in the eye when you are gone, and say what a glorious time it was, and air the library, and begin sleeping and dieting, and longing to have you back again. I hope the play didn't suffer any hurt from your absence. Mrs. Howells, whom you talked to most about it, thinks it's going to be tremendously funny, and I liked all you told me of it.

Yours ever,
W. D. HOWELLS.

XI

1877

Suggests Lowell as Minister to Spain. Barrett acts A Counterfeit
Presentment. *Mark Twain's speech at Whittier dinner. Moves to
Belmont.*

"THE Club" was again the Contributors' Club in the
Atlantic, and "my comedy" was *Out of the Question.*

To John Hay

The Atlantic Monthly, Cambridge, Mass.,
February 22, 1877.

DEAR HAY:

Many thanks for your capital ¶ for the Club—what you
said needed saying—and more yet for your letter. My wife
and I had just been talking of you, and wondering when and
how you would reappear in literature, for that you must,
we held for certain. I wish that it were to be in a story for
the *Atlantic.*—I am glad you like *The American.* The fact
that Harry James could write likingly of such a fellow-
countryman as Newman is the most hopeful thing in his
literary history, since *Gabrielle de Bergerac.* I put my joy
at your liking my comedy last, but you'll easily believe it's
first in my mind. The play is too short to have any strong
effect, I suppose, but it seems to me to prove that there is a
middle form between narrative and drama, which may be
developed into something very pleasant to the reader, and
convenient to the fictionist. At any rate my story wouldn't
take any other shape.

It does really seem as if we should have Hayes at last.
Of course I pin my faith to him, and I believe he will do
all that a very wise and just man can do to help us. But we
can't be helped against our will, and there lies the danger.
Some day I hope to come to Cleveland; your asking me is
the main inducement; but I don't yet see the hour, as the
Italians say. In the meantime, why shouldn't we exchange
fotografs, all round? I am very curious to see your family,
and don't like to wait till I meet them. Mrs. Howells joins
me in cordial regard.

Yours ever,
W. D. Howells.

Do you ever bring your babes to the seaside? We are to
be next summer at Conanicut, alongside Newport.

Horatio S. Noyes was Mrs. Howells's uncle, and a first
cousin of President Hayes, for whom he kindly left the
memorandum that alarmed the independence and delicacy
of his nephew-in-law, who, knowing the President's horror
of nepotism, was especially anxious to accept nothing for
himself.

To W. K. Rogers, Secretary to President Hayes

The Atlantic Monthly, March 13, 1877.

Dear Mr. Rogers:
   Will you do me the favor to destroy the surprising memorandum which Mr. H. S. Noyes (in the great kindness of
his friendly heart) left with you, asking that I should be
"remembered in the distribution of the minor foreign appointments"?
   I congratulate you on your relation to the President;
and it seems to me one of the pleasantest things in his good
fortune that he has such a friend as you with him.
   So far his course and bearing in all matters are like a

personal honor to all his friends. Pray remember me to him (in some unworried moment,) and tell him how proud I am to think it is no more than I expected.

Yours sincerely,
W. D. HOWELLS.

The "sister" to be "married at Quebec" was Anne Thomas Howells, who married Antoine Leonard Achille Fréchette, at that time Translator in the Canadian House of Commons, and afterwards Translator of Laws, and Chief of the Translation Branch of the House of Commons.

To Charles Dudley Warner

Cambridge, April 1, 1877.

MY DEAR WARNER:

One of few drawbacks of my visit to Hartford was that I had really no long talk with you on the many points I should have liked to discuss with you: for example, novels, what they are, and what they are for. I still don't agree with you that a novel need be long in order to be great. I believe I grow more and more contrary-minded on this point, and it seems to me that the people of the next age will look with as much amaze upon our big novels as we do upon Richardson's. The man who has set the standard for the novel of the future is Tourguénief, whom certainly you can't blame for want of a vast outlook, or sidelight, or world. And only consider a play of Shakespeare, which is of such limitless suggestion, how short it is! No, I can't believe that I should be greater with more room, or Black smaller with less. (I don't propose to speak of him, how- ever, for I've never yet read one of his books; such parts of chapters as I've read seemed to me somewhat strained and cumbrous in expression.) What one really needs is a strong *motive;* then he enlarges his territory in his reader's mind. The great art is to make your reader recur to your book with the impression that certain passages are much longer than they really are. But perhaps I'm really without desire for the sort of success you believe in for me. Very likely I don't want much world, or effect of it, in my fictions. Not that I could compel it if I did want it; but I find that on taking stock, at forty year, of my experiences, and likes and dislikes, that I don't care for society, and that I do care intensely for people. I suppose therefore my tendency would always be to get any characters away from their belongings, and let four or five people act upon each other. I hate to read stories in which I have to drop the thread of one person's fate and take up that of another; so I suppose I shall always have my people so few that their fates can be interwoven and kept constantly in common before the reader. This is merely opening the subject; some day we must talk it all out.

But I'm afraid that day is not later this spring, unless you and Mrs. Warner can come here. We are going away for the summer early in June, and before we go, I must see my sister married at Quebec, and that will take all the time I shall have for junketing. Mrs. Howells is to have Winny home in a fortnight, and then opens a grand campaign of summer's sewing. Perhaps during the summer we can contrive a meeting; but as for the apple-blossoms, I despair of seeing them in Hartford. It was a real joy to meet you and your wife again. I had to give a very full report of what you said, and how you looked, when I got home, for Mrs. Howells and I will never be divorced on account of the Warners. It's our united love that we send them now.

Yours ever,
W. D. HOWELLS.

The following letter was the original draft of one to President Hayes, to whom Howells, who had refused accepting any post for himself, suggested sending Lowell as minister to Spain.

To President Rutherford B. Hayes

The Atlantic Monthly, April 4, 1877.

DEAR MR. PRESIDENT:

You were kind enough to write me before you left Columbus that I must not let you miss anything for want of a word from me. Now I could not forgive myself if you failed to send Mr. James Russell Lowell as U. S. Minister to Madrid (where I know he would like to go) because I had kept silence. Of course he knows nothing of my officiousness.

If I *begin* with a first class foreign mission, where will I end? However, the man is so much greater than the mission.

[Crossed out with pencil, as indicated, and this added at the side:]

This is my excuse for letting you know that Mr. James Russell Lowell (who knows nothing of my writing to you) would accept the mission to Spain.

Very truly yours,
W. D. HOWELLS.

Howells had given Clemens a letter of introduction to the President, but Clemens failed in seeing him, as he and Howells had failed together in reaching the Concord centennial. Fred Douglass was then United States Marshal for the District of Columbia.

"Your play" was *Ah Sin,* a play that Clemens had written with Bret Harte. It was first given in Washington on May 7, 1877.

To S. L. Clemens

The Atlantic Monthly,
May 9, 1877.

MY DEAR CLEMENS:

I was extremely vexed at the result of your attempt to see the President who would, I know, like to have seen you. If you and I had *both* been there, our combined skill would no doubt have procured us to be expelled from the White House by Fred Douglass. But the thing seems to have been a tolerably complete failure as it was. "Try to *do* a G—— d—— man a G—— d—— kindness"—and you know how it turns out.

Your brother's letter has been a joy forever to Mrs. H. and me—and what a good kind face the poor fellow has. I 'most hate to send it back.

I'm very glad to see by the papers that your play started off well. You must have had an awful time working over it in Baltimore. I wish I could have been with you.

We all send regards to your household.

Yours ever,
W. D. HOWELLS.

To President Rutherford B. Hayes

The Atlantic Monthly, May 24, 1877.

DEAR MR. PRESIDENT:

I received your letter with the enclosure for Mr. Lowell on Monday morning, and at once carried it to him. He was extremely gratified at the form of your offer, and especially that with all your occupations you should have taken the time to write him yourself. As you expected he seemed to consider only the Austrian mission.

To my great disturbance and disappointment, however,

I found that considerations of which I knew nothing when I wrote you, made him hesitate in accepting. I still think he will accept, and I dare say that his letter of acceptance will follow hard upon this. In fact, I have every day expected to hear the decision from him. Of course he will at once write to you, but I cannot prolong my own delay, which must already have surprised you. You can understand why I felt embarrassed, after being so confident in the matter, to find that Mr. Lowell has hesitations (entirely personal to himself) of which I was unaware, and why I would gladly have deferred writing till I could announce his acceptance. But I feel now that I must not wait for that.

His reception of the honor shown him was everything you could wish, and my own pleasure at your kindness in letting me carry him your letter has been alloyed by nothing but the uncertainty in which I'm now obliged to write.

Yours very truly,

W. D. HOWELLS.

P. S. I have just received a telegram from Webb asking if I had got a letter from you dated yesterday. It has not come to hand.

"I and II" were the first instalments of *Some Rambling Notes of an Idle Excursion,* the result of Clemens's trip to Bermuda, on which he had wished to take Howells as his guest.

The play for Barrett was *A Counterfeit Presentment,* which he acted in Cincinnati on October 11th of that year.

To S. L. Clemens

The Atlantic Monthly, June 9, 1877.

MY DEAR CLEMENS:

Send on I and II as soon as they are ready, and I will have them put in type at once. If it is quite the same to you

I would rather begin printing them in the October number. This, considering that the printers now have the August copy, is not so late as it seems. But let me know if you have any prejudices or preferences in the matter.

The wretch who sold you that typewriter has not yet come to a cruel death. In the meantime he offers me $20.00 for it. I never could regard it as more than a loan, so I ask you whether I shall sell it at that price, or pass it along to you at Elmira.

Barrett offered me $25 a night for the play anywhere outside of New York, and $50 a night there, and I agreed. Perhaps I could have made better terms, but to tell you the truth I was so knocked down by his taking the play that I couldn't summon all my rapacity to my aid on the instant. Of course I have been suffering for it ever since.

We have come down (by a sympathetic simultaneity with you,) on the 6th to this island of Conanicut, near Newport, and are in a fog that carries desolation to the soul. Our address is P. O. Box 160, Newport. I know now why you wished to kill your landlord and fellow boarders when in this region. If Providence ever lets me get back to live in my own house, I don't *think* I'll leave it for a while.

I don't dare to tell Mrs. Howells how low I feel. She chipperly joins me in love to you all.

Yours ever,
W. D. HOWELLS.

I think your plan for the sketches capital.

S. L. Clemens to W. D. Howells

The Farm, Elmira,
June 14. 1877.

MY DEAR HOWELLS:

Good for you. There are no better terms than those you got, except an equal division of profits—and the latter method costs a body $2000 a year for an agent's salary and expenses and is more wear and tear and trouble than keeping hotel.

Yes, October suits me for these sketches. Shall send you the first two numbers to-morrow. I revised them to-day, and began No. 3. Isn't there some Montreal magazine I can sell or give them to, and thus beat —— Bros., thieves, of Toronto?

Sell the type-writer for $20? Yes. Do not lose this opportunity of swindling that reptile. I didn't lend you that thing; I *gave* it to you because you had been doing me some offense or other, and there seemed no other way to avenge myself; but I am placable now and am willing to take $10, you take the other ten for commission, bother, express-expenses, etc. Let us compromise on that.

We had to remain at Mother's in Elmira until yesterday, to let our youngest have a run of fever and get back her strength. But we are housed here on top of the hill, now, where it is always cool, and still, and reposeful and bewitching.

The love of we'uns unto you'uns.

Yrs ever,
MARK.

To S. L. Clemens

The Atlantic Monthly, June 30, 1877.

DEAR CLEMENS:

I have just simmered down to-day after nearly two weeks of arduous journeying and junketing. First I went to Quebec to my sister's wedding, which was a very pleasant affair, and then I got back to Cambridge in time for the President's visit to Boston, and then in Newport. Nothing can give you an adequate notion of the cordiality of his welcome, and you would have liked to see how *perfectly* he did his part. I was with his suite a great deal, breakfasted with him and met him at the Mayor's dinner.

My feeling is that on every occasion he was far the simplest and greatest man (except Longfellow and Emerson) present. His son Webb and the young ladies of the party expressed their great regret at the failure of your attempt to see him in Washington. W. said his father would have been so glad to meet you, and the family would have been pleased to have you call at the White House.

I've just been reading aloud to my wife your Bermuda papers. That they're delightfully entertaining goes without saying; but we also found that you gave us the only realizing sense of Bermuda that we've ever had. I know that they will be a great success.

The fog has cleared off, and we're in rapture with Conanicut. Would that we could bring your hill-top to our shore!

That joke you put into Twichell's mouth advising you to make the most of a place that was *like* Heaven, about killed us.

> Yours ever,
> W. D. HOWELLS.

"My play" must have been *A Counterfeit Presentment.*

To John Hay

The Atlantic Monthly, Cambridge, Mass.,
Sept. 2, 1877.

MY DEAR HAY:

Some day I shall make myself very happy by visiting you, but it will not be on the *première* of my play. Suppose the thing failed upon the stage? What would you do with my remains? No, no! I wouldn't see the play till its success was assured, even for the pleasure of seeing you—and I can't say more than that. But you and Mrs. Hay be in the claque—I am sure that if you smile upon it it *must* prosper,

—and if I am called out, you speak for me. If it *does* succeed, and you keep it in Cleveland a fortnight, why I may ac—— But this is folly.

I thank you with all my heart for the kind things you say and feel, and I present Mrs. Hay with my grateful duty. Mrs. Howells will be most glad to come with me when I come. She is now on an island near Newport, where we have all been for the summer, since June 6th. I'm afraid your friend the future Bishop may have called and found my house locked up. I shall be glad to see him if he turns up.—— I never told you how very much we liked your Astor whom you sent to me. I asked him to lunch,—to Mrs. Howells' despair. "Never mind," I said, "I'll have Smith send the lunch out from Boston." (Smith is the old colored caterer, friend of Sumner; character; sayer of things: "Madam, do you wish me to *do* it, or to *over*do it?" he asked of a lady intending a party.) Smith named over a lot of things for my lunch. "Oh, good gracious, that won't do," said I, beginning to rend my garments and looking round for ashes to strew upon my head. "I'm to have the richest man in America to lunch. Now, what?" "My dear sir," said Smith, "you want the simplest lunch that can be got." It was a success.

Yours ever,
W. D. HOWELLS.

W. H. Bishop was a friend of Howells's, whose books, *Detmold, The House of a Merchant Prince,* and *A Brownstone Boy,* are referred to in future letters. He was at this time a contributor to the *Atlantic,* and later he entered the consular service and became consul at Palermo and Genoa.

To W. H. Bishop

Cambridge, Mass., Sept. 11, 1877.

DEAR MR. BISHOP:

I wonder if I can explain to you a project of mine?

I have long wanted to find somebody in New York who

could treat the æsthetic interests of that city in a monthly paper in the *Atlantic*. I do not mean that he shall *report* literary, social, dramatic, musical and artistic events, but that he shall somehow express or distil the vital essence of those subjects, and give us that in the casual, touch and go manner of a French *chronique*. Anything in the way of *news* would be stale by the time we could print it, but what is said or thought about the news is more durable, and can be enjoyed long after the news is old. Imagine yourself still a cultivated and amiable inhabitant of Milwaukee; imagine yourself also the New York friend of your Milwaukee self. Such accounts of New York matters as you would write your Milwaukee self are probably what I should want for the magazine. Do you see?

Several have tried this, but they have all been put to death for their failure: it is one of those fabled emulations in which the penalty for failure is necessarily death, with confiscation; but if you would like to try it, I should be glad. I know it makes a man heavy to charge him to be light, but your success will largely depend upon your volatility. Cut as close to the quick as you like, but no drop of blood, mind; no hacking; and for the most, be good-natured. Also, for your own sake, be unknown; that alone can render you free. Let me hear from you.

Very truly yours,
W. D. Howells.

"That hideous mistake of poor Clemens's" was the speech he had made at the dinner given on John Greenleaf Whittier's seventieth birthday, December 17, 1877, by the staff of the *Atlantic*. In describing it in *My Mark Twain*, Howells says:

"He believed he had been particularly fortunate in his notion for the speech of that evening, and he had worked it out in joyous self-reliance. It was the notion of three tramps, three dead-beats, visiting a California mining-camp, and imposing themselves upon the innocent miners as respectively Ralph Waldo Emerson, Henry Wadsworth Longfellow, and Oliver Wendell Holmes. The humor of the conception must prosper or must fall according to the mood of the hearer, but Clemens felt sure of compelling this to sympathy, and he looked forward to an unparalleled triumph.

"But there were two things that he had not taken into account. One was the species of religious veneration in which these men were held by those nearest to them, a thing that I should not be able to realize to people remote from them in time and place. I do not suppose that anybody more truly valued them or more piously loved them than Clemens himself, but the intoxication of his fancy carried him beyond the bounds of that regard, and emboldened him to the other thing which he had not taken into account— namely, the immense hazard of working his fancy out before their faces, and expecting them to enter into the delight of it.

"Nobody knew whether to look at the speaker or down at his plate. I chose my plate as the least affliction, and so I do not know how Clemens looked, except when I stole a glance at him, and saw him standing solitary amid his appalled and appalling listeners, with his joke dead on his hands. From a first glance at the great three whom his jest had made his theme, I was aware of Longfellow sitting upright, and regarding the humorist with an air of pensive puzzle, of Holmes busily writing on his menu, with a well-feigned effect of preoccupation, and of Emerson, holding his elbows, and listening with a sort of Jovian oblivion of this nether world, in that lapse of memory which saved him in those later years from so much bother. Clemens must have dragged his joke to the climax and left it there, but I cannot say this from any sense of the fact."

To Charles Eliot Norton

Cambridge, Mass., Dec. 19, 1877.

DEAR MR. NORTON:

I send your proof, which I have read through with the freshest pleasure in your narration, familiar as the facts largely were. It is lovely. And what a sweet and graceful and gracious speech you made the other night!—All sense of that and of other things was long blotted out for me by that hideous mistake of poor Clemens's. As you have more than once expressed a kindness for him, you will like to know that before he had fairly touched his point, he felt the awfulness of what he was doing, but was fatally helpless to stop. He was completely crushed by it, and though it killed the joy of the time for me, I pitied him; for he *has* a good and reverent nature for good things, and his performance was like an effect of demoniacal possession. The worst of it was, I couldn't see any retrieval for him.

Yours truly,

W. D. HOWELLS.

To S. L. Clemens

The Atlantic Monthly, Dec. 25, 1877.

MY DEAR CLEMENS:

I was just about to ask you to let me postpone your story a month, because I found the Feb'y number overfull, and your paper had come last to hand. But I have no idea of dropping you out of the *Atlantic,* and Mr. Houghton has still less, if possible. You are going to help and not hurt us many a year yet, if you will. Everyone with whom I have talked about your speech regards it as a fatality—one of those sorrows into which a man walks with his eyes wide open, no one knows why. I believe that Emerson, Longfellow and Holmes themselves can easily conceive of it in that light, and while I think your regret does you honor and does you good, I don't want you to dwell too morbidly on the matter. Mr. Norton left a note on my table the other day, expressing just the right feeling towards you about it. One of the most fastidious men here, who *read* the speech, sees no offense in it. But I don't pretend not to agree with you about it. All I want you to do is not to exaggerate the damage. You are not going to be floored by it; there is more justice than that even in *this* world. And especially as regards *me,* just call the sore spot well. I could say more and with better heart in praise of your good-feeling (which was what I always liked in you) since this thing happened than I could before.

A man isn't hurt by any honest effort at reparation. Why shouldn't you write to each of those men and say frankly that at such and such an hour on the 17th of December you did so and so? They would take it in the right spirit, I'm sure. If they didn't the right would be yours.

Mrs. Howells joins me in cordial regards to Mrs. Clemens and yourself.

Ever yours,
W. D. HOWELLS.

"Belmont" was the country village near Cambridge where Charles Fairchild was building a house for the Howellses on his own place. McKim, Mead & White were the architects, Mead being a brother of Mrs. Howells, and it was one of the very first of the Queen Anne cottages. The style was so new that when the builder was about to put up the veranda posts with their heaviest part at the top, Mrs. Howells, with all an elder sister's distrust of her brother's firm, refused to have them placed until the architects had been consulted by telegraph.

A Counterfeit Presentment had already been given in the West, for on October 14th, 1877, Howells had written his father: "Thursday night my play, *A Counterfeit Presentment*, was given in Cincinnati. Next morning Barrett telegraphed that it was "a grand success, far exceeding his most sanguine expectations."

To John Hay

The Atlantic Monthly, Cambridge, Mass.,
Christmas, 1877.

MY DEAR HAY:

If those small pots of spot-ivy come poking along to you some time before this letter reaches you, imagine that they are from the Howellses, and express in their feeble symbolism our close-clinging regard for Mrs. Hay and yourself. We think of you and talk of you often, and we congratulate ourselves that in going to Belmont, we shall be two miles nearer Cleveland.

We have had a glorious Christmas—up to noon—and we hope you are correspondingly happy among your little ones. I wish you could have been at the *Atlantic* dinner, though your presence would have deprived me of the pleasure of reading a passage from your letter.

To-morrow night I am going to see the *C. Presentment* at Worcester. With Mrs. Howells's and my own cordial regards to both of you,

> Ever yours,
> W. D. HOWELLS.

Some honors are not pleasures. Your visit was both, in the highest degree.

XII

1878

A Counterfeit Presentment *at the Boston Museum. Translates*
A New Play *from the Spanish. Barrett acts it as* Yorick's Love.

THE "play" was "A Counterfeit Presentment," and
Clemens's letter to Longfellow was about his speech
at the *Atlantic* dinner.

To S. L. Clemens

The Atlantic Monthly, Jan. 6, 1878.

MY DEAR CLEMENS:

Your letter about the play gave me great joy, and so
did Warner's most kindly criticism in the *Courant.* I am
very happy in your liking for it. We shall yet write a play
together; but you must not expect any profit out of it if
we do. I am the champion prosperity-extinguisher. To tell
you the truth, I'm awfully discouraged at the failure of the
comedy to draw houses in New England. I don't suppose it
paid expenses in either Worcester, Providence, Springfield
or Hartford, and I shall not blame Barrett if he withdraws
it. I wonder if you had any talk with him about it?

I was with Mr. Longfellow the morning he got your
letter. He spoke of it as "most pathetic," and said every
one seemed to care more for that affair than he did. I know
you had the right sort of answer from him. I couldn't help
reading to Mr. Norton, the other day what you said of
him, and it gave him the greatest pleasure.

246

Winny will send her name. She now sends her love to your tribe with all of us.

> Yours ever,
> W. D. HOWELLS.

If Stedman sent back his poem, it was probably *Rose and Jasmine,* which appeared in the April *Atlantic* of that year.

To Edmund Clarence Stedman

The Atlantic Monthly, Jan. 7, 1878.

MY DEAR FRIEND:

Send back your poem to me, and let the public judge between us. I dare say it will find you right, and I shall be frank enough to own it. I care much more for literature than for editorial infallibility.

> Yours cordially,
> W. D. HOWELLS.

P. S. *I mean business.*

The "paper on the Lobby" was to be written for the *Atlantic.*

To Arthur G. Sedgwick

The Atlantic Monthly, Jan. 19, 1878.

MY DEAR SEDGWICK:

I like your notion of a paper on the Lobby, and I wish you would make it. The publishers would pay you $100 for it, and I had rather it were ten than fifteen pages long. $100 is not much for life's blood, but that is a thing which in these hard times can be had at panic prices: it is marked down on every hand.

I suppose we shall not go to Washington this winter,

pleasant as it would be. But after being asked to visit at the
White House, and Spartanly refusing because we could not
afford it, you see that we could not devolve upon a "lower
range of feeling" and go somewhere else without too great
sentimental discomfort. So we stay at home, and find that
sufficiently exciting and expensive.

Yours ever,
W. D. HOWELLS.

The Sign of the Savage was the hotel in Howells's story
of that name, published in the same volume with *A Fearful Responsibility.*

To S. L. Clemens

February 24, 1878.

MY DEAR CLEMENS:
I never was in Berlin and don't know any family hotel
there. I should be glad I didn't, if it would keep you from
going. You deserve to put up at the Sign of the Savage
in Vienna. Really, it's a great blow to me to hear of that
protracted sojourn. It's a shame. I must see you somehow,
before you go. I'm in dreadfully low spirits about it.

Yours ever,
W. D. H.

I was afraid your silence meant something wicked.

"My play" was *A Counterfeit Presentment,* given by
Lawrence Barrett at the Boston Museum, on April 1, 1878.
Mr. Longfellow's "old friend Greene" was G. W.
Greene, an Italian scholar. Howells says in *Literary
Friends and Acquaintance:*

"He [Longfellow] always asked me to dinner when his
old friend Greene came to visit him, and then we had an
Italian time together, with more or less repetition in our

talk, of what we had said before of Italian people and Italian character."

It was this friend, at the meetings of the Dante Club,

"who drowsed audibly in the soft and gentle heat. The poet had a fat terrier who wished always to be present at the meetings of the Club, and he commonly fell asleep at the same moment as the dear old scholar, so that when they began to be heard in concert, one could not tell which it was that most took our thoughts from the text of the *Paradiso*. When the duet opened, Longfellow would look up with an arch recognition of the fact, and then go gravely on to the end of the canto."

To William Cooper Howells

The Atlantic Monthly, March 31, 1878.

DEAR FATHER:

I am very glad of the gleam of hope you have in regard to Toronto, but I think, after your experience, that you are quite right to treat it as a gleam only. For my own part, I shall be sorry to have you leave Quebec, and I doubt if you'll find Toronto any great advantage, pecuniarily: it must be a much more expensive place. But of course you have looked carefully into the matter.

You lost nothing by my not writing last Sunday, for there was no news, and to-day there is scarcely anything but the excitement of my play, which is to be brought out at the Boston Museum to-morrow night. There is a full house in prospect, and I can't help feeling some hope that it will go off well. I have been at two rehearsals,—very strange and amusing experiences to me. A rehearsal is the bare bones merely of playing; the actors walk through their parts, with hardly any show of action or location. Mr. Long-fellow and his old friend Greene came in to the second rehearsal, and sat it well through.—I'm more and more impressed with the hardness of an actor's life. It's an extremely serious affair, with the least possible fun about it. What struck me most in regard to my own share in the business was the immovable fashion in which what I had so lightly and vaguely described had to be *realized* on the stage. A hat—just what kind of hat? A chair—precisely what sort of chair?

We were out at Belmont yesterday looking at the house, which is blossoming out into a very quaint and peculiar beauty. It is going to be something really exquisite, and, what is better, convenient. We shall be very impatient to see you after we get into it. All are well and join me in love to all.

Your affectionate son,
WILL.

This friendly note from Aldrich, written the morning after the first performance of *A Counterfeit Presentment,* gives a glimpse of its success.

Houghton, Osgood & Co.
April 2d, 1878.

Memorandum to W. D. Howells.

MY DEAR HOWELLS:

It was an awful thing to see another man so successful as you were last night. So I return Marmontel's Memoirs sadly and without comment. Wasn't it all delightful?

Yours ever,
T. B. A.

To William Cooper Howells

The Atlantic Monthly, April 3, 1878.

DEAR FATHER:

I'm glad to see by the paper of this morning that the President has sent in your name for Toronto, and I hope now that nothing will prevent the fulfillment of your highest expectations.

Your success comes upon the top of mine with my play, which has been most brilliant. The first night was a superb emotion: a gurgle of laughter from beginning to end, and a constant clapping of hands. They called me up at the end of their third act, and *roared* at me. I never had my popularity at arm's length before, and it was very pleasant. Love to all.

Your aff'te son,
WILL.

Bret Harte had fallen upon evil days and had been suggested for a consular post. President Hayes had consulted Howells privately as to Harte's fitness for such a place, and it may have been Howells's answer that sent him to Germany as American Consul to Crefeld.

To President Rutherford B. Hayes

New York, April 9, 1878.

DEAR MR. PRESIDENT:

Elinor has sent me your note from Cambridge.

I am reluctant to say anything about the matter you refer to me, but I will do so at your request. Personally, I have a great affection for the man, and personally I know nothing to his disadvantage. He spent a week with us at Cambridge when he first came East—and we all liked him. He was late about appointments, but that is a common fault. After he went away, he began to contract debts, and was arrested for debt in Boston. (I saw this.) He is notorious for borrowing and *was* notorious for drinking. This is *report*. He never borrowed of *me,* nor drank more than I, (in my presence) and yesterday I saw his doctor who says his habits are good, now; and I have heard the same thing from others. From what I hear he is really making an effort to reform. It would be a godsend to him, if he could get such a place; for he is poor, and he writes with difficulty and very little. He has had the worst reputation as regards punctuality, solvency and sobriety; but he has had a terrible lesson in falling from the highest prosperity to the lowest adversity in literature, and—you are a good enough judge of men to know whether he will profit by it or not.

Personally, I should be glad of his appointment, and I should have great hopes of him—and fears. It would be easy to recall him, if he misbehaved, and a hint of such a fate would be useful to him.

I must beg that you will not show this letter to anyone whatever, but will kindly return it to me at Cambridge.

Very respectfully yours,
W. D. HOWELLS.

"The Taylor dinner" was the farewell dinner to Bayard Taylor, of whom Howells says:

"I saw him last in the hour of those tremendous adieux which were paid him in New York before he sailed to be minister in Germany. It was one of the most graceful things done by President Hayes, who, most of all our Presidents after Lincoln, honored himself in honoring literature by his appointments, to give that place to Bayard Taylor. There was no one more fit for it, and it was peculiarly fit that he should be so distinguished to a people who knew and valued his scholarship and the service he had done German letters. He was as happy in it, apparently, as a man could be in anything here below, and he enjoyed to the last drop the many cups of kindness pressed to his lips in parting; though I believe these farewells, at a time when he was already fagged with work and excitement, were notably harmful to him, and helped to hasten his end."

"Pil" was the little name for Howells's younger daughter, who, in an effort to say Milly, had turned it into Pilla, which was often shortened into Pil.

To William Cooper Howells

The Atlantic Monthly, April 14, 1878.

DEAR FATHER:

I got home from New York yesterday morning after ten days' stay, all of which was taken up with continuous junketing. It began the night of the 4th with the Taylor dinner at Delmonico's. Next night Harper made a dinner party for me; next night Church of the late *Galaxy* dined me; Sunday I spent with Charley Mead's family; Monday morning I breakfasted with Sedgwick at the Union Club, and went out to Shepards' for the night. Tuesday I lunched with Quincy Ward, and dined with Whitelaw Reid, at whose house I spent three days. Wednesday night, I dined at the Union League Club, meeting all the New York sages in politics, literature and finance, including Tilden, Bryant, and John Jacob Astor. (The last said, "Mr. Howells, nobody has enjoyed your *Doorstep Acquaintance* more than I"—which amused me, coming from a man of his millions.) That day Reid made a dinner party for me; Friday morning I breakfasted at Ward's, and then ran out to Henry Howells's at Flushing, and got back in time to take the boat. So you see what a round it was. I enjoyed it all, for the novelty and excitement, and was glad to have it over. I met and made up all old sorrows with Dr. Holland, which I was glad to do.

I don't see what makes you think the Senate hasn't confirmed you. It seems to me I've seen the announcement of your confirmation. At any rate there can't be any doubt about the matter.

Shall you start for Toronto as soon as you are confirmed?

All join me in love to all of you.

Your aff'te son
WILL.

To Charles Eliot Norton

Boston, April 16, 1878.

DEAR MR. NORTON:

I was away in New York when your circular came. Of course I wish to subscribe for the Turner pictures, which I should like (if for no other reason) because I liked you— or because you liked them; it makes no difference which. I know they will be very useful to the artistic branches of the family, and I shall look up at them from the inferior levels of literature, and do my best to have some ideas about them.

The little drama you sent me has some very striking qualities. The dialogue is managed with great point and brilliancy: it seems really Louis Quinze Frenchmen speaking. What I can't abide is the matter between Helen and Casanova. I no longer wish to be put in pain about a woman's virtue, or to ask that suffering from others. It's odious; all the tragedy went out of that situation long ago, and only the displeasures remain. There is no reason but this for not printing the bright and shapely play, which I should otherwise be glad to have in the *Atlantic*. I will bring you the MS. in a few days.

I'm very glad that you will soon let me have a paper of your own. At Belmont, I shall be much nearer Shady Hill than I am now. It breaks my heart to have people think I'm base enough to make anything but a geographical remove from Cambridge.

Yours ever,
W. D. HOWELLS.

The experience of buying the horse and phaëton did turn into the material of *Buying a Horse;* and "my new story" was *The Lady of the Aroostook*.

"Poor Susy" refers to what Clemens had written of her on May 4th.

"Poor Susy! From the day we reached German soil, we have required Rosa to speak German to the children—which they hate with all their souls. The other morning in Hanover, Susy came to us (from Rosa in the nursery) and said, in halting syllables, 'Papa, *wie viel uhr ist es?*'—then turned with pathos in her large eyes, and said, 'Mamma, I wish Rosa was made in English.'

To S. L. Clemens

The Atlantic Monthly, June 2, 1878.

MY DEAR CLEMENS:

Ich habe Ihren herzerfreuenden Brief erhalten—or do you prefer English by this time? There is at least one American family whom your absence from the country truly bereaves, and I need not tell you your letter was truly welcome, and duly read aloud at the breakfast table the morning it came. We are still in Cambridge, and we no longer put **our** faith in joiners. The Belmont house is promised us in a month—and was so a month ago. But the weather remains charmingly cool in Cambridge, and as nobody wants to buy or to hire this house, it costs us nothing to stay in it. Just now we are excited about a horse and phaëton which we are to buy, and I suppose that by the end of a fortnight I shall be the worst-sold ass in Massachusetts. But to a literary man all these things are gain: they turn into material, as we all know. The only thing that doesn't is a displeasure with an actor: that's a thing that one likes to keep to one's self. I am working away steadily at my new story, which promises to be a long one, and I am venturing on some untried paths in it. Think of so domestic a **man as I** wrecking his hero on a coral island—an uninhabited *atoll*—in the South Pacific! There's courage for you! Till I get this done, I try not even to think of a play, though to tell you the truth I would ten times rather write plays than anything else, and I shall tackle the *Steam Generator* at the earliest opportunity. I have had a very pleasant letter from your cub-dramatist in Hartford, announcing—or rather disclaiming—all right and title to Clews.

Osgood goes abroad this month, with Waring. Aldrich spends the summer at Swampscott. John Hay is, I suppose, in Europe by this time; from a short note he sent me before sailing, I'm afraid his health is delicate. Him and O. you would like to see, and will, I dare say. Harte, you know, has got a consular appointment somewhere in Germany. So you see you are likely to be joined by the whole fraternity during the summer. I alone shall stay at home. In fact, I find that I have outlived all longing for Europe: you are now the principal attraction of that elderly enchantress, as far as I'm concerned. I hope you'll find all the hoped-for leisure there, and that you'll not be able to keep from writing for the *Atlantic*. Otherwise I must begin printing your private letters to satisfy the popular demand. People are constantly asking when you're going to begin. (That's a pleasant thorn to plant in a friend's side.) When I parted from you, that dismal day in New York, I saw that the weather was capable of anything, and I'm not surprised to hear how it used you; but I hope that by this time Mrs. Clemens is all well of her cold, and that poor Susy is more reconciled to Rosa's composition. Really, however, I could imagine the German going harder with you, for you always seemed to me a man who liked to be understood with the least possible personal inconvenience. The worst thing about any foreign country is its language, which the natives never can speak with our accent.

What a stupid letter. But give me another chance, by answering. You know that at my dullest, my heart is in the right place. Mrs. Howells joins me in love to both of you.

Affectionately,
W. D. HOWELLS.

Tell me about *Capt. Wakeman in Heaven,* and all your other enterprises.

Lawrence Barrett produced Howells's adaptation of *Un Nuevo Mundo* by Estébanez at Cleveland, Ohio, on October 26, 1878, under the title of *A New Play,* which was afterwards changed to *Yorick's Love.* Daly's version was called *Yorick.*

John Hay to W. D. Howells

Cleveland, Ohio,
October 26, 1878.

MY DEAR HOWELLS:

I went home last night moved and shaken to the core by your play, and I woke up this morning with that vague sense of calamity, with which a sorrow of the night before tinges the morning. I hardly know how to begin my report to you. If the theatre were merely a temple of art and poetry, I could congratulate you on a great and glorious triumph. I am sure I never saw Barrett play so well, with such sustained agony of passion. I went in to see him after the second act and he was haggard as a ghost, and drenched with perspiration, but he showed no diminution of energy in the last act. The play throughout had a terrible clutch upon the feelings of the audience, in spite of the young man who played Edmund, who overdid his part and left the audience behind him with no disposition to catch up. In all Barrett's scenes the attention was painfully intense, only interrupted by quick and electrical storms of applause. The audience was like your other one last year, an *Atlantic Monthly* crowd which crammed every inch of space. They appreciated the good acting and the good writing as well. The exquisite versification in the second act, for instance, was remarked upon by a dozen people about me who I should have thought would not care for such things. It was a great tragedy, nobly played, in short, and it had last night an honest and legitimate success. The success was yours too, for it was a very different play from the one I saw at the Fifth Avenue Theatre some years ago, improved almost beyond recognition. It was the best written play I have heard for a long time.

Now, shall I go on with the hateful candor of a friend, and tell you the farther impression it made on me? I do not believe that as the play stands it will ever have great runs, or make you much money. The plot is so simple, the story so sombre and heart breaking, that after the play becomes known, few people will go to see it except those who enjoy the very best things in writing and in acting. It is too concentrated, too intense. The five people in it are in such a prolonged agony that an ordinary audience would grow nervous. They must laugh once in a while, and rest once in a while, and if you do not give them the chance to do it legitimately, they will do it in the wrong places. I do not know how the Greeks managed with their awful simplicity and terror, but Shakespeare had to throw in a good deal of what I dare not call padding. Perhaps I am croaking in vain, after all. The play is magnificent—I wonder how any contemporary Spaniard could have done it. Your part of the work is, it seems to me, faultless, and Barrett's is unquestionably the stoutest piece of work I ever saw him do. (You made a great improvement in keeping Shakespeare behind the flies. He was almost grotesque in the original.) The applause was of the sharpest and most spontaneous kind, and the people were roused and moved in a very uncommon way. Perhaps I am morbid and cannot look at the prosperous side of things—but I think you will prefer to have me say what I think, even if I am wrong. I am sure I never left a theatre feeling such a sense of *tragedy* as last night, except when I walked out of the Academy of Music one afternoon and felt as if I ought to go and tell the police

that Salvini had smothered his wife and killed himself.
—Turning to brighter things. Mrs. Hay and I are starting across the ocean with Miss Blood with the assurance of
a happy voyage. The first number is delightful. It gives the
pleasure we feel at the first note of Wilhelmj's fiddle—we
know he can keep on doing it as long as he likes.

Yours affectionately,

JOHN HAY.

To John Hay

The Atlantic Monthly, Boston,

October 29, 1878.

MY DEAR HAY:

I thank you with all my heart for your thoughtful kindness in writing me about *A New Play*. But I ought, in
justice to the absent Señor Estébanez, to disclaim a good
three-fourths of your praise. The trouble with Mr. Daly's
version was that it was not Estébanez, but the tradition of
the stage. I blank-versified the more touching and noble
speeches, and here and there I helped the Spaniard out a
little; but that Hawthornian grip of the subject is his own.
He is a *great* man, if he has done nothing but this.

I haven't the least idea how far Mr. Barrett has let my
work alone. He wrote me from Chicago three weeks ago,
in quite a panic, that it was all bad, and that he should have
to "take it into his workshop" and do it over. Since then I
have not heard from him.

I see the fault (for long runs) that you speak of, and I
thank you for putting your finger on it. I could remedy it
with ease, by bringing Woodford, the author of the supposed play, into greater prominence as a comic element. Do
tell me one thing: Is there a second part of the last act, in
which Yorick loses himself in the character of Count Oc-
tavio? And does the play close with a speech of Yorick's?—
I'm glad Shakespeare was kept out. I urged that fervently,

but Mr. Barrett made no sign as to his intention in regard to it.—I do hope he will succeed with the play, for his own sake. My own stake in it is small.

It is worth while to write a story to have such praise you give *The L. of the A.* Present my regards and gratitude to Mrs. Hay.

Yours cordially,
W. D. HOWELLS.

This seems a stupid and complaining response to your letter. But let me say that I am most deeply touched and gratified, and I love you more than I could tell. What you have done is what I never could have done. I don't even know how to acknowledge it properly!

XIII

1879

The Lady of the Aroostook. *Canadian reprints sold in the States. Suggests Lowell for Minister to England. Dramatizes Longfellow's* Courtship of Miles Standish *for Barrett.*

CLARENCE KING wrote *Mountaineering in the Sierra Nevadas,* and it was upon his recommendation that Congress provided for the geological survey of a belt of Western country including the fortieth parallel and extending across the Rocky Mountains; a survey that King successfully carried out during the years of 1867–1872. In 1879 he was appointed the first Director of the United States Geological Survey.

West Brattleboro was where President Hayes's grandfather had a tavern, and it was through this grandfather's wife, Chloe Smith (a granddaughter of Parson Russell) that President Hayes and Mrs. Howells were descended from the Reverend John Russell of Hadley, Mass., who hid the regicides Goffe and Whally in his cellar for years, refusing all preferment that he might stay there to shelter them.

To President Rutherford B. Hayes

The Atlantic Monthly, Boston,
Jan. 4, 1879.

DEAR MR. PRESIDENT:

I have the honor and pleasure of introducing Mr. Clarence King, whose name in science and literature we are all so proud of. He knows everything about California especially, from suppositious diamond mines in Arizona to the last graces of the Pike dialect, and he is as you see a charming and most civilized New Englander. If you know his book, *Mountaineering in the Sierra Nevadas,* as well as I do, you must share my sole grief against him, namely, that a man who can give us such literature, should be content to be merely a great scientist.

Elinor is giving him a letter to Mrs. Hayes, and we both particularly recommend him.

Yours very truly,
W. D. HOWELLS.

P. S. You will be interested to know that Mr. King began his mountaineering, as a boy, on Round Mountain at West Brattleboro.

In the next letter Clemens told Howells of the new book he was working on—*A Tramp Abroad*—which he was keeping a secret from everyone except Twichell and Howells.

S. L. Clemens to W. D. Howells

1ᵃ Karlsstrasse, 2ᵉʳ stock,
Munich, Jan. 30, 1879.

MY DEAR HOWELLS:

It took a great burden off my heart this morning when your letter arrived and I found my 2 articles had not been lost *in transitu.* I was going to write to-day and ask about them. Ordinarily I should trouble myself but little about the loss of 2 articles, for the loss could not rob me of the chief thing, i. e., the pleasure the writing them had afforded me, —but when a body is yoked down to the grinding out of a 600-page 8-vo. book, to lose a chapter is like losing a child. I was not at all sure that I should use both of those chapters in my book, but to *have them around,* in case of need, would give that added comfort which comes of having a life-preserver handy in a ship which *might* go down though nobody is expecting such a thing. But you speak so kindly of them that I shall probably venture to use them both. I have destroyed such lots of MS. written for this book! And I suppose there are such lots left which ought to be destroyed. If it should be, it will be,—that is certain. I have rung in that fragrant account of the Limberger cheese and the coffin-box full of guns. Had I better leave that out? Give me your plain, square advice, for I propose to follow it. The back of my big job is broken, now, for the book is rather more than half done; so from this out I can tear up MS. without a pang.

You sent me 2 copies of the *first* slip of Pitcairn, but no copy of the remaining half of the article. However, I have mailed one first-slip to Chatto & Windus and asked them to send me one of their second-slips, in exchange.

I wish I *could* give those sharp satires on European life which you mention, but of course a man can't write successful satire except he be in a calm judicial good-humor—whereas I *hate* travel, and I *hate* hotels, and *I hate* the opera and I *hate* the Old Masters—in truth I don't even seem to be in a good enough humor with *anything* to *satirize* it; no, I want to stand up before it and *curse* it, and foam at the mouth,—or take a club and pound it to rags and pulp. I have got in two or three chapters about Wagner's Operas, and managed to do it without showing temper—but the strain of another such effort would burst me. (Mind, whatever I say about the book is a *secret;*—my publisher shall know little or nothing about the book till he gets the MS., for I can't trust his tongue—I am trusting *nobody* but you and Twichell. I like mighty well to tell my plans and swap opinions about them, but I don't like them to get around.) I have exposed the German language in two or three chapters, and have shown what I consider to be the needed improvements in it. I mean to describe a

German newspaper, but not satirically—simply in a plain matter of fact way. I wrote the chapter satirically, but found that a plain statement was rather the better satire. In my book I allow it to appear,—casually and without stress,—that I am over here to make the tour of Europe *on foot*. I am in pedestrian costume, as a general thing, and *start* on pedestrian tours, but mount the first conveyance that offers, making but slight explanation or excuse, and endeavoring to seem unconscious that this is not legitimate pedestrianizing. My second object here is to become a German scholar; my third, to study Art, and learn to paint. I have a notion to put a few hideous pen and ink sketches of my own in my book, and explain their merits and defects in the technical language of art. But I shall not put many in—better artists shall do nineteen-twentieths of the illustrating.

I have made a pedestrian trip up the Neckar to Heilbronn, with muslin-wound hat, leathern leggings, sun-umbrella, alpenstock, etc.—*by rail*,—with my agent,—I employ an agent on a salary, and he does the real work when any is to be done, though I appropriate his emotions to myself and do his marvelling for him—and in yesterday's chapter we have started back to Heidelberg on a raft, and are having a good time. The raft is mine, since I have chartered it, and I shall pick up useful passengers here and there to tell me the legends of the ruined castles, and other things —perhaps the Captain who brought the news of the Pitcairn revolution. I have invented quite a nice little legend for Dilsberg Castle, and maybe that is the only one I *shall* invent—don't know.

I want to make a book which people will *read*,—and I shall make it profitable reading in spots. And as soon as it is off my hands I shall take up *Wakeman in Heaven* at once.

Confound that February number, I wish it would fetch along *The Lady of the Aroostook,* for we are pretty impatient to see her again.—All right, tell me about the Pacific coast trip—I wish we were going with you.

So Aldrich is gone—but he won't go to Egypt if this plague continues to spread. I sent him a paragraph from a German paper the other day: Scientist discovered a Roman vessel near Regensburg of a sort which has long been supposed to have been used to burn fragrant herbs in during cremation of corpses, but there was no proof. He set this one on the stove one day, and presently it began to send out a sweet perfume—resumed its office after a vacation of 1500 years. Thought Aldrich could do a sonnet on it.

Write me here, to above address—for even if the plague drives us away, we shall see to it that our letters follow us all right this time.

With our loves to you and yours—

Yrs Ever
MARK.

It was Professor Samuel Pierpont Langley, the inventor of the heavier-than-air-flying machine, who gave Howells the suggestion for *The Lady of the "Aroostook."* Langley and his brother came to Venice as very young men while Howells was consul there, and told him of their voyage over with a New England girl who was the only woman on the ship. This letter from Langley confirms the fact.

Samuel Pierpont Langley to W. D. Howells

Athenæum Club, Pall Mall, S.W.,

March 23, 1879.

DEAR MR. HOWELLS:

Last year, and in Florence, I read for the first time the first chapters of *The Lady of the "Aroostook."* It seemed to me quite as though I had known Miss Blood myself, and as her Aunt lives in that city now, I asked after the niece, when I called to renew an old acquaintance.

I don't know whether your information is quite exact, for though I have not had the opportunity of reading very far into the story, it seems as though the heroine's way led through courtship and marriage.

But the living Miss —— is still Miss—Blood, and she is still a school-teacher. I wonder if she reads the *Atlantic!* However, it is such singular presumption to seem to know a child's history better than its own parent, that I should be sorry to appear guilty of it,—and yet, I am in doubt.

Sometimes I almost think I have sailed on the *Aroostook,* but then I remember that Captain —— was nothing less than paternal and that Miss —— hadn't the ministrations of so much as the small cabin-boy, who was considerately shipped for the *Atlantic's* heroine.—I am quite sure of one thing, though; that I can tell any European Critic that the (to him) incredible parts of your story are very much *under*drawn.

Then, alas! over my voyage there was none of the light that never shone on sea—or land, either—such as brightened the *Aroostook's* and on the whole, I admit that I must be mistaken.

I have been passing a very varied winter, living over all old days in Italy (except unfortunately those bright Venetian days) and spending a lonely month in December and January, among the great solitudes of the upper desert region of Mt. Etna, where I went on a scientific errand.

Since then, I have had a very agreeable time in Paris and London and shall soon hope to be home.

I wish you would think once more of the untried pleasures of the Maine woods, and then I might hope for your company in a canoe voyage this summer.

If Mrs. Howells by any chance remembers me, I beg that she will accept my respects.

Most sincerely yours,
S. P. LANGLEY.

Howells afterwards became, at Belmont, a friend and neighbor of George Fuller, who had painted the portraits of Mrs. Howells's father and brother, and wrote a biographical sketch of him for the memorial volume called *George Fuller: His Life and Works*.

To W. H. Bishop

The Atlantic Monthly, Boston,
April 12, 1879.

MY DEAR MR. BISHOP:

I have never had two minds about *Detmold:* I have thought it always a story strongly moved and with movement enough to the end; the heroine is sweet and novel; the hero a good type of good fellow; their love-making is charming; all the accessories pleased me. I have urged all this more than once; but I knew nothing of the selling qualities of the book, and I could only tell Mr. Osgood that I believed it would sell. I knew what he wrote you, and if I were you, I should make the plates and take the risk. If it sells a thousand you more than save yourself. I assure you that it shall not lack help in the *Atlantic:* I admire and like it as much as I ever did, and whatever I *don't* know of pictures, I *do* know of books.

I have had one great disappointment in your paper on the exhibition, namely, that you said nothing of Fuller's paintings: *The Romany Girl* and *She Was a Witch*. I like his work far better than that of any other American; it seems to me beautiful and interesting, with a soul as well as body. These two pictures especially charmed me. Didn't you think them good; or do you object to his methods, or did you merely pass them in carelessness or weariness? If you like them well enough to send me a page of manuscript about them, I should be glad. Fuller is one of the painters who feel and think; and most of them seem to do neither.

Yours ever,

W. D. HOWELLS.

Hay's speech was on the Negro Exodus and was made at Cleveland, Ohio, in April, 1879. In it he compared the exodus of the Negro from the South with the expulsion of the converted Moors from Spain during the reign of Philip III.

The Canadian publishers were able, under the copyright laws of this time, to print editions of American books without making any payment to the author, which they then smuggled into the United States and sold at a much lower price than the American edition. In a letter of May 11th to his father, Howells says:

"I have received the *Counterfeit Presentment* which you sent me. The worst of the Belford reprints is that they imitate the American covers, so that the wayfaring man who was intent upon the $2 edition might buy this for $1 by mistake. Of course Osgood will sell no more *Aroostooks* in Canada; but he is now in the West, and he promises that the Belfords shall sell none in Detroit. He will bring suit against every dealer in whose hands he finds them. By the way, I wish you would kindly ask some lawyer in Toronto whether I can copyright my books in Canada by residing a certain length of time—two weeks, I've heard—in the Dominion."

To John Hay

The Atlantic Monthly, Boston,

May 2, 1879.

MY DEAR HAY:

I am your debtor for a letter that touched me, and for a speech so good, so just and so manly that I felt personally obliged to you for it. How well you put the case of those wretched blacks—I wish it had been your purpose to put that of those who are black inside.

I hope you have good news of your mother, still. All sorrows but those which befall us through our parents, seem reparable. One night at eleven I got a dispatch saying, "Mother very sick—come first train." I got home three hours after her death. She had languished all summer; but because the journey was expensive and I was busy and poor, she had continually sent me word, "Tell Willy that I'm not sick—only just miserable." What tenderness was in her—what inexpressible love for her children!—I could feel for you in what you had been through at your mother's bedside and I could realize the type of character in her. It's wonderful.

My visit to my father in Toronto is postponed till the autumn. Will your sunsets keep so long? I hope so, for I want very much to see them. We shall be able then to appear in our smuggled finery—for Mrs. Howells means to buy clothes in Canada.—How very different it is when they propose to print one's book in Canada, and smuggle *that* across. It makes me feel terribly. You see they are threatening to get out a twenty-cent edition in Toronto of *The Lady of the Aroostook*. I am so glad you liked the end of the book as well as the beginning, for I thought that I had rightly philosophized the situation. Of course, South Bradfield must have the last word. As to the dialect, I am only sure that I have got the conscientiously-cunningly-reluctant, arbitrarily emphatic Yankee *manner*. Your praise does my heart good.—I have it on my soul to tell you that Barrett has paid Taylor's estate the remaining $1000, and that I judged him hastily from the delay. He is to try the play in S. Francisco. He is stale, just now with the Spanish play, which upon my word, I think the most beautiful tragedy I ever saw. I speak of the action and design.—Mrs. Hay's album has cost me no appreciable sum. Take back thy gift.

Did I tell you Whittier had written her an original poem in it?

With our love to both of you,
Yours ever,
W. D. HOWELLS.

"My book" was *The Lady of the Aroostook,* and "another story" was *The Undiscovered Country.*

To James Russell Lowell

The Atlantic Monthly, June 22, 1879.

DEAR MR. LOWELL:

Your letter made me so happy that for a while at least I felt that I must have merited so much kindness to have got it. I have a clearer mind now, but I am happy in your letter all the same. You are of course the largest part of that public of which I am conscious when I write, and if my book had not pleased you, I should not have thought it successful. —You not only praise that, but you forgive me apparently for leaving Cambridge. Do you know that at the bottom of my guilty heart, I had all along felt that my going was a sort of disloyalty to you? This grieved me, and secretly embittered Belmont. But now that you don't reproach me, I shall like the new home without a pang. We have an extremely pretty house, to which we have already welcomed most of our Cambridge friends, and we have the landscape that you know. Back of our house are lovely hill-tops, and gardened slopes, and our road frays off into the most delightful country lane to be found anywhere within a hundred miles of Boston. I hope some day to walk over it all with you. The children—especially Winny—have still keen regrets for Cambridge; but we have continued her and John in their schools there and they are not unhappy here.

House at Belmont, Mass., designed by McKim, Mead & White, in which Howells lived, 1878–1881. See the letter of June 22, 1879.

They both love the country and Bua goes in for it with all a boy's relish. His passion is for insects and he is very mortal to moths and butterflies, which he knows how to "spread," after chloroform, in a manner that moves my admiration. His sole reading is natural history. But Winny! Imagine her reading from the fact that she has kept along with me in Froude's *Cæsar;* and that Shakespeare is her favorite. She is grown up a tall girl, and is very good-looking—if I say so. Better still, she is good.—This leaves me little space to brag of the youngest, and perhaps that is just as well. But I am not ashamed of her.

I liked particularly what you said about our consciousness of England. But the matter is less serious than it may seem at a distance. Harry James waked up all the women with his *Daisy Miller,* the intention of which they misconceived, and there has been a vast discussion in which nobody felt very deeply, and everybody talked very loudly. The thing went so far that society almost divided itself in Daisy Millerites and anti-Daisy Millerites. I was glad of it, for I hoped that in making James so thoroughly known, it would call attention in a wide degree to the beautiful work he had been doing so long for very few readers and still fewer lovers. Besides, I felt that he had got his best touch in that little study. His art is an honor to us and his patriotism—which was duly questioned—is of the wholesome kind that doesn't blink our little foibles. At the end of the ends, however, I must confess that while I think our present consciousness is a fashion, we certainly are more conscious than we used to be, and are less dignified. I have come to understand fully what Hawthorne meant when he said to me that he would like to see some part of America on which the shadow of Europe had not fallen. But it's no deeper than a shadow. In the meantime it seems to me that we are in a fair way to have a pretty school of really native American fiction. There are three or four younger fellows than myself writing, and there are several extremely clever, but not too clever, young women.

You may care to know that my latest theatrical venture is a translation from the Spanish—a modern play and an extraordinarily good one. My comedy was played some thirty times, but is now in abeyance—not to use a harsher expression. They played it charmingly at the Museum, to packed houses and I in my simple soul thought it beautiful. There is no delight like seeing one's play acted. Now I have another story nearly finished.—You see I still come to you with my fond egotism. You are lucky to be beyond earshot, for you might otherwise have the story read to you.—I have sometimes wondered if you would think it quite indecorous for an Excellency like yourself to print anything. It vexes me to have you so long absent from the *Atlantic*. If you can, pray stretch a point in favor of the first inspiration.—I will do my best for the *wills* and *shalls*. You know I am not native to the right use of them; but Heaven has befriended me in much grammer hitherto, and I don't despair.—We have some hope that Dr. Holmes will begin to write largely again. I saw him the other day, and never was man on the brink of seventy more vivid.—I am glad that you still think well of the President. His action during the last three months has restored him to a favor solider if not so noisy as that which hailed his first declarations of policy. The children all send their love, and Mrs. Howells joins me in best regards to Mrs. Lowell and yourself.

Yours ever,
W. D. HOWELLS.

Aldrich and Howells must have been among the guests at Commencement, for Aldrich was given his honorary A.M. in 1896, and Howells received his in 1867. "The class of 1701" was of course figuratively speaking; Andrew Preston Peabody belonged to the class of 1826.

To Mrs. James T. Fields

Belmont, June 29, 1879.

DEAR MRS. FIELDS:

I did not know until the other day when I met Aldrich how very tedious Mr. Fields's sickness had been. Please give our love to Mr. Fields, and believe in our very cordial sympathy.

When he is able to laugh you must tell him of the majestic figure that Aldrich and I cut in the procession on Commencement Day. Of course we failed to get into line where we belonged among the guests and honorary degrees, and a young and very frightened marshall ran us up and down the ranks with no final notions in regard to us, till at last I said, "Oh, tuck us in anywhere. Here's Dr. Peabody—he won't object to our going in front of him." So we took our place in the class of 1701, and marched all round the college grounds, sharing the applause of those veterans, and going in for a full half of the honors bestowed on Dr. Peabody by the 'rahing students. Whom or what they thought us, heaven knows. Aldrich has come home very much funnier and very much fatter than ever. He is humiliated to find that he weighs a pound more than I do, and he talks violently of reducing his flesh. He says it was all the chocolate in Spain.

We have all been reading with delight Mr. Fields's witty poem on *The Owl-Critic*. It is capital, and as pat a criticism on criticism as could be. Aldrich, Longfellow, and Osgood were praising it, that day.

Don't trouble yourself, amidst your many cares, to answer this letter. We merely wished you to know that we knew of Mr. Fields's sickness and were sorry for it.

With Mrs. Howell's love,

Yours sincerely,

W. D. HOWELLS.

As it was Howells who had suggested Lowell for Minister to Spain to President Hayes, so it was again Howells who suggested him for England.

To President Rutherford B. Hayes

Belmont, Aug. 7, 1879.

DEAR MR. PRESIDENT:

At the time of the conquest of Granada there was an honest hidalgo who captured one of the Moorish kings. They called him the king-catcher, and when he attempted to seize his next prince, the Moors took *him!*

If I write you a second time in regard to a diplomatic appointment, do not let me suffer an analogous ignominy, and be sent abroad myself. I am anxious out of my love and admiration for Mr. Lowell, no less than from my regard for the national advantage, to know whether you have ever thought of him for the English mission. I believe—I don't know from him—that he would be very glad to have it offered him.

Laura Mitchell and Lilly came to us to-day for a week's visit.

Very respectfully yours,
W. D. HOWELLS.

"My story" was *The Undiscovered Country,* and Tauchnitz need not have paid anything for the books he reprinted, because the copyright laws then allowed foreigners to steal books as freely from the American authors as the American publishers stole from the foreign ones.

To Charles Eliot Norton

Boston, August 12, 1879.

DEAR FRIEND:

I have just received a note from the President, in which he says that he mentioned Lowell's name in the first talks on the subject, but hints that it may now be too late to withdraw from another direction. He adds: "But if things go so as to allow it, Mr. Lowell's name shall have a reconsideration." I gather what hope I can from this, which I would not like to have known beyond Mr. Curtis. I have reason to believe that if we had made a movement sooner, the matter could have been arranged.

I am getting well towards the end of my story, of which I once told you something. The scene of the last half is among our dear old friends the Shakers. Mr. Harrison's paper on *Sincere Demagoguery* has come, and is signally good. I have just had a letter from Tauchnitz, telling me that he has put *A Foregone Conclusion* into his edition, and means to reprint the *Aroostook*. He gilds this pretty leaf of laurel with a check for certain German marks—not a vast sum; but then he needn't have paid anything!

Yours ever,
W. D. HOWELLS.

Clemens, who had just returned from Europe and received no greeting from Howells, had written to ask if he were dead or only sleeping.

To S. L. Clemens

The Atlantic Monthly, Boston,
September 9, 1879.

MY DEAR CLEMENS:

"Sleepeth" is the matter—the sleep of a torpid conscience. I will feign that I didn't know where to write you; but I love you and all yours, and I am tremendously glad that you are at home again. When and where shall we meet? I want to see you and talk with you. Have you come home with your pockets full of *Atlantic*-able papers? How about the two books? How about all the family in the flesh and the MS.?

Thanks to your generous interest in the matter, Tauchnitz is putting one of my books into his library. He has already put *F. Conclusion* in, and the *L. of the Aroostook* goes next. He has sent me $70 for the first—and the Canadian villains, who have got out *five* editions of the *Aroostook,* never a cent.

Mrs. Howells unconsciously joins me in love to you all. We go to Toronto the first week in October to see my father. Till then we are at home, and we shall be at home about the 20th of October on our return. When do you get back to Hartford?

Yours ever,
W. D. Howells.

Clemens had proposed their writing a comedy founded on his brother Orion's character and changes of politics and religion, but this play was never written. The play they did write together was one about Colonel Sellers, which is referred to under the names of *The Steam Generator* and *Orme's Motor.* It was a failure and Clemens finally used the plot in his story of *The American Claimant.* The "longer story" was *The Undiscovered Country.*

To S. L. Clemens

The Atlantic Monthly, Sept. 17, 1879.

My dear Clemens:

We have projected a journey northward and westward, which we expect to set out on, either the first of October, or the first of November. But the date will be decided soon, and then I will make appointments for meeting, accordingly.

More than once I've taken out the skeleton of that comedy of yours, and viewed it with tears. You know I hate to say or do anything definitive; but I really have a compunction or two about helping to put your brother into drama. You can say that he is your brother, to do what you like

with him; but the alien hand might inflict an incurable hurt
to his tender heart. That's the way I have felt since your
enclosure of his letter to me. I might think differently,—and
probably should, as soon as the chance of coöperating with
you was gone. I would prefer to talk with you about the
matter. As usual my old complaint troubles me—want of
time. I am just finishing a longer story than I've written before, and I'm tempted to jump into another, as soon as that
is done, by the fact that the editor of *Cornhill* is ready to
simultane. By the way, why don't your publishers put an injunction on the sale of the Canadian ed. of *Piloting on the
M'ppi?* I have seen it for sale at the Albany depot here.
Harpers stopped a reprint of a book of theirs by suing every
man that sold it.

I have just seen Waring, who has met you since your return. That bro't us very near.

Yours ever,
W. D. HOWELLS.

Howells dramatized *The Courtship of Miles Standish*
for Lawrence Barrett, but there is no record among his
papers of its ever being acted.

To Henry Wadsworth Longfellow

The Atlantic Monthly, Boston,
October 22, 1879.

DEAR MR. LONGFELLOW:

I wish very much that you could let us have something
of yours for the January *Atlantic.* It is long since your
name appeared, and we hardly know how to begin the year
without it.

Mr. Barrett continues urgent for the drama of *Miles
Standish,* and with your kind leave I am coming soon to
look over the poem with you.

We are just returned from a long journey northward and

westward. We saw the stately Ottawa, with all her woods painted in barbaric gold and vermilion, and we saw Ohio full of corn and grapes. Such abundance I have never looked on before: those interminable levels were heaped with harvest. But after all, Belmont-that-looks-on-Cambridge, for me!

> Yours very truly,
> W. D. HOWELLS.

To S. L. Clemens

The Atlantic Monthly, Oct. 24, 1879.

MY DEAR CLEMENS:

We got home last Saturday, and though we had a glorious time in Cleveland and elsewhere, we were *glad* to get home. John Hay lives in superb style, and a lovely house, and the only thing in which I had the better of him was your letter which came there. "Why don't somebody write *me* such letters?" he sang out. "Why don't Clemens do it?" He's no end of a nice fellow, and he has a good wife and charming children. I suspect he is going to Congress next year.

Now Clemens, they are going to give Dr. Holmes a big breakfast on the 3d of December,—the *Atlantic* folks— and I want, and Mrs. Howells wants, you to come on and be our guest as long before and after that date as you can. Will you? Your invitation to the breakfast (which isn't *out,* yet,) will reach you in due time.

> Yours with our joint love to all your tribe,
> W. D. HOWELLS.

To Henry Wadsworth Longfellow

The Atlantic Monthly, Boston,
October 27, 1879.

DEAR MR. LONGFELLOW:

I am extremely vexed—for your sake—to find a newspaper paragraph stating that "Mr. Longfellow and Mr.

Howells are writing a play for Lawrence Barrett on the subject of Miles Standish." I suppose I need not say that I have never given anyone the slightest ground for making this extraordinarily foolish statement, and that I am quite mystified by it. It is too bad that your kind permission for the use of the poem should be tormented into this annoying shape.

Yours sincerely,
W. D. HOWELLS.

Hay had been appointed First Assistant Secretary of State.

To John Hay

The Atlantic Monthly, Boston,
Nov. 7, 1879.

MY DEAR HAY:

I grieve for the loss of the article, for I had made bold to announce it in our *Probabilities* for January, and was feeling rather swell about it. *Ma!*

As to that other matter, "it's like this" to my mind. I don't see any future to such an appointment. You are a far greater man than that office needs; and if you forsake anything like a completed arrangement for a Congressional nomination, don't you postpone yourself—perhaps indefinitely? This is from one whose desire for your glory is not limited by his knowledge or even his wisdom.

Yours ever,
W. D. HOWELLS.

P. S. Thanks for the key. I instantly locked Mrs. Howells's utterance with it. She had been saying that I lost it out of my pocket. Whereas it self-evidently dropped out of the keyhole on your closet floor.

President Hayes to *W. D. Howells*

Private

Executive Mansion, Washington,
22 Dec. 1879.

MY DEAR MR. HOWELLS:

Not long ago I met at Mr. Schurz's a German friend of his, formerly a resident here, and now a member of the German Parliament. He was exceedingly interesting, and a warm eulogist of yours. He was quite familiar with your writings. Among other things he said that he had heard the Russian novelist, Turgenieff, speak of your writings as superior to those of any one now living, and that he enjoyed them more than the works of anybody else.

Now put that in your pipe, and sleep if you can. If you can I'll think of you as more self satisfied than I have heretofore believed.

A Merry Christmas to Nellie and the darlings.

Sincerely,
R. B. HAYES.

XIV

1880

The Undiscovered Country. *International Copyright Treaty.*

"YOUR story" was *The House of a Merchant Prince,* which was published in 1882.

The "Siamese twins, J. and H." were James and Howells, and "my story" was *The Undiscovered Country.*

To W. H. Bishop

The Atlantic Monthly, Boston,
March 21, 1880.

DEAR MR. BISHOP:

I have been greatly interested by the inkling you have given me of your story; and I like it. You take hold of the metropolitan life at its most picturesque and characteristic point: that Fifth Avenue Sunday procession *is* New York. Your underground attachment is what gives me pause. It would be attractive and I think popular; but it might be Wilkie Collinsy or Charles Readesy. If you have grip enough on *society* to get on without it, I would, in your place. The thing is a little too far out of the common. Still, if you *like* to do it—if you would find a pleasure in it,—then you would do it well, and that would be your reason for doing it. This is a little oracular, but it is also true. Your great advantage in this New York affair is that you have the field to yourself. No one can say that you are working up the tracts of those badly assorted Siamese twins, J. and H., who happened to treat inter-continental passion (or bi-continental passion) before you, and so defrauded

Detmold of his just sales. My hope is that you will be very serious about your work, and not deal in any of those pitiful winks to the reader, with which that bad artist Thackeray has undermined most of our constitutions. You ought to treat it all as if it were history, or something truer. For heaven's sake, don't be sprightly. I am now striking all the witty things out of my work: it bolts the manuscript fearfully; but it is the right thing to do. There oughtn't be a quotable passage in a novel, unless it is dialogue. We have spoilt our readers.

My notion was not to explain anything in my story. It does not end in April (the newspapers to the contrary notwithstanding) but in July; and you will see that there are two reports of the occurrences at the tavern. I'm glad you liked that part of it. The night-walk seemed to me new and right.

Of course I knew that you did me no wrong with Gilbert.

Yours sincerely,

W. D. HOWELLS.

"Your book" was *A Tramp Abroad.*

To S. L. Clemens

The Atlantic Monthly,
March 22, 1880.

MY DEAR CLEMENS:

I have been feebly trying to give the *Atlantic* readers some notion of the charm and the solid delightfulness of your book; and now I must tell you privately what a joy it has been to Mrs. Howells and me. Since I have read it I feel sorry, for I shall not be able to read it again for a week, and in what else shall I lose myself so wholly? Mrs. Howells declares it the wittiest book she ever read, and I say there is *sense* enough in it for ten books. That is the idea which my review will try to fracture the average numskull with. Well, you are a blessing. You ought to believe in God's goodness, since he has bestowed upon the world such a delightful genius as yours to lighten its troubles.

Love from both of us to Mrs. Clemens. We wish we could come to see you, but we are many promises deep to the Warners, and our first visit must be to them. We shall hope for you here by mid-April.

Yours ever,
W. D. HOWELLS.

To *William Cooper Howells*

The Atlantic Monthly, Boston,
April 17, 1880.

DEAR FATHER:

I was glad to get your letter saying that you were in your new house, and that Henry was better. It must have been a great comfort to you in every way to have Sam with you.

We have had rather a society week. The Clemenses were in Boston, and we had them out a day and night with us. Then on Friday, I went with Winny to the Fieldses' to meet Ole Bull. We had a sit-down lunch, and uproarious story-telling gayety, and after lunch Ole Bull made his fiddle sing to us. It was wonderful: the fiddle did everything but walk round the room. Ole Bull is very white haired, and it was fine to see him as well as hear him playing. His wife was with him—an American, half his age—who accompanied him on the piano: a very gentle and charming person. This was Winny's first grown-up lunch, and might almost be said to have been made for her. She had been at a young girl's dancing party in Cambridge, the night before; and she thinks her life is very full of contrasts.

We are digging our hill-top into shape, and putting in a lot of trees this spring, especially evergreens, for which I've a great fondness. Do you know that there is an American holly, which is perfectly hardy, and keeps its leaves all winter? I'm getting that, and mountain laurel and rhododendrons.—When you come here, I expect you to take a great interest in these things. We are eager to hear about the new house, and whether you find it pleasant.—

I had a note from Goldwin Smith, the other day. Do you see anything of him? I suppose Belford is on the watch for my new book. I'm in hopes he'll find it too long to publish at the cheap rate he gets out the others.

With best love to all from all,

Your aff'te son,

WILL.

The following petition was enclosed by Clemens in a letter to Howells of March 24, 1880, in which Clemens said that he had just written Congress asking for a law making the sale of pirated books a penal offence, punishable by fine and imprisonment, like dealing with any other kind of stolen goods.

S. L. Clemens to the Senate and House of Representatives

TO THE HON. THE SENATE AND HOUSE OF REPRESENTATIVES IN CONGRESS ASSEMBLED.

Whereas, There being no provision in the Christian code of morals which justifies robbery in retaliation for robbery, but the moral law being simply *"Thou* shalt not steal," no matter what thy neighbor may do—and—

Whereas, In violation of this principle the United States has legalized the robbery of foreign authors by refusing to them the benefit of copyright—and—

Whereas, There being nothing in the Christian code of morals which justifies a man in requiring that another man shall promise to stop stealing from him before he will consent to stop stealing from said other man—

Therefore, We, your petitioners, American authors and

artists, do pray your honorable body to grant unto all foreign authors and artists full and free copyright in the
United States (upon the same terms which we ourselves
enjoy) ; and that you do this not as an act of grace or charity, but as their *right;* and furthermore that you do this
without hampering the deed with any provision requiring a
like justice at the hands of foreign governments toward
American authors and artists. We petition thus, as being
the *only* craftsmen in our country legitimately concerned in
the matter.

Believing that the infusing the spirit of God into our laws
will be something better than the empty honor of putting
His name in the Constitution, we will ever pray, etc.

SIGNED.

To William Cooper Howells

The Atlantic Monthly, Boston,
May 17, 1880.

DEAR FATHER:

Elinor and I returned from our Washington visit on
Saturday, after six charming days at the White House. We
arrived Friday afternoon of week before last, and next day
the President went with us to Mt. Vernon. Monday we
visited the Capitol, and drove out with him to Arlington;
Tuesday we drove round the city with him; Wednesday we
went down the Potomac in a steam yacht. Mrs. Hayes accompanied by Gen. Myers of the Weather Bureau, and
Bancroft the historian; Thursday I went by Mr. Evarts's
invitation to Mt. Vernon with the diplomatic corps: Elinor
was asked, but could not go. There could not have been
kinder or more attentive hosts than the Hayeses, and we
saw them as constantly as if they were private persons. He
is by all odds the weightiest man I met; and after him I
liked the Shermans the best. John Sherman remembered
and asked after you. Garfield, whom I saw twice with

Mrs. G., was full of kind inquiries and messages.—We met nearly all the distinguished people, for although Mrs. Hayes had just lost her brother, it was understood that friends would be received, and they came every night.—I can't begin to give you a full account of the visit. Of course we heard a great deal of political talk, but met no reliable prophets. I should myself greatly prefer Sherman as a candidate, and I believe his chances for the nomination are good.—Every morning before breakfast I took a long walk with the President and he talked very fully and freely with me, especially about the South. He said the Southerners had kept their word faithfully with him, and that all the trouble had come from the leadership of the Northern Democrats.

On our return we found the children all well and happy. We had a most successful visit, but how glad we are to be at home! Tell Henry that Mrs. Garfield asked particularly after him; and so she did after the girls.

With best love from all to all,

Your aff'te son,

WILL.

The "Modest Club" had been invented by Clemens, and he was, at first, the only member, as the modesty required had to be of a quite aggravated type, but upon reflection he decided that Howells was eligible, so he had held a meeting and voted to offer Howells the distinction of membership. He also thought of Hay, Warner, Twichell, Aldrich, Osgood, Fields, and Higginson, with Mrs. Howells and Mrs. Clemens, and certain others of their sex, as members.

To S. L. Clemens

The Atlantic Monthly,
May 28, 1880.

MY DEAR CLEMENS:

The only reason I have for not joining the Modest Club is that I am too modest: that is, I am afraid that I am not modest enough. If I could ever get over this difficulty, I should like to join, for I approve highly of the Club and its objects: it is calculated to do a great deal of good, and it ought to be given an annual dinner at the public expense. If *you* think I am not too modest, you may put my name down, and I will try to think the same of you. Mrs. Howells applauded the notion of the Club from the very first. She said that she knew *one* thing: that *she* was modest enough, *any* way. Her manner of saying it implied that the other persons you had named were not, and created a painful impression in my mind. I have sent your letter and the rules to Hay. But I doubt his modesty; he will think he has a *right* to belong as much as you or I; whereas other people ought only to be admitted on sufferance.

We had a magnificent time in Washington, and were six days at the White House. I wish you could have come on, as you intended, but as your friend advised, I suppose it would have been useless as far as copyright is concerned. I spoke about international copyright treaty to the President, one day; and he said that the administration would be willing to act if the authors and publishers would agree among themselves on some basis. Now, could they not agree on this basis: Englishmen to have copyright if they have an American publisher, and Americans, vice versa? Our publishers would never agree to anything else, and this would secure us our rights. If some such house as Harpers would send this proposition to all the authors and decent publishers for signature, I believe that it would be universally signed, and that if presented as a memorial to the State Department, it would before this administration goes out, become a treaty. I am going to write to the Harpers about it.

With regards to all from all,
Yours ever,
W. D. HOWELLS.

"The autobiography" was written by Orion Clemens, Mark Twain's elder brother.

To S. L. Clemens

The Atlantic Monthly,
June 14, 1880.

MY DEAR CLEMENS:

I have read the autobiography with close and painful interest. It wrung my heart, and I felt haggard after I had finished it. There is no doubt about its interest to *me;* but I got to questioning whether this interest was not mostly from my knowledge of you and your brother—whether the reader would not need some sort of "inside track" for its appreciation. The best touches in it are these which make us acquainted with *you;* and they will be valuable material hereafter. But the writer's soul is laid *too* bare; it is shocking. I can't risk the paper in the *Atlantic;* and if you print it anywhere, I hope you won't let your love of the naked truth prevent you from striking out some of the most intimate pages. *Don't* let any one else even *see* those passages about the autopsy.

The light on your father's character is most pathetic.

Yours ever,
W. D. HOWELLS.

The "document" was a memorial in favor of an International Copyright Treaty which would protect American authors from having their books stolen in Canada, and the English ones from a like piracy in America.

To John Hay

The Atlantic Monthly, Boston,
July 28, 1880.

MY DEAR HAY:

Here is a document which I have labored a good deal

to get and now I ask you to put your honored name to it, and bring to Mr. Evarts's notice, at once.

I suppose I need not say anything to you in favor of the movement. The treaty proposed by the Harpers must be on file in your Department.

Yours ever,
W. D. HOWELLS.

Björnson was Björnstjerne Björnson, the Norwegian poet, dramatist, novelist, and statesman. The separation of Norway from Sweden was due to him more than to any other man. In speaking of it years afterwards at Rome, to Howells, he said: "But it did not turn out as I wished," meaning that he had hoped for a republic.

To William Cooper Howells

The Atlantic Monthly, Boston,
Dec. 5, 1880.

DEAR FATHER:

I'm glad to hear of Henry's improvement from the Turkish baths. It's a capital idea, I should think. Winny is better than when I wrote you last, and I hope great good from the gymnasium for her. The children are all delighted with the quarters, which are beautiful.—Just now I am in all the misery of buying a horse again. Blobby, our mare, has been left stiff and useless by the epizoötic, and I have to get another horse, trusting to sell her after she gets better.— On Friday we had to lunch here the Norwegian poet Björnson, who is spending the winter at Mrs. Ole Bull's, in Cambridge. I don't know whether you've ever heard me speak of his books; but he is a great genius. Personally he is huge and very fair; and in appearance is a curious mixture of Henry and Jim Williams. I like him extremely. He is a hot Republican, and just now is in disgrace at home for having spoken disrespectfully of the king: I think he called him a donkey.

All join me in love to you all.

Your aff'te son,
WILL.

The "Two Ps" was *The Prince and the Pauper.*

Clemens had induced Howells to use a stylographic pen, with which he commenced the next letter, but at the point where he says, "No white man ought to use a stylographic pen," he renounced it for ever and returned to his ordinary one.

To S. L. Clemens

Belmont, Dec. 13, 1880.

MY DEAR CLEMENS:

I have read the Two Ps, and I like it immensely. It begins well, and it ends well, but there are things in the middle that are not so good. The whipping-boy's story seemed poor fun; and the accounts of the court ceremonials are too long, unless you *droll* them more than you have done. I think you might have let in a little more of your humor the whole way through, and satirized things more. This would not have hurt the story for the children, and would have helped it for the grownies. As it is, the book is marvellously good. It realizes most vividly the time. All the *picaresque* part—the tramps, outlaws, etc.—all the infernal clumsiness and cruelties of the law—are incomparable. The whole intention, the allegory, is splendid, and powerfully enforced. The subordinate stories, like that of Hendon, are well assimilated and thoroughly interesting.

I think the book will be a great success unless some marauding ass, who does not snuff his wonted pasturage there, should prevail on all the other asses to turn up their noses in pure ignorance. It is such a book as *I* would expect from you, knowing what a bottom of fury there is to your fun; but the public at large ought to be *led* to expect it, and must be.

No white man ought to use a stylographic pen, anyhow. You will be surprised, perhaps, that I have written you at all about the book, but Osgood sent it to me, and it took five good hours out of me on Saturday, and I think I have a right to say something. And I say it is *good*—and only long-winded in places. You ought to look out for those. The interest of the story mounts continually; there are passages that are tremendously moving; and it is full of good things.

Yours ever,
W. D. HOWELLS.

Hendon's mock—and growingly real—subordination to the prince is delightful—one of a hundred fine traits of the story.

To Arthur G. Sedgwick

The Atlantic Monthly,
Dec. 27, 1880.

MY DEAR SEDGWICK:

Your article on the theatres is indeed a noble one, and the variety of handwriting in which it is presented adds greatly to its interest. I wish you could bring it down to Barrett's performance in *Yorick's Love,* because I should like his playing to be well spoken of (if it pleased you,) and because I wish it to be authoritatively said that the play is *not* mine, as many suppose, but is merely my translation and modification. Above all, it is the Spaniard's idea (which I heartily agree with) that it isn't necessary for the young people to be "criminal" in order to feel badly; though some of the newspapers think that without carnal sin they have no occasion to be troubled.

I will write you again in regard to the paper on the F. Judiciary—perhaps within a week.

Yours ever,

W. D. HOWELLS.

XV

Places his books with James R. Osgood & Company. Resigns editorship of the Atlantic. *Degree of A.M. from Yale. Declines literary editorship of the New York* Tribune.

HENRY O. HOUGHTON and James R. Osgood of the publishing firm of Houghton & Osgood, who separated in 1880, differed in their interpretation of the agreement they had made as to authors when they parted. Howells placed his books with Osgood, who set up a new publishing house as James R. Osgood and Company, so Howells's position as editor of the *Atlantic,* which remained with H. O. Houghton, was a difficult one. Howells sent Houghton a letter in the same words as the following one to Osgood, at the same time.

To James R. Osgood

Belmont, Jan. 10, 1881.

MY DEAR OSGOOD:

I must withdraw from my proposed engagement with you; and I do this wholly of my motion, and with the full knowledge that I can in nowise be legally affected by any disagreement between Mr. Houghton and you. I have perfect confidence in your sincerity in construing your agreement as you do; but he construes it in an exactly opposite sense.

I cannot suffer myself to be made your battle-ground in fighting out your different interpretations. That is all.

I will send Mr. Houghton a copy of this letter.

Yours ever,

W. D. HOWELLS.

To James R. Osgood

Boston, Feb. 2, 1881.

DEAR OSGOOD:

When I wrote you some weeks ago that I wished to withdraw from negotiations with you, I did not expect to be in a position to make you any offer of my services. I have now, however, definitively resigned the *Atlantic* editorship, and I shall be glad to propose to you the publication of my writings hereafter.

Yours ever,
W. D. HOWELLS.

"Our relation" was that of contributor and editor.

To Horace E. Scudder

The Atlantic Monthly,
Feb. 8, 1881.

MY DEAR SCUDDER:

You break my heart! And yet I thank you for doing it, with all the pieces. You may be sure that I have enjoyed our relation as fully and thoroughly as you. I need not tell you how much I have respected your work in the magazine, how glad I was to have it there, how happy in all the personal meetings it has led to. Such a one as that of yesterday! It did me good all over. In a word, you know I love you.

But I have grown terribly, miserably tired of editing. I think my nerves have given way under the fifteen years' fret and substantial unsuccess. At any rate the MSS., the proofs, the books, the letters have become insupportable. Many a time in the past four years I have been minded to jump out and take the consequences—to throw myself upon the market as you did, *braver Mann!*—rather than continue the work which I was conscious of wishing to slight. The praise the magazine got ceased to give me pleasure, the blame galled me worse than ever. Then to see a good thing go unwelcomed, or sniffed at!—The chance came to *light soft,* and I jumped out.

I dare say I shall often regret the change—I, too, hate all changes, and this is a very great one—but I shall do my best not to regret it.

I write to you frankly, as you did to me. Dear old contributor, *salve et vale.*

Yours ever,
W. D. HOWELLS.

The *Library of Humor* was one that Clemens wished Howells to help him in editing. The "novel for Scribner" was *A Modern Instance,* but as *Scribner's Monthly* had been sold to the *Century* in 1881, the story appeared as a serial in the December *Century* of that year.

To S. L. Clemens

Boston, April 17, 1881.

MY DEAR CLEMENS:

I have written to Osgood to-day about the *Library of Humor,* and have asked him to read my letter to you; but Mrs. Howells, who has charge of my sense of decency—I wish she didn't brag so about her superior management of it—suggests that *you* ought to hear from me first. Osgood tells me that you and he are about to strike a bargain, and he wants to know if I'm ready to go to work. He also tells me that you would like to push the job through before you go to Elmira. I suppose he doesn't perhaps quite understand; but I could not agree to work at it except in the most leisurely way; you spoke of an hour a day; and I don't see how I could give more time. You see that I have to get ready a novel for Scribner by November 1st, so as to let them have the opening chapters for January; and I wish to finish it by Dec. 31, and cut for Europe. I don't know exactly how hard this work will be; but it won't be very light; and I don't know how big a book you wish to make. With the rashness of youth, I agreed to do anything, when I was at your house; but I now wish you to let me suspend my decision till I see Osgood, and get your latest ideas from him. I think also I should prefer to return to your first idea of paying me a stipulated sum—$5,000—and leave the rich possibilities of the venture to you. I believe that I could help you to that extent; but I could not afford to lose my labor if the work failed. I hope this won't seem fickle or unreasonable. The questions with me are: *I.* How many volumes and how large? *II.* Whether I can decently spring the notion of a stipulated sum on you instead of a royalty? *III.* Whether I could undertake the work experimentally and back out if I found it too hard?

Mrs. Howells is feeling badly at not having written to Mrs. Clemens and thanked her for the good time she made us have at your house. She has been in bed the greater part of the past fortnight; but she is up now, and will start the universe on the right basis again in a few days. She joins me in love to all of you.

Please write me at Belmont: we go back on Thursday.

Yours ever,
W. D. HOWELLS.

P. S. My difficulty in finishing the two-number story that I've just ended has given me a scare about loading up with more work till I see my way through the novel. If I were not able to go to Europe in December, then I should have a clear three months before I began another story, and should be glad and humbly thankful to help you on the L. of H. Or if you and Osgood can agree on terms, and leave the time blank, I can still be your man. What I dread is to enter on work that I can't decently back out from. Why don't you go on with the Etiquette Book, and let the L. of H. rest awhile? I *don't* want to give it up; but I don't want to begin it till the way is clearer to me.

The "old Eureka Mills" near Xenia, Ohio, were the grist mills that Howells's father and uncles had planned turning into paper mills, and making the centre of an ideal community. These mills were the scene of *My Year in a Log Cabin* and *New Leaf Mills*. Howells was on his way to stay with Maurice Thompson, at Crawfordsville, Indiana, to see a Western divorce case tried, so he might be sure of the details for the divorce in *A Modern Instance*.

To Mrs. W. D. Howells

5 P.M., Dayton, April 29, 1881.

DEAR ELINOR:

Our train from Xenia missed connections, and we have been here five hours, which we have spent in driving out to see the Soldiers' Home, a most interesting place—a city in itself; a sad metropolis of sickness and suffering. About 4000 soldiers there. I drove down from Xenia to the old Eureka Mills this morning, through the most beautiful country—almost as hilly as from Belmont to Lexington. The Mills almost exactly as when I left them, thirty years ago. We expect to reach Crawfordsville to-morrow morning.

Love to all.

Your

W. D. H.

"This terrible news about Garfield" was that of Guiteau's attack upon him. "Miss Porter" was the daughter of President Porter of Yale.

To Edmund Clarence Stedman

Belmont, July 2, 1881.

My dear Stedman:

With this terrible news about Garfield superseding and blotting out everything else, I hardly know how to reply fitly to your two kind letters, and tell you what a glorious time I had at Yale. I found myself in the midst of friends at once; but that did not prevent my missing you, and I enquired for you at once. I called on Mrs. Stedman, but she was not in, and I had not the pleasure of seeing her till we met at the President's reception. I was at the Commencement exercises as well as the dinner, and Lounsbury walked me all about and showed me the whole university. I topped off the next day by going to the race at New London. I learnt from Holt the fraternal interest you had taken in the high honor done me, and I wish to thank you with all my heart; and to beg you to thank my proposer for me. Do you know his address? I should like to send him my next book. The President introduced me at dinner in terms that made me blush for pride and pleasure; and I never longed so before to be able to make a speech in return. I noticed an atmosphere of enthusiasm and cordiality at Yale which seemed characteristic and peculiar, and which made me feel at once at home there. I must now write on my title-pages *W. D. H., A.M. Harv. and Yale.* At the boat-race, "I perceived a divided duty," and hardly knew whether to weep or rejoice at the defeat of my first adoptive alma mater. I happened to wear a blue neck-tie; Miss Porter noticed it, and sent to know if I wore it purposely. Good-bye. Thanks and thanks. The cloud that is over us all settled down on me again. It's terrible!

Yours ever,

W. D. Howells.

"Miss Phelps's story" was *Doctor Zay,* a novel that, to Howells's surprise, had much the same subject as his own story of *Doctor Breen's Practice* which was just appearing as a serial in the *Atlantic.* It was arranged before Howells left the *Atlantic* that *Doctor Zay* should follow *Doctor Breen's Practice* in that magazine.

At almost the same time that Miss Phelps told Howells the plot of her novel he received from a younger and less well-known authoress a story with the same outline as *Doctor Zay* and *Doctor Breen's Practice.* Taking the proofs of his novel, which was to begin in the next number of the *Atlantic,* with him in a bag, Howells went to the suburb where the young authoress lived to explain the matter to her. She received him very sternly, thinking from his bag that he was a book agent, but in spite of her discouraging manner he told her his errand and offered to show her the proofs of his story, to prevent, as he said, "all suspicion among our friends that I stole your plot," but the authoress expressed entire faith in his word and courteously refused to look at the proofs.

To Thomas Bailey Aldrich

Belmont, Aug. 24, 1881.

DEAR ALDRICH:

If the President lives, I will make a thank offering of the little paper: I wrote it when I was suffering too much with my eye to work on my story. If he dies, I shall wish to make it better.

I hardly know what to say about Miss Phelps's story. I told her that I would begin it when mine was finished, for I thought it would be a sort of card for her to follow on the same subject; and I am to write her a preface explaining that she did not get her idea from me. I see your embarrassment about the other stories: would she consent to three months' delay, so that you could get Lathrop's through, first? I will try to see you soon, and talk of the matter at length.

You were all that saved us from salting that bench with our tears.

> Yours ever,
> W. D. H.

Clemens had an idea of adding a burlesque character to *Hamlet.*

The "two rivals in the celebration of a doctress" were Miss Phelps and the young authoress who never published her story, but who the "pretty young doctress" was, it is impossible to tell.

"The P. and the P." was again *The Prince and the Pauper.*

To S. L. Clemens

Belmont, Sept. 11, 1881.

MY DEAR CLEMENS:

That is a famous idea about the *Hamlet,* and I should like ever so much to see your play when it's done. Of course you'll put it on the stage and I prophesy a great triumph for it.

You know I had *two* rivals in the celebration of a doctress; now comes a pretty young doctress who had written out her own adventures! How is that for mental telegraphy?

Osgood told me of your very generous willingness to pay me for my *Library of Humor* work in advance. I know you let him know this because you supposed I needed money; but I assure you that I do not. I am as deeply touched, though, and as grateful as if I could let you do such a thing. I can wait perfectly well till the work is ready to be done.

I have written to Hay, and he has commissioned me to

write a review of *The P. and the P.* for the *Tribune.* I'm now merely waiting for the sheets.

Winny is still trying the rest cure; but we are going to get her up as soon as the doctor comes home. If she could have been allowed to read, I think the experiment might have succeeded; but I think the privation has thrown her thoughts back upon her, and made her morbid and hypochondriacal.

You know how fond we are of you, and I needn't tell you that we were very happy in your fruitful visit here. The only trouble is that we don't meet often enough.

How fortunate Garfield's removal was! He might have been well by this time if they'd moved him a month ago.

Yesterday I wrote 30 pages on my story.

Yours ever,
W. D. HOWELLS.

When do you return to Hartford?

To Thomas S. Perry

Belmont, Mass., Sept, 25, 1881.

MY DEAR PERRY:

They are going to print my picture in Scribner, and they give me the privilege of choosing my own biographer and critic. I turn to you as a Jap gentleman does in requesting the kind services of his friend at harikari. You will not fail me? I am to be poor James's "second."

Yours ever,
W. D. HOWELLS.

To George W. Cable

Belmont, Oct. 2, 1881.

MY DEAR MR. CABLE:

I have just finished *The Grandissimes,* and I must at least try to tell you how much I like it. I had heard it called

faulty and confused in construction; that was the only blame
I had heard of it, and that is mistaken. I found it thoroughly knit and perfectly clear, portraying a multitude of
figures with a delicacy and unerring certainty of differ-
entiation that perpetually astonished me. It is a noble and
beautiful book, including all the range of tragedy and
comedy; and it made my heart warm towards you while
I had the blackest envy in it. Deuce take you, how could
you do it so well?—Aurora is one of the most delicious
creatures I ever knew. My wife kept reading me that first
call of Frowenfeld's on the Nancanou ladies, till I was in-
toxicated with their delightfulness. Oh the charm of their
English! We speak nothing else now but that dialect. Raoul,
Honoré, and the poor f.m.a.—they have our hearts, Raoul
especially. Of course you expected me to like Agricola too?
He is admirable. Bras Coupé episode most powerful; the
last chapter, exquisite—that woman left a sweet taste in
my mouth; Honoré, with his guttural r's noble and charming; all the Grandissime tribe boldly sketched, or finely suggested. The book is full of atmosphere. You are a great
fellow and we all send you homage—our love.

Yours sincerely,
W. D. HOWELLS.

The "book" was *The Prince and the Pauper.*

To S. L. Clemens

Belmont, Oct. 12, 1881.

MY DEAR CLEMENS:

I send some pages with words queried. These and other
things I have found in the book seem rather strong milk
for babies—more like milk-punch in fact. If you give me
leave I will correct them in the plates for you; but such a
thing as that on p. 154, I can't cope with. I don't think
such words as divil, and hick (for person) and basting

(for beating,) ought to be suffered in your narrations. I have found about 20 such.

Yours ever,
W. D. HOWELLS.

I'm reading your book for review.

The "Mark Twain review" was the one Howells wrote of *The Prince and the Pauper* for the New York *Tribune.*

To John Hay

Belmont, Oct. 16, 1881.

MY DEAR HAY:

Here is the Mark Twain review. I do not sign it because it isn't your custom; and it might look like advertising; whereas I have written it solely in the interest of that unappreciated serious side of Clemens's curious genius. The book has a thousand blemishes and triumphs over them. I should like to see a proof.

Yours ever,
W. D. HOWELLS.

You will have the only review from advance sheets.

The "fever" proved a serious one, and lasted for a month.

To William Cooper Howells

Belmont, Nov, 15, 1881.

DEAR FATHER:

I am down with some sort of fever—probably a short one, and though better, I am afraid I shall not be well enough to come next week. It's the result of long worry and sleeplessness from overwork, nothing at all serious.

Don't write me you're disappointed. I shall understand that, but to have you say it would afflict me.

Your aff'te son,
WILL.

Howells, who was tired of editorial work and wished to give his whole time to creative writing, must have declined Reid's suggestion.

Whitelaw Reid to W. D. Howells

New York Tribune, New York,
Nov. 29, 1881.

MY DEAR HOWELLS:

Warner told me a few weeks ago in London that you were going over soon on account of your daughter's health. Yesterday some one told me that the plan had been abandoned—which I hope means that the young lady whom I remember as a little girl so many years ago is in better health again.

Prompted by the news that you are not going to desert us, I want to renew an old suggestion. Isn't it about time for you to leave Boston and come to New York? Poor Hassard's ill-health makes it necessary for me to look about for a literary editor. I don't know just how much you did on the *Atlantic,* but I don't believe the work here would be harder. I am sure it would be free from some embarrassments you had there, and it would not be likely to be worse paid.

Is it worth considering the subject at all? I would really like very much to have you come and in many ways should feel certain that it would be pleasant for you. Think of it at any rate as favorably as you can, and write to me soon.

Faithfully yours,
WHITELAW REID.

W. D. HOWELLS, Esq.,
Care JAMES R. OSGOOD & Co.
Boston, Mass.

The proofs that Scudder corrected for Howells were either those of *Doctor Breen's Practice* that appeared in book form in 1881, or the proofs of *A Modern Instance,* which began as a serial in the December *Century* of the same year.

To Horace E. Scudder

Belmont, Dec. 12, 1881.

YOU DEAR OLD FELLOW:

How shall I thank you for your kindness? Your corrections of my proof were ideally good, and you saved me from the merciless excisions of Mrs. Howells!

I can't say I hope you will be as sick, some day, so that I may pay you up. And I'm too weak to know what I ought to say.

With love to the shy Sylvia, and best regards to Mrs. Scudder.

Yours ever,
W. D. HOWELLS.

I feel like a diluted shadow.

XVI

1882

A summer in London. A Little Swiss Sojourn. *Paper on Henry James.* A Woman's Reason. *Declines Professorship of Literature at Johns Hopkins University. Florentine Winter.*

"**YOUR** enterprise" was a biography of Whitelaw Reid that Clemens had planned after being told that the *Tribune* had made almost daily attacks upon him since Reid's return from Europe. After outlining a campaign to force a peace or get revenge, Clemens set a man to looking up the "almost daily" insults, and found they consisted of one discourteous reference to his book, two foreign criticisms, and one joke; so the biography was abandoned as Howells predicted it would be in a letter of January 20th in which he writes to Clemens:

"I told Osgood the other day, that I should write to you about—or against—your dynamitic life of Reid; but I concluded not to do so, partly because I did not know how you would take unprovoked good intentions from me, and partly because I believe you will be sick of the thing long before you reach the printing point."

"The play we once blocked out together" was *Orme's Motor* and was to be largely founded on the character of Clemens's older brother, Orion Clemens.

"The story now running in the *Century*" was *A Modern Instance.*

To S. L. Clemens

16 Louisburg Square, Boston,
Jan. 31, 1882.

MY DEAR CLEMENS:

Your letter was an immense relief to me, for although I had an abiding faith that you would get sick of your enterprise, I wasn't easy till I knew that you had given it up. It only remains now that you should see Reid some day, and have it out with him—in perfect friendliness, as I know you can—about the original grief between you. I never believed that he was a man capable of persecuting you, or systematically nagging you.

Mrs. Howells and I would like to come to your house; but for the present it isn't possible. I long to see you here, however; a thousand things are rotting in my breast for want of saying. For example, I should like to reconsider with you that play we once blocked out together. Every once in a while that seems to me a great play. What did you ever do with your amended *Hamlet?* That was a famous idea.

I am working away all the time at the story now running in the *Century*. I had written 1466 MS. pages before I fell sick, and I have had to revise nearly all that since I got up; and I have still 300 or 400 pages to write before the story is finished. I find that every mental effort costs about twice as much as it used, and the result seems to lack texture. I ought to have had a clean rest of three months when I began to get well.

My brother Joe has a boy four years old, whose favorite work is *Tom Sawyer*—"the fightingest and excitingest parts." This fact gave me an idea of fame. If you were John Bunyan, could you expect more? I wonder how long you will last, confound you? Sometimes I think we others

shall be remembered merely as your friends and corre-
spondents.

Mrs. Howells joins me in love to both of you.

Yours ever,

W. D. Howells.

William Cooper Howells was at this time United States
consul at Toronto, where he had gone from the consulate
in Quebec in 1878. After Garfield's death, he feared that
he might be removed from his consulate, but Grant's influence confirmed him in it, and he remained consul at
Toronto until he resigned in 1883.

In *My Mark Twain,* Howells gives an account of Clemens's help in securing the Toronto consularship to his
father:

"When my father was consul at Toronto during Arthur's
administration, he fancied that his place was in danger, and
he appealed to me. In turn I appealed to Clemens, bethink-
ing myself of his friendship with Grant and Grant's friendship with Arthur. I asked him to write to Grant in my
father's behalf, but No, he answered me, I must come to
Hartford, and we would go on to New York together and
see Grant personally. This was before, and long before,
Clemens became Grant's publisher and splendid benefactor,
but the men liked each other as such men could not help doing. Clemens made the appointment, and we went to find
Grant in his business office, that place where his business innocence was afterwards so betrayed. He was very simple
and very cordial, and I was instantly the more at home with
him, because his voice was the soft, rounded, Ohio River accent to which my ears were earliest used from my steamboat-
ing uncles, my earliest heroes. When I stated my business he
merely said, Oh no; that must not be; he would write to
Mr. Arthur; and he did so that day; and my father lived

to lay down his office, when he tired of it, with no urgence from above."

To William Cooper Howells

Hotel Brunswick, Fifth Avenue, 26th & 27th Sts.
New York, March 10, 1882.
DEAR FATHER:

Clemens saw Grant to-day, on your affair, and Grant made a note of it, and said he would write to the President at once in your behalf. He told Clemens that the affair could be better arranged without our going to Washington. I presume that this will settle the matter, and you need have no further anxiety.

I afterwards lunched with Grant, and found him very pleasant.

As soon as he can have heard from Washington, Clemens will write to Grant, and I will send you his reply. But I am not at all fearful as to the result.

With love to all,
Your aff'te son
WILL.

To S. L. Clemens

Boston, March 15, 1882.
MY DEAR CLEMENS:

Thanks and thanks for all your kindness in my father's affair. I have a letter from him in which he wishes me to express his gratitude to you, and I have just enclosed him yours in which you copy the Sec'y's letter to Grant. Now what can I do to show my sense of Grant's kindness. Would it be too hard on him if I sent him two of my books— *Venetian Life* and *Italian Journeys?* (I *can't* suppose he'd care for the novel-books.)

What a bare-faced pretence is that bill of $6.85! You

have got on such a string of misrepresentations in regard to your mother's visit that you can't tell the truth about *any*thing. Why, the breakfast-bacon that I ate was alone worth $6.85. But I'll settle with you! I had such a good time that I can hardly believe our mission was not an utter failure. If I hadn't been so thoroughly broken up about my work, by going away twice, I *couldn't* believe it. But that partly persuades me. You can't think what a sneaking desire I had to get into the carriage, that day, and drive home with you and Mrs. Clemens.

Yours ever,
W. D. HOWELLS.

To John Hay

16 Louisburg Square, Boston,
March 18, 1882.

MY DEAR HAY:

It is so long since you wrote to me that I hope you think you owe me a letter. But this is not really the case. When your last came, I was just crawling out of the bed where I had spent seven endless weeks, and I could only enjoy your letter and despair of answering it. That is often the effect of a good letter on me when I am in health; in fact, now when I am quite well again, and only two or three years older than I was four months ago, I begin with you on very small note, so that I can leave off at once when my courage gives out.

I will try to give your our *noticias,* first. We are planning at present to go abroad in the beginning of July, with the intention of spending the next three months in Weimar or Baden-Baden, and then of going to Florence for the winter. I want to make a book for Osgood about the smaller cities of North Italy, and I expect to leave the family at Florence and wander about myself from Parma to Modena, Verona, Vicenza, Padua, Treviso, etc., and write about them as I did about Ducal Mantua. Now what transport it would be if the Hays spent next winter in Florence, too! Is such a thing possible? Try to imagine it!—Well, Winny, who was down for nearly two years with nervous prostration, is now quite herself again, and Mrs. Howells is "usually well." The two younger children are in good state, and John is at this moment curled up on the lounge reading *Doctor Breen's Practice*. For this reason, if for no other, I could not have palpitating divans in my stories; my children are my censors, and if I wished to be wicked, I hope they would be my safe-guards. A glance at the book shows me that John is deep in the love-makingest chapter. It was not written for children, but if a child may read it without harm, it seems to me something to be glad of. I am a great admirer of French workmanship, and I read everything of Zola's that I can lay hands on. But I have to hide the books from the children! I won't try to parry the kind things you say of my work: for I do work hard, and I know that I *aim* at the highest mark, morally and artistically. There I have to leave things to others. But your words gave me a delight and courage which, if there had been any decency in me, I should have confessed to you by telegraph rather than three months afterwards.

Harry James is spending the winter only a few doors from us. (We left our country house after my sickness, and came into town.) I see him constantly, and we talk literature perpetually, as we used to do in our walks ten years ago. He is not sensibly changed, and, reflected in him, I find that I am not. He had a plan of travelling all about the country this winter and then of returning to England in April; but this has been broken up by the sudden death of his mother, and I doubt if he will stay continuously abroad again while his father lives. He and his three brothers carried their mother to her grave; it was a most touching story, as he told it to me.

I have lately been at Hartford, and have seen a great

deal of Mark Twain. We confessed to each other that the years had tamed us, and we no longer had any literary ambition: before we went to bed we had planned a play, a lecturing tour, a book of travel and a library of humor. In fact, he has life enough in him for ten generations, but his moods are now all colossal, and they seem to be mostly in the direction of co-operative literature.

Aldrich is busy on the *Atlantic* and is very fond of his editorial work. He hates writing, you know, and he likes reading and talking, and he spends six hours every day at the office where I used to put in a scant afternoon once a week. Whittier is visiting at the Claflins on Mt. Vernon street, and with Aldrich in his old house on Charles st., we are quite a literary precinct. By the way, do you read Cable's books? They are delicious: there is no more charming creation in fiction than Aurora Nancanou in *The Grandissimes*. And Cable himself is the lovliest and loyalest ex-rebel that lives. He was at Belmont last spring and took all our hearts away with him.

I could go on writing for ever, if I had the wrist for it. But now, good-bye, with love from all of us to all of you. Try to see some way of meeting us in Europe.

Yours affectionately,
W. D. HOWELLS.

The plotted comedy was *Orme's Motor*, again.

To S. L. Clemens

Consulate of the United States of America,
Toronto, July 14, 1882.

MY DEAR CLEMENS:

A letter will go by the same post with this to Norton, who will appreciate all the circumstances, and duly hold you excused. I'm glad that you're over the cause of your trouble safely, and that you're fairly off to Elmira at last. Our best love to Mrs. Clemens, and heartfelt congratulations.

The Madison Square Theatre Mallorys, having never ceased to drum me up for a play, I told them that you and I had a comedy plotted, of which the main idea would be yours, and the literature mostly mine. Whereupon they write proposing that I should let them have it for $4000 (the sum I proposed once to take for a play of my own) and pay you $1000 more for your "idea"! I have just written them that this is a totally different affair, and that they must treat with *you* for our joint comedy. Now, I suppose I could send you home the play completed from notes (which I have) and my own; but it ought to be worth the grand cash to us. I have told them to write to you, and if they want it, I hope you'll make them pay for it; and you had better have them in writing at every step. Let me know the result in London (449 Strand, Gillig's American Exchange,) and tell me whether you wish me to go on and write up the play.

Yours ever,
W. D. HOWELLS.

"Vevie" and "Mole" were Howells's niece and nephew, the children of his sister, Mrs. Fréchette. The little girl had been staying with her Howells aunts in Toronto, one of whom she called "Aunt Lili."

"The count" was El Conde de Primio Real, the Spanish Consul General in Quebec, a great friend of Howells's father and sisters.

"Elinor's brother" was William Rutherford Mead, who crossed with his sister and her family on the *Parisian.*

To Miss Victoria M. Howells

Quebec, July 21, 1882.

DEAR VIC:

I send with this a little "testimonial," which I hope you will accept in apology for itself, and for me, who intended to do something better at Toronto. My best love to you with it.

We are here in Quebec at last. We had a very pleasant sail to Montreal, where the Annie family met us, and took Vevie, who was as good as could be all the time,—and who called her mother "Aunt Lili" till she got used to her identity. Mole was on hand in great force, and the two funny little things took each other round the neck in an affecting and dramatic embrace. Achille came as far as Sorel with us, where he hurried ashore in great precipitation—after which the boat lay there an hour. Annie I found just as delightful as ever—there never was a more charming person. We had a good night, and in the morning at Quebec, I took a "colosh," and drove round hotel-ing. We all took breakfast here, and in the afternoon Annie went with her tribe to the Mountains (perhaps because the mountains wouldn't come to her). The Count's attentions began at once. He sent his *valet*, who took possession of our selves and our multitudinous trunks, with orders from the Count to pay everything. Then "his excellency" himself appeared after breakfast, and spent the whole day, driving, walking, and dining with us, and in the evening went with us to the Stewarts, who asked us to tea.—He was most affectionate in his inquiries about each of you, and he told me that father was "a man without a fault—without a fault." In fact, that seems to be the universal opinion in Quebec, and you can imagine I don't dispute it. Father never seemed to be so dear and good as on this visit. We were a solemn party for a while after he went ashore at Toronto, and poor little Pil wept.

We are gradually getting into shape for the steamer; but it is an exciting and distracting time, and to-day we shall set our faces against all "attentions." I have scarcely had a chance to speak to Annie since we reached Quebec; but she and I are going to drive down to the steamer together to-day.—Elinor's brother hasn't turned up yet, though I suppose he will be duly on hand. I am writing this at five o'clock in the morning, the flies having started me out early; and all that wonderful Quebec landscape lies before me from the window.

I went on to the steamer yesterday with the Count, and saw our rooms again. They are very good, and the purser told me he expected that we would be in Liverpool a week after starting.

I will try to send home a line from Rimouski, where some mails go ashore. With dearest love to father and all of you from us,

Your aff'te brother,
WILL.

The "charming lodgings" were those long occupied by Mrs. Procter, the widow of the poet "Barry Cornwall," and the mother of Adelaide Procter.

"The Niagara sketch" was *Niagara Revisited,* and was published in the May *Atlantic* of 1883. It was reprinted, without Howells's consent, as an advertisement for the Hoosac Tunnel Route of the Fitchburg railroad, but the author made the railroad suppress the whole edition. He afterwards added *Niagara Revisited* as a final chapter to *Their Wedding Journey.*

To James R. Osgood

18 Pelham Crescent, South Kensington,
London, S. W., August 1, 1882.

MY DEAR OSGOOD:

We are here in a very charming lodging, which James had taken for us, and in which we sat down to a dinner that was cooking for us on our way up from Liverpool. We arrived on Sunday, after a famous passage of less than eight days, free from seasickness, and as comfortable as a sea voyage could be. The ship was extraordinarily steady, and though we had rough weather the whole way, she did not roll and scarcely pitched.

I presented myself at the American Exchange this morning, and was most hospitably received both by Mr. Gillig and Mr. Tozer. They made every sort of kind offer, and I am greatly obliged to your brother and B. H. T. for commending me to them. Mr. Tozer made many inquiries about Ticknor. At the Exchange I saw Hutton who told me Barrett was at Morley's; I called there but did not find him. I have seen John Hay and wife, and we are going to Greenwich with them on Monday. I shall call on Lowell to-morrow. James has been with me to-day, and has been very kind. He said that Aldrich had proposed to offer him a great temptation in the way of price if he would write them a story for next year; but he will not write on any account for the present. I called to see Roswell Smith to-day, but he is still in Germany.

I have finished the Niagara sketch, and I shall send it to you, after getting it put in type, on Saturday. It is not a "story," though it is largely fictitious; let me know what you do with it, and what proportion of the plunder you rend from me, or assign to me. My wife, after being ashamed of our getting $500 for it, now thinks we ought to have much more! Such is the effect of prosperity on the female mind.

Remember me cordially to all hands at 211.

Yours ever,
W. D. HOWELLS.

"Mr. Herkomer" was later Sir Hubert von Herkomer.

To Charles Fairchild

London, Aug. 28, 1882.

MY DEAR FAIRCHILD:

I am asking Mr. Herkomer to take this letter to you when he visits Boston, for the pleasure that I know it will give you to make his acquaintance. He is not merely the great painter who has taken all the honors in Europe, and made everybody talk of him here; but he is partly an American: he passed six years of his boyhood at Cleveland, and is what the Cleveland *Herald* would call "a Western Reserve boy." I wish this were the place to tell you all I know of him; but I may whisper that his portraits do not sit in their frames, but walk all about the room and would shake hands with you if they were not lords and ladies: as it is they only offer you two fingers; but they are as much alive as the originals.

No doubt he will bring some of his work to Boston with him, and I hope you and Mrs. Fairchild will enjoy it as much as we have done. He has a notion of getting at American types,—especially financial heads, and I have hoped that you might help him to see the men in Boston who have done great things in money.

Yours ever,

W. D. HOWELLS.

To S. L. Clemens

London, Sept. 1, 1882.

MY DEAR CLEMENS:

You ought to have been yesterday with Osgood, Hutton and me at Oxford. We started with the intention of coming back on a Thames steamer. Of course we failed in that, but what I was thinking was that if you were along, you could have kept us, with my help, from getting to Oxford. We had a beautiful time in that beautifulest of old towns, and almost walked our legs off seeing it. We stopped at the Mitre tavern, where they let you choose your dinner from the joints hanging from the rafter, and have passages that you lose yourself in every time you try to go to your room. But you have been there. We *did* do a few miles of the Thames, in a sort of big steam launch, and if it had not rained all the way, and Osgood hadn't had the rheumatism, we should have enjoyed it. We came pretty near it, as it was.

We are in the prettiest and comfortablest kind of lodging in South Kensington (address me care American Exchange, however) where our five rooms with private dining-room and exquisite feed costs us only $50 a week (we paid $75 for *two* rooms in Boston) and here we expect to stay a month longer. We have seen lots of nice people, and have been most pleasantly made of; but I would rather have you smoke in my face, and *talk* for half a day—just for *pleasure*—than go to the best house or club in London. And yet some of these people are delightful. Boughton, for example, and Alma Tadema, above all. *What* a good fellow Tadema is. And I am sending you a card by a wonderful painter, Herkomer, who is going to America next month. John Hay has been here, and Mrs., and they are coming back in a day or two. Couldn't you and Mrs. Clemens step over for a little while? Warner lunched with us on Tuesday, and is to return from Scotland for a big dinner that Osgood gives next Thursday. W., Gen. Hawley, John Hay, Boughton, Aldrich, Tadema and W. D. H. How does that strike you as a time?

Yours ever,
W. D. HOWELLS.

"Kings and Hartes" were Clarence King and Bert Harte. "The story" must have been Hay's *Bread-Winners,* which was published anonymously in the *Century.*

To John Hay

18 Pelham Crescent,
Sept. 5, 1882.

MY DEAR HAY:
Not for Kings nor Hartes, but for yourselves alone do

we break the awful vow we made to accept no more invitations. We will come.

Aldrich says he will accept the story unsight and unseen, but he wants the author's name to go with it!

Yours ever,
W. D. HOWELLS.

The paper on Lexington for *Longmans Magazine* was afterwards reprinted with one on Shirley—the scene of *The Undiscovered Country*—and an article on Gnadenhütten, under the title of *Three Villages*.

To William Cooper Howells

18 Pelham Crescent, Sept. 10, 1882.

DEAR FATHER:

I believe that Elinor and the children have been writing quite lavishly of late, and they have probably written you all the news. The latest is that we are going to cut short our stay in London where I find myself too subject to hospitality to be able to work. I have, to be sure, written a long paper for a new English magazine which the Longmans are about to start, and have made use of our sojourn in Lexington for that purpose; but I have only done a scanty hundred pages on my story. So we leave London, Monday the 18th, and by the time you get this we shall probably be settled in a Swiss family on the Lake of Geneva—with a Mlle. E. Colomb, Le Clos, près Villeneuve, Vaud. But write as usual to the care of the American Exchange.

Last Sunday we had a lovely day at Stoke Pogis, the little churchyard on which Gray wrote his elegy. It is the prettiest and most pathetic place I ever saw. The old church dates back to 13 or 1400, and looks its age; the ivy-mantled tower is there, clothed to the very top in the vine, and there is the yew-tree. The rugged elm I could not find. Gray lies buried there in the same grave with his mother;

his monument is in the meadow adjoining. I would have given anything, father, if you could have been there with me! I could not tell you how beautiful it all was. For the rest we have been rushing hither and thither; and now we are beginning to feel the stir of travel again. But I shall be glad when we are settled, and I am fairly at work. The arrangements for travel are very bad on the continent, and we shall not get to our destination without some hard work. Imagine there being but one through train a day on the route we are to take! Whether we wish or not we must travel all night or else pick up way trains as we can, and be nearly a week about it. We expect to go through Calais, Rheims, Bâle and Berne, if you care to follow us on the map.

All join me in love to all. I'm glad Henry improves.

Your aff'te son,
WILL.

"Doctor Waldstein" was Charles Waldstein, then the lecturer on Classical Archæology at Cambridge, and "Mr. Colvin" was Sidney Colvin, at that time the Director of the Fitzwilliam Museum there.

To Charles Eliot Norton

London, Sept. 14, 1882.

MY DEAR FRIEND:

I am so bad a correspondent, that I seize myself in both hands at this last moment before leaving England, and send you any sort of line lest I should send you no sort. We have had a most charming sojourn here, and though everybody says everybody is out of town, we have met all kinds of desirable people. I must name Burne-Jones first among these: he came to a dinner with us at the Tademas, before I had the chance of making his acquaintance through your letter; and I had enough talk with him to feel his gentle and exquisite spirit, which had already delighted me in his pictures at the Grosvenor and the Royal Academy. I made interest with him at once by boasting you my friend, and he was full of affectionate questions about you, and self-reproach that he had not written you. I had not the courage to send a letter of introduction to any such fairy as a real nobleman, and your letter to Lord Reay awaits delivery till our return to England in the spring. So does that to Morley, who has been out of town. I have seen Lowell many times, and have found him sweetly and beneficently unchanged. Mrs. Lowell is astonishingly well. H. J., Jr., has been an adoptive father in housing and starting this orphan family in London. Just now he has gone to France.

Two heavenly days—one in each place—I have spent in Oxford and Cambridge: in the latter only yesterday. Winny and I were the guests of Doctor Waldstein, who says his place there corresponds to yours in the real Cambridge. He and Mr. Colvin, the curator of the Museum, were full of knowledge and praise of you. I dined "in hall" with Waldstein (King's). I met one of the Darwins (the non-American-travelled one) at Waldstein's rooms, and seemed to be in some sort at home among these people. But the strongest illusion of all was when we came to the Cambridge horse-cars. They are not so good as ours; but upon the whole their gardens and buildings are better—or at least *older*.

We start for Switzerland on Monday, and expect to spend two months by the lake of Geneva before going on to Italy.

Mrs. Howells and all the children join me in love to you all.

Yours ever,
W. D. HOWELLS.

"My story" was *A Woman's Reason*.

To William Cooper Howells

Le Clos, Villeneuve, Vaud, Switzerland,
                                Sept. 24, 1882.

DEAR FATHER:

Your letters to me and to John have come since we arrived here, and we are in possession of reasonably late news
from you. The promptness of everything is really surprising—so much greater than when we were in Europe before.
But they have still a vast deal to learn of us, especially in
railroading and in sleeping-cars. We took the bed-wagon
(as the French call it) at Calais, having crossed very comfortably at Dover, and found it but little bigger and better
than an ambulance. To satisfy the supposed passion for pri-
vacy, it was cut up into half a dozen staterooms with four
berths in each crosswise of the car, and outside of these an
aisle ran the length of the sleeper. It was badly hung, and
swayed and jolted as our cars did before we had the shiller
platform. However we got thro' to the Swiss frontier by
daylight, by way of Amiens and Rheims, and then worked
on through Berne and Lausanne by three in the afternoon.
We are delightfully placed here, within a stone's throw of
Lake Geneva and within two minutes' walk of the Castle of
Chillon, round which we all rowed in a boat yesterday.
We are with the Swiss lady to whom Edward Eggleston
recommended us before we left Toronto, and we find ourselves very comfortable. It is a distinct pleasure to be in a
Republic again; the manners are simple and unceremonious
as our own, and people stand upright in all respects. The
many resemblances to America constantly strike me; and if
I must ever be banished, I hope it may be to Switzerland.
These are my first impressions; I may change my ideas
later.—We have already entered upon a severe campaign
against the French language, but as yet without much
method, though we hope to begin with that to-morrow,

when Winny and Pillà expect to enter a girl's school and due provision is to be made for John and the rest of us. Mademoiselle is the only one in the house who speaks English besides ourselves. She is a jolly old maid of forty; and she has with her Mme. Grenier, her widowed cousin, and Mme.'s son and daughter, all nice, cultivated, friendly people, with whom we are obliged more or less to speak French. It is rough, but it is wholesome. After some terrific bouts with them, in which I trample accent and syntax into one common pulp, I stop and literally pant for breath.

We are all very well, in spite of the cold rainy weather. How good Henry's joke on the piper was. Perhaps after all, *he* will be the great humorist of the family. All unite in love to each of you.

Your aff'te son
WILL.

"The Venetian papers" were never written, and Gilder's efforts to secure Howells a professorship which R. S.— Roswell Smith—had told him of may have helped bring about the offer of the Professorship of Literature at Johns Hopkins that was afterwards made him.

To James R. Osgood

Villeneuve, Oct. 5, 1882.

MY DEAR OSGOOD:

I forgot to ask you to forward that letter of mine to Gilder. Yesterday, I received one from Roswell Smith, in which he says that he will "leave the decision to you as to whether the Venetian papers go to us, or to Harper, or to the *Atlantic*. Of course we would rather the papers went to the *Atlantic* than have them illustrated in some other periodical, but we are not strenuous about it, and we want you to do what is for your own interest." I have written him in substance what I wrote to Gilder; and now

I suppose it will be best to let this matter rest, so far as they are concerned, till I begin to write the papers—if I ever do. But if necessary, you might explain the whole affair to the Harpers.

R. S. tells me that "Gilder has been all summer trying to work up an invitation for you to take the professorship or lectureship of English literature in one of our colleges." As this scheme, which reaches my ears for the first time, may have come to your knowledge, it will interest you, I hope, to know that I have sat upon it in a sad surprise that it should have been undertaken, and have written R. S. that I would not accept a professorship if it were offered me, and that I could not understand why it should be supposed I wanted one. I would not trouble you with this detail, but I supposed you might think I was tacitly trying to detach my future from yours if you heard of it otherwise.

Yours ever,
W. D. HOWELLS.

To S. L. Clemens

Le Clos, Villeneuve, Vaud, Switzerland,
Oct. 17, 1882.

MY DEAR CLEMENS:

What you want to do is to pack up your family, and come to Florence for the winter. I shall have my story as good as done when I get there early in December, and shall be ready to go to work with you on the great American comedy of *Orme's Motor* which is to enrich us both "beyond the dreams of avarice." Its fate needn't rest with the Madison Squarers. We can get it played. We could have a lot of fun writing it, and you could go home with some of the good old Etruscan malaria in your bones, instead of the wretched pinch-beck Hartford article that you're suffering from now. I know Mrs. Clemens would like to come; and Osgood could collect that royalty for you in H., on your book. If you come, you need not kill Clarke; you could bring his material with you.

We are having a good, dull, wholesome time in this little pension on the shore of Lake Leman, within gunshot of the Castle of Chillon; but a thousand jokes rot in my breast every day for want of companionship. Think of a country where they are so proud of their manure heaps that they plait the edges of the straw that sticks out. John and I make the most of each other; but he finds me poor company.

We have now been here a month, and we have not spoken to an American soul, and to but one English, and that was a she-soul. Think of the amount of talk that must be bottled up in us! And the capacity for listening that I must have acquired. It is a great opportunity for you. Besides, nobody over there likes you half so well as I do. We are about three miles from Montreux, a little place full of half-sick, indigent English and predatory Russians, and it is worth the voyage across the Atlantic to see the gloomy splendor with which they stare at and won't speak to one another in the street. Sometimes I'm a little down-hearted, but I always cheer up when I go to Montreux.

In London, Hay and King went to hear Bret Harte read a comedy he has been collaborating with a Belgian lady. He has turned the "Luck" of Roaring Camp into a girl, and brought her to Paris, with all his Californians, where she has adventures.

All the family join me in love to yours.

Yours ever,
W. D. HOWELLS.

To William Cooper Howells

Villeneuve, Nov. 12, 1882.

DEAR FATHER:

I have just come from the village church, where I am going next Sunday to see the election, which is here not only held on Sunday, but in the church. This seems to me a great thing in the interest of order and decency; and it seems a great pity that it could not be adopted among us. What a damper it would be on repeating and shoulder-hitting if the Irish performer had to do his work in the presence of his saints! The church in Villeneuve must be nearly a thousand years old; it is of a simple and beautiful gothic inside, and is as bare as stucco and some sort of gray wash can make it. The other evening we paid a visit to the *pasteur* who lives near by on the mountain side, and passed a very pleasant evening; he is an interesting man, as I believe I wrote you before, and I had an instructive talk with him on the condition of things here. He is far superior in education and intellect to the average country minister with us; but with us the congregation would be nearer its host.

There is not much change in the family affairs—in fact, none; and I suppose we should seem rather dull to the average spectator. But it is really something uncommon to get at the life of a foreign community, which is yet so kindred in ideas and principles to ours, and I am perpetually interested.—I can now get on very well with French, so that it is a comfort to go about and talk with people, and I pry bits of information out of a great many who don't suspect it. I have a note book quite full.

It is curious to watch the approach of winter, which literally comes down upon us here; each storm, when it lifts, shows the snow a little lower on the mountains. The leaves are all gone; but the air is still mild, except at nightfall, and the roses are in bloom within two miles of heavy snow drifts.

All join me in love to all.

Your aff'te son
WILL.

The "popular history of Venice" was never written. "My paper on James," appeared in the November *Cen-*

tury of that year, and what Howells said in it of Dickens and Thackeray, while commenting on James's method of endearing some of his characters to his readers, brought a storm of abuse upon Howells from people who probably did not understand what he had said. The paragraphs referring to Dickens and Thackeray were these.

"It is a little odd, by the way, that in all the printed talk about James—and there has been no end of it,—his power of engaging your preference for certain of his people has been so little commented on. Perhaps it is because he makes no obvious appeal for them; but one likes such men as Lord Warburton, Newman, Valentine, the artistic broker in *The Europeans,* and Ralph Touchett, and such women as Isabel, Claire Belgarde, Mrs. Tristram and certain others, with a thoroughness that is one of the best testimonies to their vitality. This comes about through their own qualities, and is not affected by insinuation or by downright *petting,* such as we find in Dickens nearly always, and in Thackeray too often.

"The art of fiction has, in fact, become a finer art in our day than it was with Dickens and Thackeray. We could not suffer the confidential attitude of the latter now, or the mannerisms of the former, any more than we could endure the prolixity of Richardson or the coarseness of Fielding. These great men are of the past—they and their methods and interests; even Trollope and Reade are not of the present. The new school derives from Hawthorne and George Eliot rather than any others; but it studies human nature much more in its wonted aspects, and finds its ethical and dramatic examples in the operation of lighter but not less vital motives. The moving accident is certainly not its trade; and it prefers to avoid all manner of dire catastrophes. It is largely influenced by French fiction in form, but it is the realism of Daudet rather than the realism of Zola that prevails with it, and it has a soul of its own which is above recording the rather brutish pursuit of a woman by a man, which seems to be the chief end of the French novelist."

To Roswell Smith

Villeneuve, Nov. 19, 1882.

MY DEAR MR. SMITH:

I was very glad to get your letter of the 2d, which came to hand yesterday; for though I had written fully to Mr. Gilder in regard to the Johns Hopkins affair, I had some lingering doubts as to whether I had not seemed wanting, in my note to you, in due appreciation of his friendly interest. But that is now all settled, and we can let Johns Hopkins take care of itself for the present. What chiefly moved me in your letter was the postscript, endorsed by Mr. Gilder, which could not have been more important if it had been a lady's. Your saying, apropos of the Lexington paper, that you wished you could have for the *Century* something like a history from me, jumped with the temptation which is becoming poignant with me again, to write a popular history of Venice from the Bostonia-Chicago-New York point of view. I do think that I could make a new thing in history, and something that would be thoroughly intelligible to all your readers and thoroughly interesting. I do not know whether Osgood and you have made affairs yet for my third novel; but that need not concern the history; it will be rather in the line of it, since the scene is to be in Venice at the time of the decadence. Probably when I shall have written that third story, I shall not feel like spinning my bowels into another romance, were I ten times the spider I am; and probably I *shall* feel like writing the history. I should want to read a year for it, and then I could give it to the press as my pen ran. I should like Mr. Gilder and yourself to talk it over with Osgood; you would all have to consider that for two years' work, I must have "the grand cash." The work was something that I wished very much to do for the *Atlantic* at one time; I even collected some material for it, but I found that I had not the time to read for it, and edit the magazine, and so I gave it up.

I suppose you will have seen that I have stirred up the English papers pretty generally by what I wrote of Dickens and Thackeray in my paper on James. I don't remember just what I said, but so far as they have quoted me, I stand by myself, and should only wish to amplify and intensify the opinions that they object to. I knew what I was talking about, and they don't know at all what they are talking about.

I am glad that *A Woman's Reason* pleases you, so far. I find it as I go on a most difficult and delicate thing to handle, but I hope to make it justify itself. I don't expect everybody to agree with it, but I shall try to interest everybody, and to give them something to think about. If the perplexities of the story cause me to modify the plan of the Italian papers I will let you know: in any case I shall have work cut out for Mr. Pennell when he comes. In about a week we shall start for Florence, and I hope there to finish the story by January. But if I don't, how would you like, instead of the Minor City series, a series of semi-historical studies of Florence and the formerly dependent cities of Pisa, Sienna, etc.?—which I could gather the material for without interrupting my work on the story. That series might have a more continuous interest than the other. I suggest it as something that I might wish to turn to in extremity.

Yours sincerely,
W. D. Howells.

President Gilman had offered Howells the Professorship of Literature at Johns Hopkins University.

To Daniel Coit Gilman

Villeneuve, Dec. 3, 1882.

MY DEAR MR. GILMAN:

I do not know what to say in answer to your most kind and gratifying letter of the 14th ult., and I feel the disadvantage of trying to talk the matter over with you at this prodigious distance. I am afraid in the first place that you do not know how rich and various are my disqualifications for such a position as that you offer me; and I am most anxious, before the negotiation goes farther, to be perfectly frank about them. I have a literary use of Spanish, French, German and Italian, and I have some knowledge of the literature and the literary history of those languages; but I have not a *scholarly* acquaintance with them, and could not write any of them correctly, not even Italian. Greek literature I know only by translations, and not fully; under *peine forte et dure,* I might read Latin. As to English literature, why of course I know it in a sort of way, but rather in the order and degree of preference than thoroughly and systematically. And I do not even know our own language scientifically,—that is from the Anglo-Saxon up; and I might often be unable to give a philological reason for the faith that was in me.

Nevertheless, I do feel strongly and deeply, the art of literature, and I believe I could make others feel its beauty and importance. I have fancied myself confronting a class of young men,—and also young women,—and I have thought that I should begin by making each one tell me what he had read, in whatever language. Then I should inquire into his preferences and require the reasons for them. When I had acquainted myself fully with the literary attainments and opinions of the class and come perfectly into *rapport* with them, I should want to see their work, to criticize it with them and correct it—not in detail but "by sample." All the time I should be giving illustrative readings and lectures, which would be rather to the point of what we were doing than in any order of time, or critical or historical sequence. Often I should read a poem, or an essay or passage from a novel or history, and prove to them —for such things are perfectly susceptible of proof—why it was good or bad; but I should always give them the first chance to analyze: I should seek at every step to make them partners in the enterprise, and not treat them as bottles to be filled with so much literary information and opinion. Sometimes I should turn to one literature and sometimes to another; if a new book were making much talk, I would read it and talk about it with them. In every way I would try to emancipate them from the sense of drudgery, and yet teach them that work—delightful work —was perpetually necessary in literary art as in every other. My idea is that the sum of this art is to speak and to write simply and clearly, and I should labor in every way to make them feel that this was also to write beautifully and strongly. Is any such system or no-system practicable with you? I could not and would not *teach* by any sort of *text-book* in any branch.

Now, how much of my time must I give to such work? How many hours a week?

I am by trade and by affection a writer of novels, and I cannot give up my trade, because, for one reason, I earn nearly twice as much money by it as you offer me for salary. But I feel the honor and distinction of being connected with such an institution as yours, and I own that your offer tempts me.

Yours sincerely,
W. D. HOWELLS.

P. S. If it were at all possible to leave this matter open till my return next August, it would be best. I don't see how we can arrive at each other's ideas clearly and fully by letter.

While Howells was in London, various mutual friends were anxious to have him meet Robert Louis Stevenson, with whom he had exchanged some letters as editor of the *Atlantic*. It was arranged that they should see each other on the Continent, but before that could happen Stevenson read *A Modern Instance,* which he took for a general condemnation of divorce, and wrote the following letter, to which Howells made no reply.

Robert Louis Stevenson to W. D. Howells

> Campagne Defli, St. Marcel,
> Banlieue de Marseille,
> Dec. 4th, 1882.

W. D. HOWELLS, ESQ.

DEAR SIR,

I have just finished reading your last book; it has enlightened (or darkened?) me as to your opinions; and as I have been sending, by all possible intermediaries, invitations speeding after you, I find myself under the unpleasant necessity of obtruding on your knowledge a piece of my private life.

My wife did me the honour to divorce her husband in order to marry me.

This, neither more nor less, it is at once my duty and my pleasure to communicate. According as your heart is, so will the meaning of this letter be.

But I will add this much: that after the kindness you showed me in your own country and the sympathy with which many of your books have inspired me, it will be a sincere disappointment to find that you cannot be my guest.

I shall bear up however; for I assure you I desire to know no one who considers himself holier than my wife.

With best wishes, however it goes, believe me

Yours truly,

ROBERT LOUIS STEVENSON.

"No. 3" must have been *Silas Lapham,* "No. 2," *A Woman's Reason,* and "the new book," *A Modern Instance.*

"The skull-cracking" was the criticism and abuse resulting from what he had said in his article on Henry James.

To James Russell Lowell

Hôtel Minerva, Sta. Maria Novella,
Florence,

Dec. 17, 1882.

DEAR MR. LOWELL:

You have so often stood my friend that I easily forgive myself for troubling you about a matter which is troubling me a great deal. It looks like fortune, but who knows Fortune's real face? I am offered the Professorship of Literature in the Johns Hopkins University, and I am given to understand that I can make the place what I like. But I am forty-five, unused to personal influence and probably without the presence that would affect young people. I should have to unset and reset myself; I should have to rub up my general ignorance in all directions and try by some sort of swift magic to transmute it into general knowledge. I believe that I could give students ideas of literary art, and could criticise their work usefully, and that is what I am expected mainly to do. But I wished to ask of your experience how much of a distraction from my own literary work the contact with a class twice or thrice a week, and the inevitable preparation for the encounter, would be. Should I not be spoiling a fair-to-middling novelist in order to make a poor professor? I hate to leave Boston, and the notion of a new calling is a cold bath to my imagination. The advantages of the position are a salary that would keep the printer at bay, and leisure (I suppose) to do something besides novelling, if I ever felt inclined. I can only present my misgivings crudely and vaguely, but I know you can divine them, and I am sure you can trust me not to hold you responsible for any but a good result from your comment.

We are here, all very much flattened out by a change from three months of Swiss air to the mawkish tepidity of this climate; but we hope to get used to it.

Mrs. Howells commends herself to the kind remembrance of Mrs. Lowell and yourself, and I join her in hoping that you are both well and have not forgotten,

Your affectionate
W. D. HOWELLS.

To James Russell Lowell

Florence, Dec. 27, 1882.

MY DEAR MR. LOWELL:

Even if you had not advised me exactly as I wished, I believe I should have been grateful for your kindest of letters. It came in the morning and in the afternoon I sent off my respectful refusal to President Gilman. You can imagine what a load went with it; I ought to have paid at least a ton of postage on that letter.

I think once I might have had the making of a scholar, even of a professor, in me, but it is too late now to inquire practically, and I should only have placed myself in a false position if I had taken the place; and should have known that I was suffering justly when the shame of my failure came. There is so much bitter in every man's cup, that whatever comes, I shall always be glad to have foregone that draught. I am not afraid of the future, as long as I can stand up to it; I have known smaller things than I know now, and I can go back to them without a pang, if need be, of which there seems no present sign. In fact, the affair was so thoroughly settled in my mind, that I believe I was obliged by the oracle's kindness even more than by his wisdom, though heaven knows how glad I always am of that.

We are here in Italy again, in the old soft air, under the same mild old sky, out of which all snap and sharpness have gone as out of the mood of a man too much experienced to be eager about anything. I don't know whether the old charm is here or not: it is by brief surprises, and all sorts of indirection, I suppose. At least there is something that faces me afar, and flits and comes again in the distance. But I perceive that it will no longer be intimate and constant; perhaps it finds me rude and cross.—I found Switzerland immensely to my liking. If I were to live anywhere in Europe, I would choose to live there: the Swiss are a kind of anterior New Englanders, with the very Yankee wit. One of the old peasants said of the grim season just past, "The winter has come to spend the summer with us." With the family love to Mrs. Lowell and yourself,

Yours sincerely,

W. D. HOWELLS.

XVII

1883

Tuscan Cities. *Venice revisited. Home of the "Quaker How-ellses" in Wales. Return to Boston.*

To Charles Dudley Warner

Siena, March 4, 1883.

MY DEAR WARNER:

If I were not dead to shame I sh'd now be feeling a lively self-reproach for neglecting your kind letter so long. It reached me in the midst of a foolish round of "pleasure" in Florence which almost spoiled my business there, and has kept me hard at work here for the last month trying to "catch up." Siena is a good place to work, but that is the least of its merits. It is the most medieval town I've ever seen, not excepting Quebec, and is almost as picturesque as Quebec. For the last three days, however, it has been giving us a tramontana unexampled out of Hartford: it makes me feel as if I were at Mark Twain's with my handkerchief in my hand to keep those steel door knobs from snapping all my electricity out of me.

But the cold pressure in regard to Thackeray and Dickens, which prevailed all over the region of my pericardium at the time you wrote, has quite passed away. I don't know how you ever got the notion that I was going to hurry to "explain" what I said, unless it was from that extraordinary and unauthorized statement in the *Athenæum*. I wrote Gosse that when I got time I should like to say my say of D. & T.; but I am far too lazy and too busy to see the hour of doing it. Sometimes I think it would be amusing to go over the whole affair, not omitting special consideration of the *Quarterly Reviewer*, who jumps up and down with rage.

Our plans are to go to Florence again for three weeks, and then to Venice, where we expect to spend April and the greater part of May. (By the way I tried to see Mrs. Harris in Florence, but she was not at home.) I hope to be writing there on my Tuscan cities, and to finish up the job by the time I get home at the end of the summer. If I were at leisure I should like extremely to see something of English society; but there is little hope of that, now. I shall go to some quiet place in England, and work hard on the Italian papers. How would Oxford do? At Cambridge I know people.

The family are all enriching themselves in experience; but I think even the insatiate Mrs. Howells is nearly satisfied. John is going to Rome with Pennell (who is to illustrate me) but the rest of us joyfully refrain. The idea of the Colosseum makes me sick, and I am satisfied that the dome of the State House is good enough for me. I wish I could see it, this minute. John Hay and his wife were a week with us in Florence, and again in Siena. The young Baron Rothschild has taken a fancy to Clarence King (as if that man had not luck enough already!) and wants to live with him. Mrs. Howells joins me in love to both of you.

Yours ever,
W. D. HOWELLS.

Perry's book was *English Literature in the Eighteenth Century,* which had just been published.

To Thomas S. Perry

Florence, March 13, 1883.

MY DEAR PERRY:

I am delighted to hear of the book, and I hope it will reach me while I'm still in Florence, so that I may be able to show it to Carl Hillebrand, whom I have met. I have also met here Dr. Hamberger, who wrote so kindly of my books in the *Rundschau* and the *Mag. für die Lit. des Auslandes,* and I shall want to send him yours. I hope it will have the luck it merits, and I trust for your own sake that you have touched the British lion,—who seems to have been born, like Prince Leopold, without a cuticle,—in such a way as to make him roar. It is only necessary to have insinuated that all English novels are not perfection. One of my London friends actually asked me if I didn't hate Thackeray and Dickens because they were English! But I don't consider the English clamor over that business so shameful as that of our own people, who are clearer-witted (really) and ought not to have been so stupid as to misunderstand what I really said in the paper on H. J.

Your kind words are not the less welcome because—to my own surprise—I have been scarcely if at all troubled by the row about me, and have been chiefly vexed because it includes James. As to what I've done in novels I'm not alarmed: my only trouble is about what I shall do hereafter.

We are back here after three weeks in Siena, which is a most fascinating old town, and medieval to the marrow of its bones. I think that there one really conceives of a little Italian Republic, and what it was like. When I fairly consider of it, I'm glad not to be a little Italian Republican. But all this remains for print.

I wish you could have scraped me up a little news, if there is any in Boston. We have done a great deal of society in Florence; but this time we shall keep out of it, partly because it interferes with the proper business of sight-seeing. I have been turning over a good many books, and putting myself in rapport with Italy again. But I'm not sure that it pays. After all, *we* have the country of the present and the future.

Yours ever,
W. D. HOWELLS.

The enclosed letter was one from Wm. H. Mallory of *The Churchman,* and of the Madison Square Theatre, that recalled their correspondence about *Orme's Motor* and said that he was anxious to attach Howells's name to the Madison Square Theatre, as he was trying to keep only American plays on its stage.

To S. L. Clemens

Venice, April 22, 1883.

MY DEAR CLEMENS:

I enclose a letter just come from Madison Sq. Theatre people, with a note which you can forward if you like. If you can get the right terms from them, with absolute surety as to pay in the event of success, it would be worth our while to give the month of October to working on that play. There is the making of a good comedy in it without any doubt—something that would run like Scheherazade, for *A Thousand and One Nights.* But they ought to be made to understand that we could not fool away a month's time for nothing: I for my part should want to be assured a Thousand Dollars, whether they ever put the play on the stage or not. Then if they did produce it, the grand cash should be ours. Please let me know whether you write them, and if you do, what, and with what result.

There was a Prince Edward's Island woman in our pension at Siena, who was of Sienese origin, and had returned to her native city after twenty years' misery in the British Provinces. She had brought from our hemisphere two books: the Bible and—*Roughing It;* which she appeared to think equally inspired and binding. When we told her that we knew you, the effect was much as if we had said we knew St. Matthew. I give you the bare bones of a feast, on which I'll enlarge when we meet. She said she often took the book —*Roughing It*—and showed the pictures to her Italian friends.

You won't expect me to say anything about Venice, merely because I'm here, will you? The idea of being here is benumbing and silencing. I feel like the Wandering Jew, or the ghost of the Cardiff Giant. I used sometimes to dream of having come back, but nothing was ever so strange as this reality, for it isn't strange at all—so far as I'm able to express it.

Winny, who had been drooping in Florence, and getting so that she could not sleep, has recovered in her native air as if by magic; she takes the deadly romantic view of Venice, and doesn't hesitate to tell me that I did the place great injustice in my books. It is quite amusing. She thinks it is *all* beauty and gayety; but for my part, the poor old place is forlorner and shabbier than ever. I don't think I began to see the misery of it when I lived here. The rags and dirt I witnessed in a walk this morning sickened me.

All join in regards to you all.

Yours ever,

W. D. H.

The "Crown Princess of Germany" was afterwards the Empress Frederick.

"The Virginia scheme" was William Cooper Howells's plan, which his son did not view very hopefully, of taking up farming in Virginia at the age of seventy-six. He first hired a farm in Goochland County, and in 1884 he bought one at Westham, Henrico County, on the James River near Richmond, where with characteristic optimism he planted a vineyard, peach and pear orchards, and made a carp pond. The farming part of the venture proved a failure, and he retired with his family to Jefferson, Ohio.

"My Edinburgh publisher" was David Douglas, who became Howells's friend as well as publisher.

To William Cooper Howells

Venice, May 6, 1883.

DEAR FATHER:

The children have been writing to you lately, and I think I've only sent you one letter from Venice. The time is passing rapidly and not very profitably with me, for I find myself unable to write here: my head has stopped like a watch that's been dropped; and we shall perhaps hurry away a little sooner, to England, on that account. We hate to leave, too, for Winny is feeling better here than she has been anywhere else on the continent. However, she was very well in England. The children are all delighted with Venice, though the weather is bad for the most part, and our excursioning is a good deal limited by that.

A curious thing has happened to me here. The Crown Prince and Crown Princess of Germany have been in Venice for the last fortnight, and last night I received a letter from an American lady who wrote that the Crown Princess was "very anxious to meet me," and begging that I would go with her to Sir Henry Layard's. There was of course no refusing under the circumstances, and I went and was duly presented. The Crown Princess, you know, is Queen Victoria's oldest daughter, and I should think she had all her mother's good and kindly qualities. She was dressed with extreme simplicity, and her manners were utterly unaffected and amiable. I was quite at my ease from the first word, and we talked for some ten minutes; then Lady Layard came up, and the Princess passed with her into the next room.—I gave as full a report of the interview as I could, to the children, but it didn't at all meet their expectations. *"Didn't you say 'So please your majesty' even once, Papa?"* asked poor Pil. Winny has drawn a caricature of the meeting: me on my knees, kissing the hand of the princess, who wore a crown, and had her train borne by two dwarfs.—John has concluded, after all, to be a writer; he sees no chance of an architect being asked to meet a crown princess. I write this solely to the family, and I shall be very greatly damaged if it gets into print from my letter. Be very careful about it, please.—The Crown Prince and the young ladies of the family were present, but I had no further introductions.

We have not heard from you for some time, and I am interested to know how the Virginia scheme prospers, with you. I'm becoming extremely restive with my stay abroad, and long to be at home and quietly at work again. I find that I can't write while shifting about so much, and there is no happiness for me in anything else.

My Edinburgh publisher is here; a very nice old gentleman, whom I like very much, and who is very enthusiastic about my books.

All join me in love to all.

Your aff'te son
WILL.

To James Russell Lowell

51 Upper Bedford Place,
June 19, 1883.

DEAR MR. LOWELL:

I believe it has all been distinctly arranged about the dinner next Tuesday: I am to come, as the only member of my family who had the forethought to keep his good clothes for London instead of sending them home from Venice in a box, though I really think it would have been better to let Mrs. Howells represent my literature; she seems always to understand it so much better, and as people have told me, looks it so much more. I have qualifications for sitting down in your study and letting you smoke to me and talk to me which I feel might be better employed in that way.

I do not know what you have been saying about me in the book to Lord Dufferin, but if you were of a mind to attack me savagely sometimes, I believe it would make life a little easier. What am I ever to do with the long arrears of kindness I have had from you? And it seems never to stop! I can only remain fully and inadequately but ever,

Affectionately yours,

W. D. Howells.

William Cooper Howells was born in the Welsh town of Hay, which is on the river Wye just above Hereford, and was brought to the United States when he was a year old.

To William Cooper Howells

Swan Hotel, Hay, June 21, 1883.

Dear Father:

You see I have kept my promise at last, and am here in your birthplace. I came down this morning from London thro' lovely English country—Swindon, Gloucester, and Hereford—and among the first low hills of the Welsh border. The Hay lies in the lap of these, on the banks of the pretty Wye, a shallow stream, turbid with recent rains. It is made up chiefly of low stone houses in winding crooked streets, with here and there a handsomer and larger dwelling. Hay Castle, where I have been to call for information about the local births and deaths, is a fine old Norman pile, just back of the town. But I will send you a pamphlet giving you all the history and topography and will come at once to business. In the bookstore where I stopped to buy it, I told the wife of the owner that my great-grandfather once owned a flannel mill here, and she said, "Oh, then this must be the place," and when I returned later, her husband took me back of the store up into the old factory, which you'll be amused to know is now a printing-office— book and job in a small way. It has deep stone walls, and is very strongly built, but is not of imposing size: about as big as your Toronto house. Mr. Harden thinks there could never have been power looms in it. His wife told me that this inn was kept by people of the name of Howells, and though I had taken a room at the other hotel, I came here on that account. I have my doubts of the bed, but one must do something for one's ancestors, and the landlady is a very nice and pleasant old body, with whom I've had some talk. Her husband, John Howells, died last year; they were first from Peterschurch, near here, but have been a long time in Hay. She says she remembers your Aunt Sweatman very well: a spry, sharp little old lady, who lived and died a Quaker; some of her children and grandchildren, the Trust-its, are still in the region. In the churchyard I find the graves of three of our name, and Watkinses *galore*, but so far I haven't found your grandfather's last resting-place. The Quaker chapel here was torn down only last year, but it had no churchyard. Canon Bevan, of the Castle, has promised to look up the records with me to-morrow, and then I shall write you again, and in the morning, I'm to interview a very historical barber, who is said to embody all the information about the past of the town and its in-habitants. So far, our ancestry does not impress me as so splendid as our posterity will probably be. It seems to have been a plain, decent, religious-minded ancestry enough, and I wish its memory well, but I'm glad on the whole not to be part of it—in fact to be above ground in America. Our landlady's daughter, by the way, has just gone out to Paisley, in Ontario, with her husband, to farm. At Hay there is apparently no sort of manufacturing business, now; and the bridge-keeper told me the farms were not very rich. But it is neat, and looks not unprosperous—it looks more like an Ohio river town than anything else I can compare it to, and the drunkards on the street don't detract from the resemblance. The people are very familiar; they bow to the stranger, and they speak upon small provocation; two of them have wished to sell me things on the streets; and the grocers' windows are full of American canned goods. Living is said to be very cheap, and if you find Virginia too dear, perhaps you will come here. I please myself with the notion of writing my first letter to you in your latest home from your earliest, and I hope my letter won't spoil everything by going astray. I left the family well this morning in London, where I am almost consumed with engagements. Last night as I was quietly getting into bed came a card from Lady Rosebery for her reception and a letter from the Lord Chancellor's daughter asking me for Friday night, as her father "would be glad to make my acquaintance." The night before, Lowell took me to Gladstone's reception and next week he dines me to meet swells, who it seems wish to see me. Of all vanities these are the hollowest, and I contrive in every possible way short of rudeness to avoid them; they make me acutely miserable. But thank goodness we sail the 5th of July! We got your first Virginia letter yesterday and I'm delighted that you're so happy. Love to all.

Your aff'te son,
WILL.

To William Cooper Howells

London, Upper Bedford Place,
June 24, 1883.

DEAR FATHER:

I will resume the story of my explorations in Hay. The morning after I wrote you there, I had, to begin with, a breakfast at the Swan, of bacon, and fresh trout from the Wye. Then I went out and pumped Mr. Games, the barber, to the lure of tuppence for putting my razor in order. He remembered your Aunt Sweatman, and showed me the "ironmonger's" close by where she kept her draper's shop. He told me further that your grandfather had three mills: one where the printing office is, one "just above the Blue Boar's inn," and one "down on the Bank" (of the Wye). I heard later from the bookseller that the Blaney's, who kept the last, probably had some of their manufactures to sell, and I went to see. I found a quaint stone pile of buildings in a weedy enclosure on the slope of the river, and in a sort of little shop by the mill door a very friendly and sensible old woman. Dear, dear! And was I the son of that Mr. Howells? No, his great-grandson. "Well, sir, this is the very spot; he built this mill his self, sir, and we had an old Weaver—his name was Prosser, sir, who remembered him well, sir, and used to be always talking about him." But Prosser had been dead two years, and I turned to and bought from her a woollen bed-cover, which is woven and dyed like a very heavy shawl, and which I'm going to give you as a memento of the place. Mrs. Blaney showed me the mills, and from the antiquity of the machinery, I should say the bed-cover might have been woven on the looms your grandfather set up there. "Many a time 'e's trod this path, sir," she said, going to open the door. From the mill she showed me that we stood in the corner of three counties: Brecknock, Radnor, and Hereford; and a lovely, mildly picturesque region it is, all about. The Blaney mill isn't very prosperous, since Mrs. Blaney's "master" or husband died: an exemplary man, by her accounts; but she keeps up the business, carding, dyeing, spinning, and weaving bed-covers, coarse shawls, linsey-woolsey, and Welsh flannels, a bit of which last I got for a specimen. At 12 o'clock I kept my appointment with Rev. Canon Bevan at the Castle, and after showing me over the fine old house he went with me to the church and examined the records there. But as our people were Quakers, there was no record of their births or deaths. Every one to whom I mentioned them, said, "Oh, the Quaker Howellses!" and then spoke of the Sweatmans and Trustits. The tradition of Thomas Howells was perfect, even to his going to America and returning; but I could nowhere find his grave, nor learn certainly whether he died in Hay. The little rose-embowered post-office is kept in the house where your Aunt Sweatman lived. I had an hour at Hereford, on my way up to London, and I drove through the town to see the cathedral. The verger showed me the seat in the choir where the minor canon, Rev. Edward Howells, sat. "Many's the 'alf crown I've 'ad from 'im, sir."

I found the folks all well in London, when I got back from my pilgrimage, and now we are all eager for our departure on the 5th of July. We go to Quebec—our passage having been engaged in April. All join me in love to the family.

Your aff'te son,
WILL.

To James Russell Lowell

Moville, July 6, 1883.

DEAR MR. LOWELL:

I gave Gosse a note of introduction to you, mindful of the kindly feeling you expressed for him, and of his advantage. In this I hope I did not presume too far, and that I am not wrong in asking you to remember him in connection with the Lowell Lectures.

But if I were capable of shame I should blush to ask anything of you after all your unasked kindness.

The Johns Hopkinses are after me again tempting me to try it for a year!

All the family join me in love to you and Mrs. Lowell.

Yours affectionately ever,
W. D. HOWELLS.

How delicious your speech at the Irving dinner! Every phrase melted on my tongue.

"The Gerhardts" were a young sculptor and his wife whom the Clemenses had befriended, and sent to Paris so that the husband might study there.

To S. L. Clemens

S. S. *Parisian,* off the Straits of Belle Isle,
and about 180 miles from Greenland.
July 10, 1883.

My dear Clemens:

We saw the Gerhardts in Paris. I took a fiacre and drove literally hell-wards to the region of the Boulevard d'Enfer, near which they live, and found the little woman preparing asparagus for their dinner in his studio. There was a stove in the middle of the room, a lounge-bed for the nurse and baby at one side, and a curtained corner where I suppose the Gerhardts slept. It was as primitive and simple as all Chicopee, and virtuous poverty spoke from every appointment of the place. Gerhardt was off at work somewhere, but the next day they both came to see us at our hotel, and Mrs. Howells took a great liking to them. She thought Mrs. G. thoroughly good and honest and very ambitious for her husband, and she thought that he was looking a little worn with overwork. I should think he had used the time you've given him very conscientiously, and that he had studied hard; it seemed to me also that they were keeping a good conscience about living economically, in a city which seems to me rather more expensive than New York. I don't know how far your beneficence is to extend to them; but if you are still paying their way it wouldn't cost any more to let them run down into Italy for three or four months than it would to keep them in Paris—not as much—and Gerhardt needs some sort of outing, and he could learn while he was resting in Italy. He seems to be a man of delicate and refined genius; the little medallion which he exhibited of you in the Salon was full of this, and seized your best points; it was artfully concealed from the public in the catalogue as the portrait of "M. Marc Swain," but it was favorably noticed by the critics. You are those poor little people's god—I don't know but they'd like me to write you with the large G.

If you answer this letter, you can write me to the care of Osgoods in my own blessed Boston, so nearly are my wanderings over, I hope; for we are now supposed to be within three days of Quebec. When we meet I'll tell about my experiences in England and with the English elsewhere; on paper I might seem to brag.—One night I met Thomas Hardy, the novelist, at dinner; and he said, "Why don't people understand that Mark Twain is not merely a great humorist? He's a very remarkable fellow in a very different way," and then he went on to praise your *Mississippi* in a manner that justified all the admiration I had ever felt for his books.

The family join me in love to both Mrs. Clemens and yourself.

Yours ever,
W. D. HOWELLS.

To William Cooper Howells

Memphremagog House, Newport, Vt.,
July 15, 1883.

DEAR FATHER:

We arrived at Quebec Friday night on the *Parisian,* which left Liverpool eight days before. We had perfectly smooth seas and no sickness, and are now struggling hard to realize that we are once more in our own country. We came down last night, and shall stay at this hotel till to-morrow morning. It is a lovely spot here, as beautiful as in Switzerland, and so much better for being in America.

I hope you are all well. As yet I don't know when I can come to see you; but I will try to arrange some plan after we get settled, and your Virginia summer has had a chance to cool off.

All join me in love to all.

Your aff'te son
WILL.

To John Hay

Boston, July 30, 1883.

MY DEAR HAY:

I am ashamed that with all your trouble and ill-health you got in before me with a letter. We have been two weeks in Boston, in a frenzy of house-hunting, and so there is a little more excuse for me than usual; but not excuse enough. The rest must come from your familiar kindness. It truly grieves me to hear the bad report you give of yourself; but I am not surprised, for I expected something of the kind from what you have undergone. What can a friend say to you that will seem least futile and insulting? I wish you better with all my heart.

How good you always are about what I write. But I don't like your undervaluing *The Bread-Winners*. I saw that story in MS. and it strikes me as even more fascinating in print. I thought—but probably I was mistaken—that the description of the heroine's pull-back had been toned down, and some physical sense of her thereby lost. But the story reads very evenly, and if it is a new hand, more power to it I say. I see it already well-spoken of by the press. The relation of the heroine, with her robust romance of marrying a sick man, to the pale, thin Azalia, strikes me as uncommonly good.

I haven't yet read all of James's paper, but what he said of Warner's theory of fiction was all gospel. As to *Nana,* I don't think it perfect, and its bad art in one respect arose from the bad French morality. Think of a mother, who in order to reconcile her daughter to her husband's falsehood, cold-bloodedly tells her, with the father's consent, that her idolized father had also been false. It's atrocious.

We had a lovely time in England, where the hospitalities of London pressed us hard. I could have boarded around for a year on the invitations I had in a fortnight. Certain little books seemed to be known in quarters where their author never expected to find them; and from the bookstalls he had to turn his modest eyes away. I could celebrate at length, but you won't care. Something that happened to me may interest you: President Gilman of Johns Hopkins renewed that offer to me with such kind insistence and concession that I am presently much tempted to go to Baltimore three or four months of the winter. It will depend upon whether the President and I can come to an understanding about the time and length of time. We have all come home in pretty good trim, though Winny is not quite well yet.

We join in love to all of you.

Yours affectionately,

W. D. HOWELLS.

"Your method of English history by the running foot" was one just invented by Clemens for the benefit of his daughters. He had measured off eight hundred and seventeen feet of his road at their Elmira farm and then subdivided it with pegs, putting one in at the beginning of every reign and allowing a foot to each year of it, so that their comparative lengths could be taken in at a glance.

To S. L. Clemens

4 Louisburg Square, Boston,
Aug. 12, 1883.

MY DEAR CLEMENS:

What I've done to you is to launch a lord at you. The Earl of Onslow, now eating breakfasts at Newport, was one of our fellow-passangers on the *Parisian,* and I gave him a letter to you, because I liked him and he liked you. He seemed a simple, quiet, gentlemanly man, with a good taste in literature which he evinced by going about with my books in his pockets and talking of yours. That is the whole story: and knowing that you liked "good" Englishmen, I ventured. He will be in Hartford about January and February; so you will have time to get settled before he comes. Mrs. Clemens will like his Countess, who is very pretty and agreeable, and not at all unlike a pleasant sort of American. The Earl is out of health, I believe, and is here to get it back. He's a light of the Beef-steak Club in London, and seems to know a lot of artists and literary men. I dare say we shall meet before you see him, and then I can post you further, if I can think of anything else.

I admire your method of English history by the running foot, and predict a success for it. You had better patent or copyright it before some one else gets hold of it; I see the newspapers have exploited it.

By the way, do you want to go in for a pair of grape-scissors which my father has invented? They are for gathering grapes, and enable a man to do it with one hand and convey them without bruising to the basket he carries in the other; and they have been patented.

We have taken this house for a year, and you can't come to see us in it any too soon. We wish that Mrs. Clemens could come with you, and we both long to see you both. Mrs. Howells joins me in love to all of you.

Yours ever,

W. D. HOWELLS.

"Your MS." was *The 1002ⁿᵈ Arabian Night,* which was never published. In it Scheherazade continues her stories until she talks the Sultan to death.

To S. L. Clemens

4 Louisburg Square,
Sept. 18, 1883.

MY DEAR CLEMENS:

Osgood gave me your MS. to read last night, and I understood from him that you wanted my opinion of it. The opening passages are the funniest you have ever done; but when I got into the story itself, it seemed to me that I was made a fellow-sufferer with the Sultan from Scheherazade's prolixity. The effect was like that of a play in which the audience is surprised along with the characters by some turn in the plot. I don't mean to say that there were not extremely killing things in it; but on the whole it was not your best or your second-best; and all the way it skirts a certain kind of fun which you can't afford to indulge in: it's a little too broad, as well as exquisitely ludicrous, at times.

You're such an impartial critic of your own work that I feel doubly brutal, and as if I were taking a mean advantage of your magnanimity when I fail to like something of yours. But I fail so seldom that I have some heart to forgive myself. At any rate I feel bound to say that I think this burlesque falls short of being amusing. Very likely, if you gave it to the public, it might be a great success; there is no telling how these things may go, and I am but one poor, fallible friend of yours.

You are back in Hartford again, and I mean to see you there before long, on my way to visit my father in Virginia. Mallory of the Madison Sq. Theatre has asked me to meet him here on Thursday and talk play. Perhaps I shall have something to report.

You're all well enough to stand the shock of our united affection, I hope.

Yours ever,
W. D. HOWELLS.

"Sellers inventions" were for use in the play Clemens and he were writing.

"Arnold" was Matthew Arnold.

Clara's "calf" was one to which she was devoted under the impression that it would some day grow into a pony.

To S. L. Clemens

Boston, Nov. 19, 1883.

DEAR CLEMENS:

I enclose a scrap or two from a newspaper with valuable suggestions for Sellers inventions. I have just been talking with Mrs. Howells about when I can go to Hartford for the revision, and I have about concluded to postpone it till I can see a week clear before me. The trouble now is that I am so tired—actually brain-weary—with our work on the play already that I couldn't do anything on it that wouldn't hurt it for five or six days at any rate. Then Cable comes here to read next Monday, and in decency I ought to be present. By the first of December Arnold is to be here again with a lecture that he has several times told me he has put me into, and so I ought to be on hand to hear that. I don't believe, therefore, that I can get to Hartford with a solid week before me and a good conscience behind

me till two weeks from to-day. But the time needn't a moment of it be lost. We are perfectly sure to make that play
just what you want it and you can push on the negotiations
with Raymond on that understanding. As soon as you have
the typewriter copy complete, send it to me and I will doctor all the dialogue except the Sellers speeches. When we
meet we can go over them together and my corrections, and
decide about them.

I have been about half dead to-day from eating and
laughing yesterday. I hope that having got rid of me, you
got safely off from the ——'s. That was a terrible moment, yesterday, when she consented to let you go to Norton's with me, and never did a wish fulfilled bring me so
little joy. None but the pitying angels will ever know what
Mrs. Howells said to me when she got me out of doors.
She began by saying that I was always very lenient to *her*
when she committed a blunder, and so she was not going to
be hard on me. But I think the enormity of my crime must
have grown upon her as she painted it to me. At any rate,
I never wish to be *spared* again.

This is done on the new type writer I told you of. You
see how distinctly it writes. I can use it with a fair degree
of speed, and I shall give it fair trial. I have hired it for a
month, paying $10 which goes as a payment on the machine
if I keep it. It is only to cost $40 in all.

Mrs. Howells sends her love with mine to all your house.
Pilla is very anxious to go back with me and see your
girls. Tell Clara not to neglect that calf.

Yours ever,

W. D. Howells.

Howells would not submit his work to editors but offered them an outline of his idea for a story or article, for
them to accept or decline on the strength of his other writings, usually before the thing was written.

To James R. Osgood

4 Louisburg Square, Boston,
Nov. 28, 1883.

MY DEAR OSGOOD:

Please say to Mr. Alden, that I cannot submit the story to him for his approval. I know what his general wish is; and I can conform to it; for the rest, if he wants a story from me he must leave me to be entirely responsible for it.

Yours ever,

W. D. HOWELLS.

XVIII

1884, 1885

A Little Girl Among the Old Masters. *Writes Opera,* A Sea Change, *with Georg Henschel. Buys house on Beacon Street.* The Minister's Charge. The Rise of Silas Lapham. *James R. Osgood & Company fails. Connection with Harper & Brothers.*

"YOUR friend's book" was Hay's novel, *The Bread-Winners.*

"Pilla's book" was *A Little Girl Among the Old Masters.*

To John Hay

4 Louisburg Square, Boston,
Jan. 7, 1884.

MY DEAR HAY:

Let me tell you at once that we have scarlet fever in the house, so that although I write at the bottom of it, and poor John lies at the top,—not very sick—you may burn this letter as soon as you please, if you think it necessary, on account of your children.

I think the storm about your friend's book is flurry which will pass, and let justice have a chance later. Of course I know the annoyance he must feel; but you can tell him from me at least that I don't think any less of his work because it is being jumped on. Maud Matchin will live because she *does* live, and he has added a type new, true and difficult to draw, to our own fiction. If I were to make any printed defence of his book I should insist that it courageously expressed a fact not hitherto attempted; the fact that the workingmen *as* workingmen are no better or wiser than the rich *as* the rich, and are quite as likely to be false and fool-ish. It certainly didn't strike me that the author was assail-ing them as a class. I still think that the result of the mur-der is too little moralized: it ought to be shown (not in words) that Sleeny was a homicide who would probably beat Maud, and that she was a huzzy who would deserve it; that they were bad and *bound* to be wretched. I would not have let her face wear any "happy" look, the slut! That is the grand literary and artistic shortcoming of the story; if I had been proof-reading for the author I should have markt what I thought some minor ones. Some of the things about the story are preposterous—as for example that Maud is made miserable because she was found poor, and Farnham made happy because he was found rich. She is supposed to have been virtuous because she told him she would only be his wife! In her heart she was just as ready to be his harlot if she could make sure of as much money and splendor. I've no patience with such twaddle. It is as well, perhaps, that the author suppressed the dedication, for it would have got me in for more fight than I've leisure for; I certainly should have spoken out, if I had been hit along with him.

We got your very kind note about Pilla's book from New York, and your praises were most grateful to both of us. It has had a very fair little success, and would have had more if there had not been a very long break between the two editions. We had not forgotten the interest you and Mrs. Hay took in the little drawings, and counted on your liking the book. Of course, it was something hazardous, as concerned Pilla; but we knew her unspoilableness. The only ugly thing said of the book was in the *Tribune,* where there was a little paragraph as mistaken in point of view, as it was insulting in terms. But Reid expressed his regret to me about it, and so it's all right, as far as he's concerned.

Mrs. Howells distractedly joins me in love to you both.

Yours ever,

W. D. HOWELLS.

The play was finally offered to Raymond, who declined it as not reviving his *Colonel Sellers,* but as presenting a lunatic.

To S. L. Clemens

4 Louisburg Square, Boston,
Feb. 11, 1884.

MY DEAR CLEMENS:

The copy of the Library went to Osgood by your direction last November, so that he might estimate the quantity. I have no doubt he will let me have it again if you ask him, and I should be glad to complete my work on it, and have it off my hands.

If you have got any comfort in regard to our play, I wish you would heave it into my bosom. Of course the widow's thirds offered us by the Mallorys were ridiculous; but it appears now that even they are not to be had. I rather think that we have got to wait for Raymond: wait till he has worn out his present success and then let him have the play at our figures.

What is the matter with Cable? If you had got sick in our house, Mrs. Howells would have killed me. She would have killed *you, any* way.

I am having dreams, now, that are worth having. Last night at eleven I laid the foundations of a horror in a potato salad full of onion, and at nine this morning I was still carrying round a human head which from time to time I wrapped up in brown paper, flattening the nose down to make a neat roll. This object was bestowed on me by the wife of *two* of my friends; she seemed to be not exactly of good repute, and I had to escape from her premises with the ignominy and virtue of Joseph, and then I found myself furnished with that hideous thing. I couldn't get rid of it; at times I explained that it was "merely the head of a cadaver," which at first seemed very satisfactory, and then not so much so.—The night before I was shinning round all night trying to get the deputy sheriff to give me up the writ for John's execution. It was painful.

Yours ever,
W. D. HOWELLS.

It was through Howells's efforts that Edmund Gosse was invited to lecture by the Lowell Institute, and while the lectures were being given he and Mrs. Gosse stayed with the Howellses.

The "Johns Hopkins course" was secured for Mr. Gosse, and he also lectured at Yale. His lectures were afterwards published under the title of *From Shakespeare to Pope.*

To Mrs. James T. Fields

Feb. 15, 1884.

DEAR MRS. FIELDS:

Thank you all the same. I have written to Dr. Gilman at Baltimore, hoping to get Gosse the Johns Hopkins course also.

I wish something might be done for him at Cornell! The six Lowell Lectures only give him $750, and that would be too little to come so far on.

Yours sincerely,
W. D. HOWELLS.

The story that Mr. Alden, as editor of *Harper's Monthly,* was considering was *The Minister's Charge,* which afterwards appeared as a serial in the *Century.*

To James R. Osgood

4 Louisburg Square, Boston,
May 12, 1884.

DEAR OSGOOD:

I suppose you will see Mr. Alden in New York, and I wish you would tell him that I have had it in my mind to answer his last letter ever since I came away. In that he said that he would like to reconsider the plan of my story if I would make more of the hero and heroine; and I could easily do this, for I never meant to make what he seemed to think I would—that is, something farcical or comical. In the first place, I don't believe in heroes and heroines, and willingly avoid the heroic; but I meant to make a simple, earnest, and often very pathetic figure of my country boy, whose adventures and qualities should win him the reader's entire sympathy and respect. It seemed to me that I had indicated this purpose both in my opening chapters and my sketch, but I must have failed, since Mr. Alden understood something so different. Nothing in a story can be better than life, and I intended to make this story as lifelike as possible. But I look at life as a very serious affair, and the tendency of the story would be to grow rather tragical than comical. I do not see how I could re-write the plan so as to present to Mr. Alden's mind the image of a more considerable hero; I can only give him the assurance that he will be anything but a trivial or farcical figure. If he wishes to reconsider the idea with this light upon it, and this assurance, I shall be glad to write the story, to his order, and keep his wish in mind; but neither you nor I wish him to take it with a faltering faith in my ability to make it important and attractive.

Perhaps you will show him this letter. He appeared to think that I had some poet *manqué* like gifted Hopkins in mind; but I had nothing of the sort. I believe in this story, and am not afraid of its effect before the public.

Yours ever,
W. D. HOWELLS.

"The Story of a C. Town," was *The Story of a Country Town,* by E. W. Howe.

Often after Clemens's death, Howells used to say, longingly, "I wish I could have a talk with Clemens!"

To S. L. Clemens

Boston, May 23, 1884.

DEAR CLEMENS:

Mr. Dana was unable to tell me just how much the pay would be, but he said it would be more than American authors had ever received before, and so I promised him that luckless play of mine which the Mad. Sq. refused. In working it over, I struck a snag, and went down with it beyond the present reach of any diving-bell, and so I am not to do anything for the *Sun,* after all.

I've been writing an "open letter" to the *Century* about *The Story of a C. Town.* "But Lord," as Pepys says, how I wish there was a telephone that would let me talk to you, these days. There is just one other man—Perry—whom I can reason with beside yourself. I would give any thing if we lived within tongue-shot of each other. Why not both of us remove to Washington? W. is running powerfully in my head these days.

Yours ever,
W. D. HOWELLS.

"My opera" was *A Sea Change,* for which Georg Henschel wrote the music. It was to have been given at the Bijou Theatre in Boston; but the manager who had accepted it fell off the end of a pier one night and was killed, and the opera was never produced.

To William Cooper Howells

Boston, June 8, 1884.

DEAR FATHER:

I let John write the last letter for me, being occupied with the making of the prompt-book for my opera. I believe we have told you that it has been taken by the Bijou theatre here. They will produce it the day after Blaine's defeat, and if it succeeds, it will be a very nice thing for me. But I have made my fortune in the theatre too often to be elated of this chance.

Talking of fortunes makes me think of grape scissors. You mustn't suppose I'm neglecting the matter. I'm looking after it most vigilantly; but there seems to be a hitch somewhere in Lowentrant. He reported the batch ready for stamping three weeks ago, but they are not yet finished. Joe and I have got everything in trim for advertising and selling.

All join me in love to all.

Your aff'te son
WILL.

"Here" was the house he had just bought at 302 Beacon Street.

To William Cooper Howells

Boston, Aug. 10, 1884.

DEAR FATHER:

I came down here last Monday, to put the house in order —or rather my books—leaving the family at Kennebunkport, Me. (I seem to have written you all this before.) And here I have been hard at work, and lonesome of course. There is not only nobody else in the house, but nobody else I know sleeps in town. Altogether the effect is queer. There are miles of empty houses all round me. And how unequally things are divided in this world. While these beautiful, airy, wholesome houses are uninhabited, thousands upon thousands of poor creatures are stifling in wretched barracks in the city here, whole families in one room. I wonder that men are so patient with society as they are.

Aurelia's letter came Thursday, and I was glad that the poor child was pleased. Tell her not to be restricted by any suggestions of mine in the use of the money. You must be patient about my not bringing many of the family with me this fall. It is a long journey, and neither Elinor nor Winny is quite strong enough for it. I am sorry you are so far off, but that can't be helped. I will do the best I can. It's pleasant to know that you're arranging your house to suit you.

Lowentrant sent an inquiry for the shears from some one in Bridgeport, which I forwarded to Joe—the first he's had. L. has behaved badly about finishing them up in time. If they succeed we must get some one else to make them.

With love to all,

Your aff'te son

WILL.

"The circus" was Clemens's proposal that Aldrich, Howells, Cable, and himself should tour the country in a private car, lecturing as they went.

To S. L. Clemens

Boston, Aug. 10, 1884.

DEAR CLEMENS:

If I had written half as good a book as *Huck Finn,* I shouldn't ask anything better than to read the proofs; even as it is I don't. So send them on; they will always find me somewhere. I'm here in town for the present; but I'm going to Kennebunkport where the family are on Tuesday, and then to Campobello, N. B. Back to Boston the last of the month.

I see that the circus has been finally reduced to Cable and you. That is right. The public wants to hear both of *you;* but I should have been a drag.

That was funny about the Mark Twain fotograf and the sick women's comprehensive censure of authors. I'm looking up, for my new story, facts about the general lack of literature in people, and I asked the teacher of a first-class ladies' school here how little literature a girl could carry away from her school. "Some go barely knowing that Shakespeare was an Englishman. One who had read all the 'love-part' of your (my) novels, didn't know that you were an American or a contemporary. We have to fight in eight months against fifteen or twenty years' absolute ignorance of literature."

I've got a mighty pretty house here on the water side of Beacon st., and Mrs. Howells wants Mrs. Clemens and you to consider yourself engaged for a visit to us when my opera comes out in November.

> Yours ever,
> W. D. HOWELLS.

The story that Howells was writing was *The Rise of Silas Lapham,* and his opera was *A Sea Change.*

To Henry James

> Kennebunkport, Maine,
> Aug. 22, 1884.

MY DEAR JAMES:

It is very good of you to write me when I've so long owed you a letter, and to make my buying a house "on the water side of Beacon" the occasion of forgiving my neglect. The greatest pleasure the house has yet brought me is this; but it is a pretty house and an extremely fine situation, and

I hope it is not the only joy I shall have from it. I have spent some desolate weeks in it already, putting my books on their shelves, while the family were away at mountainside and seaside, and I can speak confidently and authoritatively of the sunsets from the library-windows. The sun goes down over Cambridge with as much apparent interest as if he were a Harvard graduate: possibly he is; and he spreads a glory over the Back Bay that is not to be equalled by the blush of a Boston Independent for such of us Republicans as are going to vote for Blaine.—Sometimes I feel it an extraordinary thing that I should have been able to buy a house on Beacon str., but I built one on Concord Avenue of nearly the same cost when I had far less money to begin with. In those doubting days I used to go and look at the cellar they were digging, and ask myself, knowing that I had had barely money to pay for the lot, *"Can* blood be got out of a turnip?" Now I know that some divine power loves turnips, and that somehow the blood will be got out of the particular turnip which I represent. Drolly enough, I am writing a story in which the chief personage builds a house "on the water side of Beacon," and I shall be able to use all my experience, down to the quick. Perhaps the novel may pay for the house.

I am just back from a visit of a few days at Campobello, which is so far off that I feel as if I had been to Europe. It is a fashionable resort, in spite of its remoteness, and I saw many well-dressed and well-read girls there who were all disposed more or less to talk to you, and of your latest story, *A New England Winter*. Generally speaking I should say that its prime effect had been to imbue the female Boston mind with a firm resolve to walk on the domestic roof at the first opportunity. The maiden aunt gives universal satisfaction, especially in her rage with her nephew when he blows her a five-fingered kiss. I myself having the vice of always liking you, ought perhaps to be excluded from the stand, but I must bear my witness to the excellence particularly of some of the bits of painting. In just such a glare of savage sunshine I made my way through Washington street in such a horse-car as you portray, the day I read your advance sheets. Besides that, I keenly enjoyed these fine touches by which you suggest a more artistically difficult and evasive Boston than I ever get at. The fashionableness which is so unlike the fashionableness of other towns—no one touches that but you; and you contrive also to indicate its contiguity, in its most ethereal intangibility, to something that is very plain and deeply practical. It is a great triumph which Pauline Mesh embodies. The study pleases me throughout: the mother with her struggles—herculean struggles—with such shadowy problems; the son with the sincere Europeanism of an inalienable, wholly uninspired American. As for the vehicle, it is delicious.

I don't know whether I've bragged to you of all the work I've done the past winter. One piece of it was an opera which Henschel set to music, and we had a contract with the Bijou Theatre for its production in November. The other night the manager with whom we contracted, in trying to get aboard his yacht in the fog, fell and fractured his skull, poor man. He died, and with him our legal hold upon a potential future. I dare say the Theatre will still want it; but I wait the return of the puissant Osgood, who put our contract through, before knowing. The Madison Square people have bought the London dramatization of *A Foregone Conclusion,* and have sent it to me for revision. As yet we have not got beyond the point of having refused to do it for next to nothing. Sometime, when we meet, I will tell you how these gifted brothers led me on protesting over the same path you trod to the same flowery pitfall, with another play. I really begin to admire them; they are masters of no common skill.

We are expecting the Gosses at our house early in December, and have plans for making them like this country, which ought to succeed at least so long as they are in it.

There is no literary news to give you in this dull season, at this little seaport, where loverless maidens superabound in the hotels and the row-boats on the river in such numbers as would furnish all the novelists with heroines indefinitely. The family joins me in love.

Yours ever,

W. D. HOWELLS.

1885

"The last 'Portfolio,' " was a number of *The New Portfolio* by Holmes, which began in the January *Atlantic* of 1885.

To Oliver Wendell Holmes

302 Beacon St.,
Feb. 5, 1885.

DEAR MR. HOLMES:

I deprive myself of an excuse to bore you in person by sending this magazine; but I can't let it go without some word of my delight in the last *Portfolio,* which I've just read. I tasted every particle of it with ecstasy, but the morsel that had most relish in it for me is that formed of the paragraph about "our childhood's horizon" and the paragraph following. In the friendliness for simple and homely things there expressed you will let the poor average human soul come very near you and add to your lovers everywhere.—That is beautiful about Dr. Clarke, too.— What is there in the paper that isn't beautiful? The thoughts about becoming part of the people that one ponders and writes about are a wholly fresh contribution, and interested me intensely. Pray forgive this chatter!

Yours sincerely,

W. D. HOWELLS.

The Authors' Reading where Clemens and Howells had appeared was given for the Longfellow Memorial Fund.

"Osgood's break" proved a final one, and Howells's next book was published by Ticknor & Company.

To S. L. Clemens

Boston, May 5, 1885.

MY DEAR CLEMENS:

I am exceedingly glad that you approved my reading, for it gives me some hope that I may do something on the platform next winter. It *seemed* to me that I was making the audience understand, and with a little more practice and ease I believe that I could do what I want. But I would never read within a hundred miles of *you*, if I could help it. You simply straddled down to the foot-lights, and took that house up in the hollow of your hand and *tickled* it.

I don't see how a *reasonably selfish* author could have refused to read there. Wasn't it our own interest we were promoting? Cable ought to have thought that his books were to gain as much as any one's. And Warner failed, too! Well, the show netted $1700, Lathrop tells me.

I had to go out into the country just after the thing, and I left while you were still talking.

I guess Osgood's break is not a bad one,—not the worst, any way. If he can resume I suppose I shall go on with him; if not I shall lapse to somebody else. Fairchild thinks there won't be any loss. But in the meantime, till something is concluded, I am my own lord as well as master.

It's all right about the *Library of Humor* copy. That is at Osgood's house, and I shall have it to-day.

Yours ever,

W. D. HOWELLS.

"Imogene" was the younger daughter of *Silas Lapham.*

To Thomas Bailey Aldrich

Wells Beach,
Aug. 4, 1885.

MY DEAR ALDRICH:

You needn't hope, after galling my pedant-pride through three pages, to soothe it by asking me a flattering question about an Italian superlative. Italian I care nothing for, but my Russian I am proud of, and I think I know my Tourguénieff. However, I *am* glad you like Imogene, for she seems pretty good to me, and I do value your good opinion. If I were to speak of her as a distinctively beautiful American, I believe I should say *la bella Americana,* rather than *bellissima,* though I believe it's perfectly right to say that. I remember the Venetians used to speak of Mrs. Ruskin as *la bella Inglese,* as if she were so extremely; and it seems to me that the superlative would weaken the qualification.

We are off to-morrow morning for the White Mountains, but I hope to see you in Boston before the end of the month.

Yours ever,
W. D. HOWELLS.

Clemens had written that he had just been reading Part II of *Indian Summer* and that to his mind there wasn't a waste line in it, or one that could be improved; so "the story" must have been that one.

To S. L. Clemens

Ranlet House, Bethlehem, N. H.
Aug. 9, 1885.

MY DEAR CLEMENS:

I was glad you could find it in your heart to write me that kind letter, for it did me a world of good. What people cannot see is that I analyze as little as possible, but go on talking about the analytical school which I am supposed to belong to; and I want to thank you for using your eyes. I am in hopes you will like the story all through, though it is all a variation of the one theme.

Did you ever read De Foe's *Roxana?* If not, then read it, not merely for some of the deepest insights into the lying, suffering, sinning, well-meaning human soul, but the best and most natural English that a book was ever written in. You will find it in the Bohn library. I wish to goodness that you could take a week off and run up to this White Mountain village. I think the landscape would be a revelation to you, and if we were not always insulting our maker you would be amazed at the affront offered him by the ugliness of the little Yankee town dropt into the beauty of his everlasting hills.

We had a funeral service for Grant, here, yesterday, and all the time while they were pumping song and praise over his great memory, I kept thinking of the day when we lunched on pork and beans with him in New York, and longing to make him feel and see how far above their hymns he was even in such an association. How he "sits and towers" as Dante says.

Mrs. Howells sends love to both of you with me.

Yours ever,
W. D. HOWELLS.

Howells had placed his work with Harper & Brothers and his contract with them forbade his writing for anyone else.

Mark Twain wrote in response to this letter that he could not publish the *Library of Humor* without a very responsible name to support him on the title page, so his decision was simply to pigeonhole the Library, and wait and see what new thing Providence would do about it.

To S. L. Clemens

302 Beacon St., Boston,
Oct. 16, 1885.

MY DEAR CLEMENS:

You will have heard from the din of the newspapers that I have contracted to take all of Harper & Brothers' money in return for certain literary services. They want as a slight condition that I shall not let my name appear except over their imprint, and this concerns the *Library of Humor.* I have got the copy all ready, as you know, except some dozen short biographical notes, and I could soon prepare it for the printers, if I had the facts for these. The introductory essay is unwritten, but that is something which you could easily knock together. I propose, therefore, to sell out to you at a sacrifice, and let you call it "Mark Twain's Library of American Humor"—a capital selling title—suppressing my name altogether. You have now paid me $500 on account, and if you will send me your check for $2000 more—just half the price agreed on for my co-operation—I will call it square.

You know I have the copy, which is always and in any event at your service.

Yours ever,
W. D. HOWELLS.

To Thomas S. Perry

Auburndale, Mass., Oct. 30, 1885.

MY DEAR PERRY:

Anna Karénina is a wonderful book. I seem to live in it, I don't think it is so great as Tourguéniff's, but the subtlety of the observation in it is astounding, simply. The way the

Karénine's passion is treated—I've only got through Part I—is a little superstitious? Or am I older than I was? That looks like the only bit of convention yet. But how good you feel the author's heart to be; and what a comfort, what a *rest* that is!

Yours ever,
W. D. HOWELLS

Please let me have the English criticism again, with this letter.

The following letter from Francis Parkman is one of the many letters Howells received about *The Rise of Silas Lapham.*

Francis Parkman to W. D. Howells

MY DEAR HOWELLS:

My sister has just been reading *Silas Lapham* to me, and I cannot help writing to tell you how much I have been interested and delighted. It is admirable portraiture, realistic in the best sense of the word. It must touch the consciousness of a great many people, and—as we descendants of the puritans are said to be always on the look out for a moral—it will teach the much needed lesson that money cannot do everything.

I think I have never admired your genius more than in this capital book.

Yours faithfully,
F. PARKMAN.

Jamaica Plain
6 Nov. '85.

The following letter was the beginning of one of

Howells's queer literary experiences and formed the suggestion for his story of *Fennel and Rue,* many years later.

Elizabeth C. Meader to W. D. Howells

Mr. W. D. Howells,

Dear Sir,

For many months past I have been an invalid whose only means of keeping her mind from "preying upon itself" has been reading. The fact that I cannot live during this winter —that indeed my death is always rather more probable than my continuance in life—has been so long known to me that it was with something like relief that I heard my doctor finally decide definitely as to the limit of my time. You will doubtless be surprised at the singular request which this induces me to make of you.

I have been reading *Indian Summer* with a degree of interest which I cannot attempt to express. From the singular naturalness of the style of the story—and from my mode of life, (the absence of all *real* event about me) the novel and its characters have become to me by far the *realest* things in my life.

The thought that I shall probably never live to know its conclusion has become perfectly insupportable to me. Is there any way in which it could be arranged? A single statement—a brief summary of the facts would seem unreal—I want the circumstances as they naturally unfold,—the words of the characters themselves. Is there *any* way in which I could see the advanced sheets?

With the *sincerest* thanks, my dear Mr. Howells, for all the *interest* which your books have given to my monotonous life—I am

Very truly yours,
Elizabeth C. Meader.

To Mrs. Elizabeth C. Meader

Lee's Hotel, Auburndale, Mass.,
Nov. 18, 1885.

DEAR MADAM:

I have written to the editor of the magazine, asking him to send you the advance sheets of my story, and I have no doubt he will do so. We shall know of course that they meet only your eyes, and shall rely upon you to destroy them as soon as you have read them.

I cannot tell you how sincerely and humbly grateful I am to be the means of lightening the moments of sickness to you, and this book of mine will always have a peculiar interest to me because it has interested you at this time.

My wife joins me in cordial regards and sympathy.

Yours sincerely,
W. D. HOWELLS.

MRS. MEADER.

Henry M. Alden, then editor of *Harper's Monthly,* to whom Howells had sent "Elizabeth C. Meader's" letter, consulted Mr. Osgood and Mr. J. Henry Harper about it, and they advised inquiring into the matter: so he wrote to Mrs. Meader that her request was one that could not usually be granted, but, if she would send her physician's written confirmation of her situation, the advance sheets of the story would be sent her for her eye alone. Alden's letter resulted in one of apology from "Elizabeth C. Meader" to Howells, which confessed there was really no such person, but the writer of her letter had been so impatient for the end of *Indian Summer* after reading the latest number of it, that she had said to her friends, "I believe I'll write to Mr. Howells and tell him I'm dying and simply can't wait." The friends had thought it a good joke, so the letter had been written and sent under an assumed name.

"Webster's check for $2000" was one Clemens had sent him for his share in *The Library of American Humor.* Clemens felt that the Library contained so many extracts from his own writings, selected by Howells, that it could not fittingly appear under his name alone; and Howells's suggestions are meant to cover this difficulty. The book was finally published in 1888 under the title of *Mark Twain's Library of Humor.*

"The Grant book" was General Grant's autobiography, just published with enormous success by Clemens's firm of Charles L. Webster & Company.

"The unsuccessful campaign" was Clemens's *A Campaign that Failed,* which appeared in the December *Century* of that year.

To S. L. Clemens

Lee's Hotel, Auburndale,
Dec. 5, 1885.

MY DEAR CLEMENS:

I have got Webster's check for $2000, but I have a difficulty about keeping it, which I must lay before you. If we have no definite plan for publishing the book, the money does not belong to me. I do not believe the Harpers will consent to my name with another imprint willingly till it has been identified with theirs by several publications—that is, a year or two hence. You may not wish to wait so long, and I certainly could not ask you to do so. Is there not someone else whose name you could associate with yours on the title-page? Or couldn't I reduce the number of selections from you so as to sort of fig-leaf your editorial nakedness? Or couldn't we get over it in some joking way in the introduction (which I'm to write) and say that the selections from you had been committed to your friend Howells, who had betrayed your confidence? Wouldn't Uncle Remus, for the other half of the $5,000, or Warner, or Aldrich, or Cook, or Blaine, or Cleveland, or somebody, go on the title-page with you in my place? How would Beecher do? Think the misery over again.

I'm more rejoiced than I can tell you at the gigantic triumph of the Grant book. I should like to see you in these days of wild excitement. How you must smoke and swear!

I read your piece about the unsuccessful campaign with the greatest delight. It was immensely amusing, with such a bloody bit of heart ache in it, too.

Yours ever,
W. D. HOWELLS.

XIX

1886, 1887

Failure of play written with Mark Twain. Declines Smith Pro-
fessorship at Harvard. First President of Tavern Club. Trial of
Chicago Anarchists. Winter in Buffalo.

To Thomas S. Perry

> Auburndale, Mass.,
> Jan. 28, 1886.

MY DEAR PERRY:

Don't come Sunday because there's to be someone else
that day, and I want you all to myself. Can't you come
Monday, if fine, and have a walk? Or foul, and a talk? Of
course you're right: no one invented realism; it came. It's
perfectly astonishing that it seems to have come everywhere at once, and yet not in England. They always had it
there, though, and were ashamed of it.

Be sure to bring your manuscript, I want to hear it.

This time I made the Study mainly about Tolstoi, Gogol,
and Valdés. But isn't it strange that in all this vast land
there should not be one intelligent voice besides yours on the
right side? How does history account for that?

> Yours ever,
> W. D. HOWELLS.

"Perry's book" was *English Literature in the Eighteenth*
Century. In another letter to Perry of February 10th,
Howells writes of his book again and says of Louis Dyer
—then Professor of Greek and Latin at Harvard, and very

near-sighted: "Dyer came round to me with a sort of scared expression in his glasses, 'Perry has read everything!' But he said he had enjoyed talking with you immensely, and longed to see your book."

To Thomas S. Perry

1408 H st., Washington,
March 3, 1886.

MY DEAR PERRY:

Mr. David A. Monroe of Harper & Bros., "one of the powers behind the throne" as Osgood tells me, is a devoted friend and admirer of yours. He is here, and to-day he asked me, "Do you know Perry's book?" and testified the most lovely and lively sense of its excellence. I told him in general terms that I lived upon it, and that *I had learned from you* the new and true way of looking at literature.

A roaring good book (Schoenhof's) is Ernest Dupuy's *Grands Romanciers Russes*—Gogol, Turgénief, Tolstoi. Read it, little father.

This is a crazy place, but amusing. I wish you were here. To-day I called on some Southern ladies; one of them said to me, "Resume your seat, sir," just like a person in Sir Walter Scott.

I've got a new book of Valdés's—*José*.

.With regards to Mrs. Perry,
Yours ever,
W. D. HOWELLS.

As Howells had contracted to write only for Harper & Brothers, and Whittier had promised his biography to Ticknor & Company, Howells could not do what Whittier suggested in the following letter.

John G. Whittier to W. D. Howells

Oak Knoll, Danvers,
Mar. 18, 1886.

MY DEAR FRIEND HOWELLS:

I thank thee for the translation of *Light and Darkness* by the Spanish Minister to our Government. I am glad the translation fell into such able hands.

I am following with peculiar interest the future of *The Minister's Charge,* not without some painful reflections that I may have good-naturedly done as much harm as the minister, to unfortunate versifiers who come to me with their wares.

As is natural at my age, I have been thinking of the approaching close, and of the probability that somebody will write my biography. I would greatly prefer that nothing should be said, but I suppose that is not to be expected. I am tempted to ask, as a very great favor, that thee would do it. My relative, Mr. S. T. Pickard of the Portland (Me.) *Transcript* would take the trouble to look over my papers, collect letters, etc., and prepare the material of the book, and make thy task as light as possible. Ticknor & Co. would see that the thing was not altogether a labor of love. Indeed I am sure, from a conversation with Mr. B. H. Ticknor they will be very liberal in the matter. I have not, of course, mentioned thy name to him or to any one. Will thee think of it, and if necessary consult Mr. Ticknor. I do not wish to urge it. Even now I am almost sorry I have mentioned it at all.

With thanks for all the pleasure I have derived from thy writings and with every good wish I am thy friend,

JOHN G. WHITTIER.

John G. Whittier to W. D. Howells

Oak Knoll, Danvers.
3rd Mo. 23, 1886.

MY DEAR FRIEND:

How shall I thank thee for thy prompt and kind response to my request? Had I known of thy business engagement I should not have ventured to suggest it. As it is, I fear I may not be able to avail myself of thy generous proposal to confer with the Harpers, as I had agreed to give the publication of the *"last word"* to Ticknor & Co., the publishers of Longfellow's Biography. Ticknor and his father were my publishers at a time when I was unpopular and unprofitable, as an anti-slavery agitator. I am afraid this will be a serious difficulty, in thy present position, and a *very* great disappointment to me. I supposed at the time I made the agreement that T. & Co. were thy publishers and that it would be all right in that respect. I do not think they would now release me from the engagement. In any event, I thank thee, from my heart, for thy willingness to do me the great favor, if possible. I do not know now to whom I can look to take the place I had hoped thee might occupy. I see no other way than to leave my papers, letters, etc. with Mr. Pickard and my niece. It is possible I may think of some-one yet.

The long, hard winter has given place to signs of Spring. The bluebirds have come, and were never more welcome.

I am very gratefully thy friend,

JOHN G. WHITTIER.

"The 3d Act" was of the "claimant" play about Colonel Sellers, which A. P. Burbank, a well known elocutionist and actor, was thinking of producing.

To S. L. Clemens

Boston, May 5, 1886.

DEAR CLEMENS:

I've just read over the 3d Act, and reviewed the whole play in my mind, and I must say that I think it will fail. It *is* a lunatic whom we've pictured, and while a lunatic in *one* act might amuse, I'm afraid that in three he would simply bore. I suspect that the play hasn't success in it, on that account, which is the point that Raymond made against it; he wouldn't have given it up if that were not fatal. The real motive—the claimant business—isn't developed; and there is nothing in the play but the idea of Sellers' character, and a lot of comic situations. That is the way I feel about it *now,* after having firmly, furiously believed in it. Neither of us needs the money it might make, very badly, though we would like it, and it won't make us any reputation, even if it succeeds.

Think it over again before closing any arrangement with Mr. Burbank. I write solely from my own cogitations and without advice from any one.

Yours ever,
W. D. HOWELLS.

Burbank had the idea of impersonating Raymond as Sellers, so making the play a double burlesque, and Howells and Clemens had agreed to let him have it, hiring the old Lyceum for a week at seven hundred dollars for its production: but Howells decided the play was impossible, and after a consultation they agreed to pay for the theatre, take the play off, and release Burbank from his contract. Howells gave up all rights in the play, and Clemens financed it for a week of one-night stands, but it was never given in New York.

To S. L. Clemens

Boston, May 18, 1886.

DEAR CLEMENS:

Your indictment is perfect, but the trodden worm remembers details that escape the recollection of the boot-heel. That fatal Burbank-Sunday, I came in after my visit to the Asylum (where they ought to have locked me up) and found you lying on that lustrous-rugged lounge in the library, I said, when you told me that B. was to go on, "Well, now you know *two actors* have refused the play, and we haven't been able to get any manager to take it. Do you think it's going to succeed with a reader? Hadn't we better consider?" And you answered that you had done it in the face of that fact that there were 9 chances out of ten it would *fail*. This reassured me.

Burbank *is* splendid. I wish I could do something for him, too. If he gets a play that needs any literary tinkering, I'll tinker it.

Well, this experience is good, but it has almost killed me. The nervous strain of that awful Monday is something I haven't got over yet. It's perfectly lurid, the retrospect.

Yours ever,

W. D. HOWELLS.

"The pathetic story" was one Clemens had written about his mother in a letter to Howells. When she was eighty-two she had insisted upon going to a convention of the old settlers of the Mississippi Valley, held at a distance from her home. When she arrived she asked the hotel clerk if Dr. Barrett was there and was told that he had returned to St. Louis. She went back to her home in silence, and then told her children that she and this man had loved each other when they were young but had been parted through a misunderstanding. She had not seen him for sixty-four years, and had gone to the convention because she had seen in the papers that he was to be there.

The "new story" was *April Hopes.*

To S. L. Clemens

Boston, May 23, 1886.

MY DEAR CLEMENS:

I never read a more pathetic story than that you tell me of your mother. After all how poor and hackneyed all the inventions are, compared with the simple and stately facts! Who could have imagined such a heartbreak as that? Yet it went along with the fulfillment of every day duty, and made no more noise than a grave underfoot. I doubt if fiction will ever get the knack of such things. How could it represent them?

I'm worrying away at the start of a new story, which I haven't fairly got on its legs after a month's trying. And to-morrow I have to switch off and do a "Study." What a fool I was to undertake that! But oh! how much better it all is than to be waiting for the axe to-morrow night! I would rather be the lessee of a theatre any time than the author of a new play.

Yours ever,
W. D. HOWELLS.

The next letter was laid aside by Charles Eliot Norton when he was going through Lowell's letters to Howells, which had been sent him for use in Lowell's Life. It has Norton's own note on it, and also one by Howells about the offer of the Smith Professorship of the French and Spanish Languages and Literatures at Harvard that was made him through Lowell.

(This letter I do not print. It belongs to Howell's "Life," and may it remain long unprinted! With H's note attached it is an interesting memorial of both J. R. L. and himself,—characteristic of both.—C. E. N. 26 Nov. 1892.)

James Russell Lowell to W. D. Howells

Deerfoot Farm, Southborough, Mass.
24th Dec., 1886.

MY DEAR BOY:

I am glad you were pleased, but think you are right in refusing. But since you were pleased I feel uneasy under the credit your affection (which is very precious to me) gives me for it.

I didn't make the suggestion. It came from the President himself. When he spoke of it to me I made the same objections which I made when you consulted me about Johns Hopkins and which you now make. After talking it over with him and getting his allowance for every possible elbow-room for you, of course I became a warm convert to his view of the case. This is my only merit in the affair. I should have been mightily pleased to see you in my gown and so would Longfellow. When you talked to 'em about Chaucer, you would have had only to add a hood to it to give 'em as good a piece of realism as ever you could wish. Go to the Public Library and look at Occleve's (I think 'tis his) portrait of the dear old fellow and you will see that I am right—as I always am, have you ever noticed it? Show it to Mrs. Howells with my compliments, and *she* will say I am right.

Much as I should have liked it, however, I think you are right in your decision.

I wish you to like a bit of humour and sentiment which will be in the February *Atlantic*. Do you hear? When you told me the other day you had been reading my poems, I stupidly let go my chance to make you uncomfortable by asking you how you liked 'em. The February *Atlantic*

("Febuary," as Amanda Grier would have called it) will make it good to me.

With kindest regards and a Merry Xmas to Mrs. Howells and the weans (where did the two girls get those lovely eyes?)

Affectionately yours,
J. R. LOWELL.

I have written to Eliot. Yes, I had rather have one novel of yours than cords of lectures—even of my own!

> (He came in one afternoon to me in Beacon street, and with the sweetest graciousness told me the President of Harvard had asked him to learn if I would accept the professorship that he and Longfellow and Ticknor had held. I thought it over a night and then decided that I could not do justice to the position. This offer, precious as it was to a man of my self-lettered life, was less precious than his way of making it.—W. D. HOWELLS, 1891.)

"The book" must have been *The Rise of Silas Lapham* or *The Minister's Charge*. James's "new story," was probably *Louisa Pallant,* which appeared in the February *Harper's Monthly* of 1888.

"Duveneck" was Frank Duveneck, the artist, who had married Miss Boott.

To Henry James

302 Beacon Street, Boston,
December 25, 1886.

MY DEAR JAMES:

I'm ashamed to send you a typewritten letter; but I'm almost obliged to do so, for my wrist has weakened again and my handwriting has gone all to pieces. This sort has at least the merit of clearness; and you can forgive something to mere modernity in me.

Your most kind letter from Milan caused great excitement and rejoicing in this family. What could I ask more, even if I had the cheek to ask half so much? One doesn't thank you for such a thing, I suppose, but I may tell you at least of my pride and pleasure in it. I'm disposed to make the most of the abundance of your kindness, for in many quarters here the book meets with little but misconception. If we regard it as nothing but an example of work in the new way—the performance of a man who won't and can't keep on doing what's been done already—its reception here by most of the reviewers is extremely discouraging. Of all grounds in the world they take the genteel ground, and every

> Half-bred rogue that groomed his mother's cow,

reproaches me for introducing him to low company. This has been the tone of "society" about it; in the newspapers it hardly stops short of personal defamation. Of course they entirely miss the very simple purpose of the book. Nevertheless it sells, and sells bravely, and to my surprise I find myself not really caring a great deal for the printed animosity, except as it means ignorance. I suspect it's an effect of the frankness about our civilization which you have sometimes wondered I could practice with impunity. The impunity's gone, now, I assure you.

But all this is too much about myself. The other day the Harpers told me they had a new story from you which they seemed immensely pleased with. I understood that it was on international ground, and I was glad they seemed disposed to rejoice with me that it was so. I took occasion to say to them that I hoped you would never allow yourself to be disturbed by any outside influence. It is pre-eminently and indefeasibly your ground; you made it, as if it were a bit of the Back Bay; and the character that must pass under your eye is increasingly vast in quantity. I feel myself a recreant in not yet having read your two last books; I now read a good deal for reviewing, or whatever my work in *Harpers* may be called; and I leave the books till I have the occasion to talk of them. I know certain passages and characters in *The Bostonians* quite well, and I think Olive Chancellor miraculously good; but the Princess Casamassima I don't know at all yet. Lowell goes about proclaiming it your best, and I've heard only good of it on all hands.

I see Perry every other day, and we talk literature perpetually. Pellew has come back to town, and I find him very interesting. He's a very able fellow, and distinctly a literary promise. Another man whom you will hear of is a Mr. John Heard, a Paris-born Bostonian, whose later life has been passed in Mexico; he writes equally well in French and English, and has contributed to the *Revue Internationale* of Florence. These, with a young Russian, are the people I see most. Into Boston society I'm asked very little and go less. I would like to go oftener to Cambridge, but it's very far off; and I'm looking forward to our escape next summer to Paris, where John is to go on with his architectural studies in the Ecole des Beaux Arts if he can get in. He's a youth of parts, and has hitherto done what he's attempted. Just now, he's very much absorbed in his first dress-suit which he gets into every night after dinner for some social occasion.

We expect to be two years in Paris, and when we return, I hope that we can contrive to spend the year pretty equally between Washington and Cambridge. Certainly I think we shall always winter hereafter in Washington; if it hadn't been for John's going into the Tech., here, we should have been there this winter.

I see Aldrich more rarely than I should like, these days, for the comfort of mere old friendship is very great.

I'm sick of this confounded machine, and you shall have the rest through the pen.

Last summer, which I spent in my house, here, I went several times to see Grace Norton, always gay company, and full of the literary interest which I care for almost alone. She gave me news of you, and sometimes read passages of your letters, which always amazed me by their excellent abundance. How can you get time to write them? By the way, I find your *Little Tour in France* delightful reading: it's a more absolute transference to literature of the mood of observation than anything else that I know.

We have been having a decently merry Christmas, and the children have enjoyed it; but I notice a decadence from the more robust and resolute Christmas of the old Dickens days, when holly was such a panacea. If one came back to Boston fifty years from now I fancy he would find it even soberer than now on Christmas. That reminds me, I shall be fifty my next birthday, the first of March. I've heard people say that they are not conscious of growing old; but *I* am. I'm perfectly aware of the shrinking bounds. I don't plan so largely as I used, and without having lost hope I don't have so much use for it as once. I feel my half century fully. Lord, how it's slipped away!

Our Winny, who's been ailing so long, seems at last to have got her feet on the rising ground again. I wish you would give all our loves to your sister, and give us some good news of her when you write. The family join me in affectionate regards to yourself, whom we count upon seeing next year. If this letter follows you to Italy, salute the Arno and the Grand Canal for me; the Tiber I don't feel quite up to. Salute also the Bootts and their Duveneck, and believe me

Ever yours,
W. D. HOWELLS.

1887

"This" was the proof of the Editor's Study for the May *Harper's Monthly* of 1887, which dealt with various books, and in doing so said:

"That is all we can ask of fiction, sense and truth; we cannot prophesy that every novel that has them will have the success of *Innocents Abroad* or *Roughing It,* but we believe recognition wide and full will await it.

"Much of the best fails of recognition, but enough of the best gets it to make us hopeful that when literature comes close to life, even ordinary minds will feel and know its charm. We think there is proof of this in the vast popularity of one humorist, in the fame of the greatest whose pseudonym is at this moment as well known, in America at least, as the name of Shakespeare. We need not blink any of his shortcomings in recognizing that his books are all masterpieces of humor; they are so, and yet our public does care for them in a prodigious degree, and it cares for them because incomparably more and better than any other American books they express a familiar and almost universal quality of the American mind, they faithfully portray a phase of American life, which they reflect in its vast kindliness and good-will, its shrewdness and its generosity, its informality which is not formless; under every fantastic disguise they are honest and true."

To S. L. Clemens

302 Beacon St., Boston,
Feb'y 13, 1887.

MY DEAR CLEMENS:

This has to lie over from the April to the May Study, but I can't help showing it to you now. Don't let it be seen out of the family.

Say: if I could get a publisher to take that *Library of Humor* off your hands, what would you ask for it? You know the work is almost wholly Clark's and mine; and it would appear under my name, if I could get the pub. It

grinds me all the time to think you should have paid me
$2500 for work that you don't expect to use.

Yours ever,
W. D. HOWELLS.

In 1884 Howells was chosen for the first president of the
Tavern Club, which had grown from the meetings of some
of the younger artists, musicians, writers, and professional
men, at the Carrolton Hotel. When they became a club
they took rooms in a building at the corner of Park Square,
under those of Frederic P. Vinton who had William Hunt's
old studio there. At Mrs. Vinton's invitation they held
their entertainments in her husband's studio, as their own
rooms were small and bare. When the club grew larger
they decided to move to a house of their own on Boylston
Place, and it was at the time of their moving there that the
next letter was written.

To Mrs. Frederic P. Vinton

Tavern Club, 1 Park Square,
April 21, 1887.

DEAR MRS. VINTON:

In behalf of the gentlemen of the Club, I have to beg
your acceptance of the accompanying pieces of silver as an
expression of their sense of the graceful hospitality they
have long enjoyed at your hands. Without the generous
and unfailing welcome which they have found in the Vinton
Studio, and which they gratefully ascribe to your inexhausti-
ble patience, no festivity of the Club could have been complete, and with it each has been an increasing success. The
whole Club therefore regards you as in some sort the inspiration of its fortunes, and honors itself with the hope
that you will share its regrets in parting. We never expect
again to find neighbors so charmingly sympathetic as your-

self and Mr. Vinton, and we are sure that you will find none more devotedly appreciative than your obliged friends of the Tavern Club.

Yours sincerely,
W. D. HOWELLS.
President.

What Howells saw of the Natural Gas in Findlay, he afterwards used for Fulkerson's background of Moffit in *A Hazard of New Fortunes.*

To S. L. Clemens

Joy House, Findlay, Ohio,
May 27, 1887.

MY DEAR CLEMENS:

They are going to have a Natural Gas Jubilee in this wonderful place on the 8th or 9th of June, and they are going to ask you, of course. I think if you will come you will enjoy a No. 11 astonishment, and it will fit you comfortably. The wildest dreams of Col. Sellers are here the commonplaces of every day experience. I wish I could blow off a gas-well in this note, for then you would have some notion of what a gas-well is. But I can't, and so you had better come, and see what thirteen of them all going at once, are.

Yours ever,
W. D. HOWELLS.

Mr. C. C. Howell, who came within an S of being a cousin of mine, would put himself in charge of you, and you would be in good hands.

Winifred Howells was still an invalid, and her parents and sister had gone with her to the Sanatorium at Dansville in the hope of its benefiting her health.

Howells felt so strongly that the "Chicago Anarchists" had not been fairly tried that he risked, as he believed, his reputation and his livelihood in trying to save them. His wife, in spite of her anxiety for their children, and especially for their invalid daughter, faced the possible loss of his position with him, and upheld him in his efforts. Whether he was right or wrong in his view of the case does not affect the fact of his courage in hazarding everything for what he thought the right.

Judge Roger A. Pryor was the leading counsel for the "Chicago Anarchists" before the Supreme Court.

To Judge Roger A. Pryor

The Sanatorium, Dansville, N. Y.,
Sept. 25, 1887.

MY DEAR SIR:

I am glad you have taken the case of the Chicago Anarchists, and that you see some hope for them before the Supreme Court, for I have never believed them guilty of murder, or of anything but their opinions, and I do not think they were justly convicted. I have no warrant in writing to you except my very strong feeling in this matter, but I am not quite a stranger to you. I had the pleasure of meeting Mrs. Pryor and yourself at Mr. Mead's, in Washington Place, in the spring of '86.

I venture to call myself to her remembrance; and to wish you all success in your effort to save these men.

Yours sincerely,
W. D. HOWELLS.

Judge Pryor's reply to Howells's letter of September 25th states his legal view of the trial.

Roger A. Pryor to W. D. Howells

18 Wall Street, New York,
3rd October, 1887.

MY DEAR MR. HOWELLS:

A temperate claim on behalf of the Anarchists—that however guilty they have a right to a fair trial and a *legal* conviction; that the most atrocious criminal cannot be convicted but in conformity with law; that an illegal conviction of such criminal breaks down the securities which the law provides for the protection of innocence; that there is grave doubt whether, in the whirlwind of passion which swept over Chicago, the Anarchists have had a fair and legal trial; that they claim that they have been doomed to death contrary to the guarantees of the Federal constitution; that they desire to test this claim before the Supreme Court of the United States; that if the claim be sustained, clearly they should not hang, while, if refuted, their execution will be delayed but for a brief period, and the country will then be satisfied of the legality and righteousness of their punishment; that their execution under a sentence of doubtful legality, will propitiate sympathy for them, and for their doctrines,—such an appeal to the public, under the *imprimatur* of your name, cannot but be of wholesome and happy effect.

The enclosed extract from the judgment of the U. S. Supreme Court, in Milligan's case, 4 Wallace's Reports, p. 132,—a case in which they annulled the sentence of death pronounced by a military commission against a traitor in the war of secession—states clearly and authoritatively the great and salutary principle that even the worst and most notorious criminal has an inviolable right to a *legal* trial.

I anticipate great pleasure for myself and Mrs. Pryor from the promised meeting with you and your wife.

With many and heartfelt thanks for your generous concern for the fate of my unhappy clients, I am

Most sincerely yours,

ROGER A. PRYOR.

P. S. I mail you the speeches made by my clients on being
called for sentence; from which you will have some idea of
the sort of men they are. Please return the document after
you have read it.

R. A. P.

John P. Altgeld, Governor of Illinois, in his *Reasons for
Pardoning Fielden, Neebe and Schwab,* gives this brief and
clear account of the case.

STATEMENT OF THE CASE

On the night of May 4, 1886, a public meeting was held
on Haymarket Square in Chicago; there were from 800 to
1,000 people present, nearly all being laboring men. There
had been trouble, growing out of the effort to introduce
an eight-hour day, resulting in some collisions with the police, in one of which several laboring people were killed,
and this meeting was called as a protest against alleged
police brutality.

The meeting was orderly and was attended by the
mayor, who remained until the crowd began to disperse and
then went away. As soon as Capt. John Bonfield, of the
police department, learned that the mayor had gone, he
took a detachment of police and hurried to the meeting
for the purpose of dispersing the few that remained, and
as the police approached the place of meeting a bomb was
thrown by some unknown person, which exploded and
wounded many and killed several policemen, among the
latter being one Mathias Degan. A number of people were
arrested and after a time August Spies, Albert R. Parsons,

Louis Lingg, Michael Schwab, Samuel Fielden, George Engle, Adolph Fischer and Oscar Neebe were indicted for the murder of Mathias Degan. The prosecution could not discover who had thrown the bomb and could not bring the really guilty man to justice, and, as some of the men indicted were not at the Haymarket meeting and had nothing to do with it, the prosecution was forced to proceed on the theory that the men indicted were guilty of murder because it was claimed they had at various times in the past uttered and printed incendiary and seditious language, practically advising the killing of policemen, of Pinkerton men and others acting in that capacity, and that they were therefore responsible for the murder of Mathias Degan. The public was greatly excited and after a prolonged trial all of the defendants were found guilty; Oscar Neebe was sentenced to fifteen years imprisonment and all of the other defendants were sentenced to be hanged. The case was carried to the supreme court and was there affirmed in the fall of 1887. Soon thereafter Lingg committed suicide. The sentence of Fielden and Schwab was commuted to imprisonment for life and Parsons, Fischer, Engle and Spies were hanged, and the petitioners now ask to have Neebe, Fielden and Schwab set at liberty.

The several thousand merchants, bankers, judges, lawyers and other prominent citizens of Chicago who have by petition, by letter and in other ways urged executive clemency, mostly base their appeal on the ground that, assuming the prisoners to be guilty, they have been punished enough, but a number of them who have examined the case more carefully, and are more familiar with the record and with the facts disclosed by the papers on file, base their appeal on entirely different grounds. They assert,

FIRST—That the jury which tried the case was a packed jury selected to convict.

SECOND—That according to the law as laid down by the supreme court, both prior to and again since the trial of this case, the jurors, according to their own answers, were not competent jurors and the trial was therefore not a legal trial.

THIRD—That the defendants were not proven to be guilty of the crime charged in the indictment.

FOURTH—That as to the defendant Neebe, the state's attorney had declared at the close of the evidence that there was no case against him, and yet he has been kept in prison all these years.

FIFTH—That the trial judge was either so prejudiced against the defendants, or else so determined to win the applause of a certain class in the community that he could not and did not grant a fair trial.

Judge Pryor refers to a letter from Howells to him about the "Anarchists" that he suggested publishing, but which Howells decided not to print.

Roger A. Pryor to W. D. Howells

18 Wall Street, New York,
1st November, 1887.

MY DEAR MR. HOWELLS:

The present is the first opportunity I have had, to answer your last letter. I think, *now*, you did well to suppress the publication; because I am satisfied that, while your chivalry might have somewhat compromised you, it could do no good to the condemned. In the ardor of my zeal for my clients, the possible detriment to yourself escaped my consideration; but that fact, as well as the no effect of the publication, are obvious on cool reflection. No man should challenge public obloquy without a commensurate object.

Still, I am satisfied that an appeal by you for Executive clemency, would not be ineffectual. And, I am afraid that such appeal is our last resource. The Court should grant us the writ—of which the effect is only to bring the judgment below up for review on Federal questions, but I believe it will be denied. However, you will know by Thursday next, at farthest.

I have to beg that when you come to New York, you will apprise me of your presence,—to the end that I may do myself the honor of proffering you the hospitalities of my house.

Very sincerely etc.
ROGER A. PRYOR.

The sentence of the "Chicago Anarchists" was affirmed by the Supreme Court in Washington on November 2, 1887. The New York *Tribune* of November 3, says:

One of the first to hear the news was General Roger A. Pryor, the leading counsel before the Supreme Court for the men. "I am somewhat disappointed," he said to a *Tribune* reporter, "I had reason to expect that the Supreme Court would decide in my favor. However, I told my colleagues in Washington that I was afraid the writ would be denied us. Yesterday I thought the chances were in my favor. I got a request from Washington for the twelve additional points that I raised, and I had to scurry around to get them. I sent them to Washington and I supposed the request for them looked favorable to the case. Nothing is left for the men but the interference of the Governor. I hope he will use his prerogative and commute their sentences. The law has been vindicated.

"Outside of my professional capacity as attorney for the men, I fully believe that they were innocent of the crime charged. If there was a plot in existence do you suppose that they would have had their wives and children there?"

The letter from Howells appeared in the New York *Tribune* of November 4, 1887.

CLEMENCY FOR THE ANARCHISTS

A Letter from Mr. W. D. Howells

To THE EDITOR OF the *Tribune:*

SIR: I have petitioned the Governor of Illinois to commute the death-penalty of the Anarchists to imprisonment and have also personally written him in their behalf; and I now ask your leave to express here the hope that those who are inclined to do either will not lose faith in themselves because the Supreme Court has denied the condemned a writ of error. That court simply affirmed the legality of the forms under which the Chicago court proceeded; it did not affirm the propriety of trying for murder men fairly indictable for conspiracy alone; and it by no means approved the principle of punishing them because of their frantic opinions, for a crime which they were not shown to have committed. The justice or injustice of their sentence was not before the highest tribunal of our law, and unhappily could not be got there. That question must remain for history, which judges the judgment of courts, to deal with; and I, for one, cannot doubt what the decision of history will be.

But the worst is still for a very few days reparable; the men sentenced to death are still alive, and their lives may be finally saved through the clemency of the Governor, whose prerogative is now the supreme law in their case. I conjure all those who believe that it would be either injustice or impolicy to put them to death, to join in urging him by petition, by letter, through the press, and from the pulpit and the platform, to use his power, in the only direction where power can never be misused, for the mitigation of their punishment.

WILLIAM DEAN HOWELLS.

Dansville, N. Y., Nov. 4, 1887.

Brand Whitlock in *Forty Years of It,* says of Howells's letter in the *Tribune:*

"My work in the office of the secretary of state involved the care of the state's archives. . . . It was a tedious and stupid task, until we came one day to file what were called the papers in the anarchist case. Officially they related to

the applications for the commutation of the sentences of
the four men, Spies, Engle, Fischer, and Parsons, who had
been hanged, and for the pardon of the three who were then
confined in the penitentiary at Joliet, Fielden and Schwab
for life, and old Oscar Neebe for fifteen years. Fielden and
Schwab had been sentenced to death with the four who had
been killed, but Governor Oglesby had commuted their sentences to imprisonment for life; Neebe's original sentence
had been for the fifteen years he was then serving. The
papers consisted of communications to the governor, great
petitions, and letters and telegrams, many sent in mercy, and
some in the spirit of reason, asking for clemency, many in a
wild hysteria of fear, and in a hideous hate that is born of
fear, begging the governor to let 'justice' take its course.

"There were the names of many prominent men and
women signed to these communications; among them a request signed by many authors in England requesting clemency, but there was no appeal stronger, and no protest
braver, than that in the letter which Mr. Howells had written to a New York newspaper analyzing the case and showing the amazing injustice of the whole proceeding. Mr.
Howells had first gone, so he told me in after years, to the
aged poet Whittier, whose gentle philosophy might have
moved him to a mood against that public wrong, and then
to George William Curtis, but they advised him to write
the protest himself, and he had done so, and he had done
it better and more bravely than either of them could have
done out of the great conscience and the great heart that
have always been on the side of the weak and the oppressed,
with a mercy which when it is practised by mankind is always so much nearer the right and the divine than our crude
and generally cruel attempts at justice can ever be. But all
these prayers had fallen on official ears that—to use a grotesque figure—were so closely pressed to the ground that
they could not hear,—and there was nothing to do, since
they were so many and so bulky that no latest-improved

and patented steel filing-case could hold them, but to have a big box made and lock them up in that for all time, forgotten, like so many other records of injustice, out of the minds of men.

"But not entirely; for injustice was never long out of the mind of John P. Altgeld, and during all those first months of his administration he had been brooding over this notable instance of injustice, and he had come to his decision. He knew the cost to him; he had just come to the governorship of his state, and to the leadership of his party, after its thirty years of defeat, and he realized what powerful interests would be frightened and offended if he were to turn three forgotten men out of prison; he understood how partizanship would turn the action to its advantage.

"It mattered not that most of the thoughtful men in Illinois would tell you that the 'anarchists' had been improperly convicted, that they were not only entirely innocent of the murder of which they had been accused, but were not even anarchists; it was simply that the mob had convicted them in one of the strangest frenzies of fear that ever distracted a whole community, a case which all psychologists of all the universities in the world might have tried, without getting at the truth of it—much less a jury in a criminal court.

"And so, one morning in June, very early, I was called to the governor's and told to make out pardons for Fielden, Neebe, and Schwab."

Francis F. Browne was the founder and editor of the *Dial,* who felt with Howells about the "Anarchists."

To Francis F. Browne

Dansville, Nov. 11, 1887.

MY DEAR FRIEND:

It is all right. My pride suffered some twinges when I saw my letter in the *Tribune,* with the insulting head-line the night editor had given it; for I perceived that what was written for the eye of a friend was somewhat hysterical in print. But if you and other humane persons believed that it might do good,—even so little where so much was needed —you did right, and I approved and adopt your action.— I don't know yet what the governor has done. While I write that hideous scene may be enacting in your jail yard —the thing forever damnable before God and abominable to civilized men. But while I don't know, I can still hope.

Miserable Lingg! I'm glad he's out of the story; but even with his death, it seems to me that humanity's judgment of the law begins. All over the world people must be asking themselves, What cause is this really, for which men die so gladly, so inexorably? So the evil will grow from violence to violence!

Sometime I hope to meet you and exchange with you the histories of our several experiences in this matter. The last time we met I remember we disagreed about a man named Blaine and a man named Cleveland. How trivial the difference between them seems in this lurid light.

Yours sincerely,

W. D. HOWELLS.

To William Cooper Howells

Dansville, Nov. 13, 1887.

DEAR FATHER:

I've had no letter from you this week, but I suppose you got my last. I sent you the *Tribune* with my unavailing word for the Anarchists. All is over now, except the judgment that begins at once for every unjust and evil deed, and goes on forever. The historical perspective is that this free Republic has killed five men for their opinions.—I have had many letters thanking me for my words. The Pres't of the American Press Association, (which supplies Joe with his stereotype photos?) says, "Your stand in regard to the Anarchists meets with my most cordial approval. Society will commit a great blunder—a great crime would be the better term—if the Anarchists are hung." Harriet Prescott Spofford writes, "Great as your work is, you never wrote more immortal words than those in behalf of these men who are dying for free speech." So it goes. Of course I get abuse in print; but that doesn't matter.

With love to all,
Your aff'te son,
WILL.

The Upper and the Nether Millstone became *Annie Kilburn*.

To Mrs. Achille Fréchette

Hotel Niagara, Buffalo,
Nov. 18, 1887.

MY DEAR ANNIE:

It's a very, very long time since I've heard from you, and it's my own fault, for I'm afraid I've neglected your letters. I hope you are all well, and that your lovely and interesting children are getting into the winter without too much trouble of mind or body. I know that Mole must have a great deal to preoccupy him; but I hope he hasn't forgotten his Uncle Will; and the manful struggle we made together in the cause of ameliorative table-manners when we last met. And dear little Vevie, how much I'd like to see her, and take up our common interests with her. What does she study? What does she read? *Can* she be as cunning as ever? Do tell me about yourself, and Achille, whom I think it one of the misfortunes that I can't see every day. He and father seem to me two perfect gentlemen, always.

I want to tell you how charming we all thought your story in *St. Nicholas* was. Pilla, especially, was delighted. I wish you could write more.

I suppose you wouldn't be much surprised at getting a letter from me in the moon; but I ought to try to explain why we're in Buffalo. For the last two months we've been at the Sanatorium in Dansville, where we took Winny when we left Lake George. I think she'll get well there if anywhere, and the doctors have judged it best that we should be away from her. So, we've come to this wonderful new hotel, the most exquisite place of the sort that I ever was in. In daresay Aurelia has told you about it. She it really was who found it, for she read me the advertisement when she came on with Pil and me in October, and she passed a day here with us. We've now been here three days, and we expect to stay till into February, if we can stand the climate, and all goes well with Winny. There's a good Art School, where Pil can study, and she can get French and dancing. To-night she's gone with a party of young girls to the Dickens' reading. I think I shall have time for work, and it is pleasant to be so near dear old father. (Isn't it nice, Willy naming his boy for him?) I hope to have him here, and go to see him more than once during our stay. The only objection we have to the place is a queer one, and I'm afraid you won't think it's sincere. Elinor and I both no longer care for the world's life, and would like to be settled somewhere very humbly and simply, where we could be socially identified with the principles of progress and sympathy for the struggling mass. I can only excuse our present movement as temporary. The last two months have been full of heartache and horror for me, on account of the civic murder committed last Friday at Chicago. You may have seen in the papers that I had taken part in petitioning for clemency for the Anarchists, whom I thought unfairly tried, and most unjustly condemned. Annie, it's all been an atrocious piece of frenzy and cruelty, for which we must stand ashamed forever before history. But it's no use. I can't write about it. Some day I hope to do justice to these irreparably wronged men.

I'm busy with another story, which will deal rather with humanity than with love. I think I shall call it *The Upper and the Nether Millstone*, and the hero to be a minister who preaches the life rather than the doctrine of Christ. Have you read Tolstoi's heart-searching books? They're worth all the other novels ever written.

Elinor is well, and joins me in love to you all. I'm well, too, except for turning my ankle, the other day. That has kept me indoors since. Very best love to Achille, the children, and yourself.

Your affectionate brother,
WILL.

Howells greatly admired the work of Valdés and they often wrote to each other, Valdés in Spanish and Howells in Italian.

A. Palacio Valdés to W. D. Howells

Oviedo, Spain,
Nov. 26, 1887.

MR WILLIAM DEAN HOWELLS

Dear Sir:

I have read an Editor's Study for this month in Harper's Magazine, and I am very glad to see that we agree on these esthetic questions on which the opinions are so varied. I believe that a mysterious current of sympathy joins our hearts and minds across the ocean—the same things impress or disgust us. I believe that we must think the same on many other subjects besides art.

If for any reason we should bless civilization, it is because with it man is not isolated, and at hundreds of miles distance he finds brothers with whom he can live in agreeable communion of thoughts and feelings. You have the blessing of living in a civilized country, I have the misfortune of living in a semi-barbarous country, but even then, we both live in an ideal country, we are both citizens of a heavenly city where all difference of race and selfishness disappear.

You do not forget me in your articles. Why don't you remember to write me a letter? I wish you would tell me of your private and public life, what you do, what you think, what you love. I believe I told you that I am very anxious to meet you. The hope of going some day to that prosperous nation, and of shaking your hand, does not abandon me. Thanks to you, I am not unknown to the American public. If my business affairs run smoothly, I may take a pleasure trip to America. It may prove profitable if I describe it in a book. We shall see.

Now I am writing a book whose subject is the Spanish aristocracy. Unfortunately it is sufficiently corrupted, and the book cannot be as clean as the others, unless I should misrepresent, something I would not do for any consideration.

I thank you again for your article. Believe me always your true friend. Please write to me.

A. PALACIO VALDÉS.

I have just received a letter from your friend, William Henry Bishop. He asks for my picture and some facts about other Spanish writers. He is a very pleasant man, and I am very grateful for the visitor whom he sent in his place.

XX

1888, 1889

Goes to New York. A Hazard of New Fortunes. *Death of Winifred Howells. Back to Boston.*

"YOUR land tenure idea" was also Henry George's, of whom Garland was a disciple. In explaining this Garland says:

"As often as I dared, I tried to win Howells to a belief in the single tax. He gave it his allegiance to the point of saying, 'It is good as far as it goes but reforms should go further.' In other words he was more socialistic than I. We never *argued*—we just stated our theories and convictions."

To Hamlin Garland

The Niagara, Buffalo, N. Y.
January 15, 1888.

DEAR MR. GARLAND:

I am glad to have your letter and to know what you are doing and intending. Your time must come for recognition, but you are already a power, and that is more than a name, which is sometimes a hindrance to full use of one's strength.

I'm interested by what you say of the drama and if you can fit your character play to some character actor, you'll succeed. But I'm still more interested by what I will call your appeal to me. You'll easily believe that I did not bring myself to the point of openly befriending those men who were civically murdered in Chicago for their opinions without thinking and feeling much, and my horizons have been indefinitely widened by the process. Your land tenure idea

407

is one of the good things which we must hope for and strive for by all the good means at our hands. But I don't know that it's the first step to be taken; and I can't yet bring myself to look upon confiscation in any direction as a good thing. The new commonwealth must be founded in justice even to the unjust,. in generosity to the unjust rather than anything less than justice. Besides, the land idea arrays against progress the vast farmer class who might favor national control of telegraphs, railways, and mines, postal savings-bank-and-life-insurance, a national labor bureau for bringing work and workmen together without cost to the workman, and other schemes by which it is hoped to lessen the sum of wrong in the world, and insure to every man the food and shelter which the gift of life implies the right to. Understand, I don't argue against you; I don't know yet what is best; but I am reading and thinking about questions that carry me beyond myself and my miserable literary idolatries of the past; perhaps you'll find that I've been writing about them. I am still the slave of selfishness, but I no longer am content to be so. That's as far as I can honestly say I've got.

You ought to get acquainted with Robertson James (a brother of the novelist) who lives at Concord, and is an ardent Georgeite.

We shall be leaving Buffalo in about a fortnight, for either New York or Boston; but my address is always with the Harpers.

Yours cordially,
W. D. HOWELLS.

Stedman had sent Howells a review of Howells's work by Mme. Cavazza, and in a letter written to her at the same time Stedman says:

"For some time I have felt that Tray, Blanche, and Sweetheart had yelped quite enough at a thoroughly sincere, modest, hardworking author—who has the courage of his convictions. What success he has gained has been gained neither by envy nor by self seeking, but by steady performance according to his lights. Howells is a *man,* at all events, and has been taunted after an unmanly fashion. I am glad you and a few others are calling a halt."

"The poem you wanted" was *The Song the Oriole Sings.* Stedman was collecting to bind in his own copy of his *Poets of America* autograph poems by the poets included in that book, and he had asked Howells for one; but Stedman was never able to carry out his plan for this volume.

To Edmund Clarence Stedman

Jefferson, Ashtabula Co., Ohio,
Feb. 4, '88.

MY DEAR STEDMAN:

How kind of you to write me that long friendly letter! It dropt into a moment of my life when it seemed as if I were a literary Ishmael, and it made me feel at once like the legitimate seed of Abraham,—after a good bargain. I was so glad of it, that I can't yet be sorry I almost extorted it from your overworked hand and brain. I'm obliged to you also for Mrs. Cavazza's review. People take me so viciously awry, and think (or say) that I have no serious meaning when my whole trouble has been to sugarcoat my medicinal properties; and she not only feels all my meaning, but puts it with greater distinctness and aptness than I could myself if I tried to phrase it. And how extremely clever her little parting sting was!

We have had a very interesting winter in Buffalo (every inch of this America is interesting) and Thursday my wife and daughter went East to Boston, and Friday I came here to visit my dear father, now eighty, but young as ever in his concern about human affairs and his whole intellectual life.—I wish I could meet you some time, and have a long talk about literature, and about the economic phases which now seem to me so important. I fancy we might find ourselves on common ground, where we now appear to differ. At any rate you would not find me wanting in honor for the hand that has kept the Lamp alight and aloft above all the dust and din of commerce these many years. I send you the poem you wanted—the one I now like best of mine.

Yours ever,
W. D. HOWELLS.

"The book" was *April Hopes.*

To Hamlin Garland

46 West 9th st., New York,
March 11, 1888.

DEAR MR. GARLAND:

I read your criticisms with great interest and respect. I supposed that the social intent of the book—the teaching that *love is not enough in love affairs,* but that there must be parity of ideal, training and disposition, in order to ensure happiness—was only too obvious. I meant to show that an engagement made from mere passion had better be broken, if it does not bear the strain of temperament; every such broken engagement I consider a blessing and an escape. To infuse, or to declare more of my personality in a story, would be a mistake, to my thinking: it should rather be the novelist's business to keep out of the way. My work must take its chance with readers. It is written from a sincere sense of the equality of men, and a real trust in them. I can't do more.

I wish I had seen your papers in the *American*—one extract in a newspaper greatly pleased me. *Zury* slipped through my fingers—I hardly know how; but sometime I shall get round to it.

Yours sincerely,
W. D. HOWELLS.

I'm glad of the success of your lectures, as the papers report it.

One of "your two essays" must have been *Knights of Labor,* which was written in 1887 but never published; what the other one was it is now impossible to tell.

To S. L. Clemens

46 West 9th st., N. Y.,
April 5, 1888.

My dear Clemens:

I have read your two essays with thrills almost amounting to yells of satisfaction. It is about the best thing yet said on the subject; but it is strange that you can't get a single newspaper to face the facts of the situation. Here the fools are now all shouting because the Knights of Labor have revenged themselves on the Engineers, and the C. B. & Q. strike is a failure. No one notices how labor has educated itself; no one perceives that *next* time there won't be any revenge or any failure! If ever a public was betrayed by its press, it's ours. No man could safely make himself heard in behalf of the strikers any more than for the anarchists.

By the way have you seen Rev. Kimball yet? When you do, give him my regards.

Yours ever,
W. D. Howells.

The Rise of Silas Lapham was published by Hachette et Cie in French.

John Durand was the friend and translator of Taine.

J. Durand to W. D. Howells

16 rue Littré
April 10, 1888.

MY DEAR MR. HOWELLS:

The arrangement for the publication of Silas Lapham in book form by Hachette & C. are completed. Only it will be eight or ten months before it is issued—when I hope to send you 500 francs for the copyright. In bringing this about Mr. Taine helped it along with the following in a note to Hachette & C.

"J'apprends que vous songez à publier en français le roman de Howells intitulé *Silas Lapham*. Je l'ai lu en Anglais avec le plus grand plaisir et avec beaucoup d'admiration; c'est le meilleur roman écrit par un Américain, le plus semblable à ceux de Balzac, le plus comprehensif. Silas, sa femme et ses deux filles sont des types nouveaux pour nous, très solides et très complets."

Faithfully yours,
J. DURAND.

"Father Fay" was the Rev. Hercules Warren Fay, a friend of both Perry and Howells.

"The Adventure book" was the *Library of Universal Adventure* which Perry and Howells had compiled together.

"Pellew" was William George Pellew, who won the Bowdoin prize at Harvard for his essay on Jane Austen's novels, and who later wrote *In Castle and Cabin* and the *Life of John Jay*.

"Sidney Luska" was the Jewish pseudonym of Henry Harland, under which he wrote his first novels, *As It was Written, Mrs. Peixada,* and *The Yoke of the Thorah.*

To Thomas S. Perry

46 West 9th st., New York,
April 14, 1888.

DEAR PERRY:

It's a long time that I've had you on my conscience, and now you're both a duty and a privilege, of which I was freshly reminded, the other day, by getting these *Figaros* from the good Father Fay. I read with some mystification about the decadents; how could I read myself easiest into some knowledge of them? Are they possibly the Next?

We have been two months in New York, in this flat (where you must not address me, but continue to direct % Harper's) and I have been trying to catch on to the bigger life of the place. It's immensely interesting, but I don't know whether I shall manage it; I'm now fifty-one, you know. There are lots of interesting young painting and writing fellows, and the place is lordly free, with foreign touches of all kinds all thro' its abounding Americanism: Boston seems of another planet.

I enclose my letter about the Anarchists, which I wrote just before their civic murder. I came to that mind about it through reading their trial, in which they proved themselves absolutely guiltless of the murder charged upon them; but it was predetermined to kill them. They died with unsurpassable courage. Of course I had nothing to do with their opinions, though some of the papers abused me as heartily as if I had proclaimed myself a dynamiter. I wish I could go fully into the subject.

You'll be glad to know that the Adventure book is about printed, and that they will begin taking subscriptions in May. The subscription man is full of hope and energy.

Lowell talked here last night to the Independents, but I couldn't—or didn't—go. I care little for either party. Sometimes I think that if there were a labor party, embodying any practical ideas I would vote with it; but there's none. Very soon, I'm afraid, we shall have trouble with that element, and partly thro' the fault of those who won't deal fairly with it. The C. B. & Q. strike has been badly managed by the road; though you won't hear a hint of this in the press. It is through the forbearance of the Engineers that the road isn't ruined, for they could refuse its cars on every other line.

There isn't much in literature that's new. Pellew's going to have a paper in the *Forum* on fiction. He did a most generous thing by me in a letter to the Boston *Post,* and I think has really turned the tide of contumely, in several places. I'm treated quite decently now.

To-night I go to dine at an Italian place with W. H. Bishop, Boyeson and "Sidney Luska"—a delightful fellow, and a most ardent convert to realism.

I've had two charming letters from Fay, with word from you, and I read with great interest what you said of Tolstoi's play. How I wish I could have seen it!

I hope Mrs. Perry keeps well in the midst of her happiness and usefulness, and that you, dear fellow, are gorging whole libraries without a pang of indigestion.

You'll see James's extraordinary *tour de force* about Stevenson in the *Century* for April. It is really the most remarkable piece of shinning round the question I ever saw. I fancy it was something he was asked to do.

My wrist is played out—not my love.

Yours ever,

W. D. HOWELLS.

Howells had written of Cawein's first book, *The Blooms of the Berry,* in the Editor's Study, and "Your lovely little book" was *The Triumph of Music.* Cawein was then a clerk in a "betting house" in Louisville, Kentucky.

To Madison Cawein

Revere House, Boston,
May 27, 1888.

MY DEAR MR. CAWEIN:

Your lovely little book has followed me here from New York with your letter, and I hardly know how to thank you for the gratifying inscription of the volume. My family have been reading it with the delight that your other poems gave, and I expect soon to share their pleasure.

I was greatly touched and interested by what you told me of yourself. Of course I understand your uneasiness in your present situation, and I can't think any relation to a "betting-house" fortunate. But your conscience is in your own keeping, and so long as that is unspotted, you have nothing that ought really to make you unhappy. You have youth, and you have already shown mastery in verse. A life of success is before you, and it is for you to make it beautiful and beneficent or not.

I expect to be near Boston all summer, and I shall always be glad to see you. My address is in care of Harper & Bros., N. Y.

.With cordial regard,
Yours sincerely,
.W. D. HOWELLS.

"My story" was *Annie Kilburn*.

"Eddy Mead" was Edwin D. Mead, a cousin of Mrs. Howells; he edited the *New England Magazine* and was afterwards Chief Director of the World Peace Foundation. Mead was a friend, as well as a cousin-in-law, of Howells, for they shared many literary and social interests.

To Edward Everett Hale

Little Nahant, Aug. 30, 1888.

DEAR FRIEND:

It was very, very kind of you to think of writing me about my story, and I needn't tell you I'm glad of your praise. But if you read it to the end you'll see that I solve nothing, except what was solved eighteen centuries ago. The most that I can do is perhaps to set a few people thinking; for as yet I haven't got to *doing* anything, myself. But at present it seems to me that our competitive civilization is a state of warfare and a game of chance, in which each man fights and bets against fearful odds.

Eddy Mead has sent me your paper on *Wealth in Common,* which I shall read, and I'm anxious to see your books. John will gladly join your Tolstoi Club. He's read a great deal of Tolstoi, and has had him much talked into him. Of course, I should like to join, though I suppose I shall be in New York in the winter. I hope to get intimately at that vast mass of life.

Yours cordially,
W. D. HOWELLS.

Box 311, Lynn, Mass.

To Henry James

Little Nahant, Massachusetts,
October 10, 1888.

MY DEAR JAMES:

I found your letter here when I came home this morning from a house-hunt in New York. I write at once, or I shall never write, to say that it gave me great joy to know from you that I had given you pleasure. These things needed to be said, and I was glad to say them; I wish I could have said them more at length; and I want to tell you now that I think your *Partial Portraits* wonderfully good work. It makes all my critical work seem clumsy and uncouth. Surely you were born with the right word in your mouth; you never say the wrong one, anyway. Of course the *bestialità* will keep being said; but I think there is distinctly a tendency to a better sense of you here, if you really care for the fact. I'm not in a very good humor with "America" myself. It seems to be the most grotesquely illogical thing under the sun; and I suppose I love it less because it won't let me love it more. I should hardly like to trust pen and ink with all the audacity of my social ideas; but after fifty years of optimistic content with "civilization" and its ability to come out all right in the end, I now abhor it, and feel that it is coming out all wrong in the end, unless it bases itself anew on a real equality. Meantime, I wear a fur-lined overcoat, and live in all the luxury my money can buy. This non-ended summer it bought us the use of a wide-verandahed villa in forty acres of seclusion where poor Winny might get a little better possibly. The experiment isn't wholly a failure; but helplessness and anguish still remain for her; and this winter she will go to New York with us, for such doctoring as we can get there. I've found an apartment in two floors, in a huge old house overlooking Livingston Place, where we shall dwell in some rooms of rather a European effect (I have mainly in mind a metal framed mirror). I fancy the place would please Gosse, whom kindly tell with my love of our whereabouts. I'm glad he's half one of us, and rather sorry he denies us a great poet; he's a great American poet himself on his mother's side, it seems.

Pilla draws in a life class in New York, and that is one of the larger reasons why we go there. But at the bottom of our wicked hearts we all like New York, and I hope to use some of its vast, gay, shapeless life in my fiction. I suppose our home—such as it is—will be there hereafter in the winter, though we expect always to drift back to this good Boston region for the summer.

Mrs. Howells charges me to say that her heart was in all those words of mine that pleased you; and that she reads no one else with half so much pleasure.

Yours cordially,

W. D. HOWELLS.

"Vacations" was *Mr. Tangier's Vacations,* and "the Boss" was *My Friend the Boss,* both written by Hale. "Another novel" was *A Hazard of New Fortunes.*

To Edward Everett Hale

Little Nahant, Oct. 28, 1888.

MY DEAR HALE:

I am afraid that I am going away to New York for the winter without seeing you, for which I am truly sorry. The summer has been one of worrying work; and of harassing cares for my wife and me with our sick daughter; then there has come with the little leisure much fatigue. I needn't bother you, though, with excuses for what is my own loss; only, don't think me insensible of it.

I read the *Vacations* going out to Ohio, and I take the *Boss* with me. I value all you do in that direction, and admire the charm you give the evident intention. It is work that no one else can do, and it teaches me patience with conditions that I believe wrong, but that must be borne, with all the possible alleviations, till they can be very gradually changed. I do not think there is any fixed hope of justice under them, but then I know from myself—my own prejudices, passions, follies—that they cannot be bettered except through the unselfishness you enjoin, the immediate altruism dealing with what now is. I know this, while I am persuaded also that the best that is in men, most men, cannot come out till they all have a fair chance. I used to think America gave this; now I don't.—I am neither an example nor an incentive, meanwhile, in my own way of living; I am a creature of the past; only I do believe that I see the light of the future, and that it is this which shows me my ugliness and fatuity and feebleness.—Words, words, words! How to make them things, deeds,—you have the secret of that; with me they only breed more words. At present they are running into another novel, in which I'm going to deal with some mere actualities; but on new ground—New York, namely; though I take some of my characters on from Boston with me. I hardly dare ask you to look me up in any spare moment you may have there; but I am to be found at 330 East 17th st.

Yours sincerely,
W. D. HOWELLS.

To Hamlin Garland

330 East 17th st., New York,
Nov. 6, 1888.

DEAR MR. GARLAND:

I feel a good deal like the clergyman who had preached a sermon against Atheism and was complimented on it by a parishioner, who added, "But parson, I do believe there *is* a God."

Annie Kilburn is from first to last a cry for *justice,* not *alms;* i Peck's failure and death, even, it is that; and you and the *Standard* coolly ask me why I do not insist upon justice instead of alms. Really, I hope you will read the story in justice, if not alms to the friendless author. Read Mr. Peck's sermon. It could hardly have been expected that he should preach the single tax, but short of that, what more could you have?

Yours sincerely,
W. D. HOWELLS.

"The Arnold paper" was the Editor's Study for July, 1888.

To John Hay

330 East 17th st., New York,
Dec. 18, 1888.

MY DEAR HAY:

I have ventured to give a card for you to Mr. Wm. Grey, an Englishman, and as nearly a brother as may be: nephew of Sir George Grey, formerly governor of New Zealand and of the South Seas generally, and himself to be Earl of Stamford, if he outlives an aged and ailing uncle. He loves convicts, bishops and paupers, and is apparently a good and able man, with a fine head, though Solomon was perhaps better dressed on state occasions.

And how are you? And will you go to England if they ask you? Misery has been our meat with regard to Winny's invalidism for a year past, but now she's better. You can never know what a bitter moment that hand-kiss about the Arnold paper thrown from your Westward Pullman last spring, sweetened for me.

With the family love to you all,
Yours ever,
W. D. HOWELLS.

1889

This letter to Aldrich, who was then editing the *Atlantic,* is characteristically thoughtful of others.

To Thomas Bailey Aldrich

330 East 17th st., N. Y.,
Jan. 10, 1889.

MY DEAR ALDRICH:

Don't you want to order a little paper or something about something or other from ——, who is now in Paris?

Art, I fancy, might be his best hold. I happen indirectly to know that an increase of family has brought him a disproportionate decrease of fortune—the decrease is as triplets to twins. Of course, this is necessarily very confidential, and I write only in the hope that you may be really wanting something from ——, but hadn't thought of it. If you should, and will send me the money, I'll forward it to him.

Yours ever,
W. D. HOWELLS.

P. S. Of course you ought to be free even of my knowledge whether you act on my suggestion or not. So I open this, to say that ——'s address is ——, and if you have anything to say you can write him directly.

To *William Cooper Howells*

New York, Jan. 13, 1889.

DEAR FATHER:

I wrote to Aurelia in reply to her letter about the box of clothes, which I think she distributed very wisely and generously. I am sorry she had to be troubled about them.

I have not much news. President Hayes has been in town, and spent two evenings with us. He talked of Harrison whose ability he rated very high. He laughed at the rumor that he was going into the cabinet.

Friday night I went to a Socialist meeting, at the American Section. It was as quiet and orderly as a Sunday School, and people whom the reporters represent as violent conspirators were poorly dressed, well behaved listeners to a lecture which dealt patiently with hard facts. The lecturer told them that the way to national control of business was already opened by the great "trusts." One gets life in curious slices in N. Y. Friday afternoon I went to two fashionable teas, as a preparation for this Socialist meeting. One very rich young fellow, whose family has a house at Newport, is a member of this "Section."

We hear good news from Winny.

With love to all from us all,
Your aff'te son,
WILL.

The "fact that now seems so incredible" was the death of Winifred Howells on March 3, 1889.

The Scudders had been endlessly kind in arranging for the services and burial in Cambridge.

To Horace E. Scudder

330 East 17th st.,
March 11, 1889.

MY DEAR SCUDDER:

I found the family all well last night, and in one of those cheerful moods which express the inability of life to accept the fact of death. We have had our tears, our moments of insupportable heaviness, but we have begun to live on, and I suppose we shall live into some consciousness of the fact that now seems so incredible. I wrote as usual, Pilla went to her drawing, and my wife busied herself with her many cares. It must be best to do so; at any rate it is the best we can do.

We are keeping John over night, but he goes back to his work in the morning.

I write merely to send our love to Mrs. Scudder and yourself, dear, kind friends!

Yours ever,
W. D. HOWELLS.

Howells's "new book" was *A Hazard of New Fortunes*.

Björnson's works were in the order in which he writes of them, *Det Flager i By og i Havn, Over Aevne,* and *Geografi og Kjarlighet.*

Björnstjerne Björnson to W. D. Howells

Paris, rue Faraday 15, Ternes
13 Mar. 89.

DEAR MR. HOWELLS:

It was with great pleasure that I received your long letter, and it is with joy, that I look forward to your new book. In your way you are one of the greatest psychologists of your age in my eyes; that will say, that you perhaps are the greatest now living in the sphere, where you have your kingdom and realm.

Just now I am treating a very rich subject, namely, how of a strong, rough, sensual family after generations a man comes forth, who founds a girls' school and gets at the head of the moral work in his town. All these transitions amuse me. As soon as this is finished, probably in May, I begin a novel called *God's Ways*. It has three collisions between a clergyman and a physician, the first, when the both are boys at school, the second, when the both are at the university; the future clergyman is victorious in both by his greater moral earnestness; the third, when the both are ready, and then the physican is victor, for now he stays inspired by humanity and science, far superior to the clergyman's narrow theological doctrines. The principal battles take place before some bed-ridden persons and before some conversions from drunkenness, where the physician does what the clergyman can not do. At last the clergyman reverently says, that God's ways are more numerous than the theolog did know of. A Swedish physician, Dr. Munthe is assisting me with the last part; he is very interested in the subject, and wonders that there not earlier is written about the collisions between a clergyman and a physician before the sick-bed and else in the community. When this is finished I will get on with *Over Aevne* (beyond our means, above our power).

It is namely my opinion, that there is something "above means" in all of us, and that it shows itself in many ways and not only in our religion fanatisme. It is first now, that we really begin to see, how we far more are swayed by prejudices, imagination, traditions, sanguine hopes and customs, than by common sense and clear calculation. Then I have a divorce (which *not* becomes a divorce!) called *Geography and Love*. The husband is geograph, with heart and soul a geograph, and neglects his younger wife entirely; acknowledges that it is wrong, but can't let the geography go either. It is a comedy!

I do not think I can be ready with all this before two years, and I will probably stay here in Paris all the time.

My best wishes for your spiritual wife, your children and for Professor Horsford's kind family.

Your affectionate friend
BJÖRNST. BJÖRNSON.

My address is now rue Faraday 15, Ternes, Paris.

To Edward Everett Hale

330 East 17th st., April 5, 1889.

MY DEAR FRIEND:

I cannot quite tell you how very sweet and good I find it of you to have written me, and to have tried to see me. God knows how humbly grateful I should have been for the help that I think I might have got from meeting you. Truly, I feel quite beaten into the dust, from which I do not know how to lift myself. The blow came with terrible suddenness, when we were hoping so much and fearing nothing less than what happened. The most that I can say to myself is that she could not have died out of her time, unless all that exists is a shabby mockery unworthy even humanity. I account for the fact upon this ground, and I am trying, as I can, to imagine her well and happy somewhere. I wish to think of her as not only freed from her long pain, but emancipated from what is clumsy and cruel and uncouth in all earthly conditions. But at the end, I come back sore from head to foot and grovel in the mere sense of loss. Never to hear, never to see, never to touch, till time shall be no more! How can I bear that? And that is what I must bear. It makes one mass of anguished egotism of me, and shuts me up from all the things outside of myself in which I have been lately interested, so that I do not know how to acknowledge fitly the fact you tell me about the Tolstoi Club. But some day I shall be glad of it; and I suppose ashamed of these groans and cries. What you said of your children, those you have and those you have lost, went to my heart.

Yours sincerely,
W. D. HOWELLS.

Miss Alice James was the sister of Henry James, who lived with him in England.

In a letter of March 30th to John Hay, Howells says: "James wrote me 'To be young and gentle, and do no harm, and pay for it as if it were a crime.' That is the whole history of our dear girl's life."

To Miss Alice James

330 East 17th st., New York,
April 26, 1889.

DEAR MISS ALICE:

I have not yet had the strength to reply to your brother Harry's beautiful letter about Winny; but I must try to send you some word of thanks for yours. It is strange, and not strange, either, that the greatest help and kindness in this bewildering grief of ours, should have come from your father's children; for your brother William said something that more than anything else enabled our hearts to lay hold on faith again, and supplemented with a hint of hope those perfect terms in which Harry had expressed our loss. And now your message, with its memory of another world, completely past, is an intimation that we may somewhere else survive that of to-day, too, and of all earthly morrows. I cannot tell you with what tenderness I recurred to those Sundays, when you mentioned them, and with what vividness your dear father and mother's presence was with me again. I was greatly privileged to know such a man as he, and things that he said have enriched my life with a meaning that did not all appear in the moment. It consoles and encourages me that such a mind as his held fast to such a belief as his.

Our dear girl is gone—we begin to realize it, to yield, almost to consent. But whether we consent or not, we are helpless. I conjure her back in gleams and glimpses of her old childish self, presently obscured by the sad phantom of the long suffering before the close. It is useless; we shall go to her, but she will not return to us. This fact has changed the whole import of death and life; they seem at times almost convertible. I wish I could say something fit about her. I cannot. Only this I say, that she now seems not only the best and gentlest, but one of the wisest souls that ever lived. It is hard to explain; but she was *wise,* and of such a truth that I wonder she could have been my child. Pilla and her mother are well. We shall go to the vicinity of Boston for the summer, to have John with us as long as possible. You know he is now a Harvard Sophomore.

The family join me in love, and in the warmest wishes for your welfare.

Yours sincerely,
W. D. HOWELLS.

To S. L. Clemens

Mt. Auburn Station, Cambridge,
July 21, 1889.

MY DEAR CLEMENS:

I am extremely sorry not to have been able to come to you, but one trivial thing after another—of the sort that we let kill the real pleasures and interests of life—hitched on. Besides, we had long promised a visit to Mrs. Fields at Manchester—Pilla and I—this week, and I could not make two absences from home so near together. I can see how my wife depends upon me almost momently. I have denied myself a great deal; I would rather see and talk with you than any other man in the world, outside my own blood.

Yours ever,
W. D. HOWELLS.

"Your book" was *A Connecticut Yankee at King Arthur's Court.*

To S. L. Clemens

Mt. Auburn Station, Cambridge,
Oct. 17, 1889.

MY DEAR CLEMENS:

This last book, about the King's and Boss's adventures, is all good; and it's every kind of a delightful book. Passages in it do my whole soul good.—I suppose the Church will get after you; and I think it's a pity that you don't let us see how whenever Christ himself could get a chance, all possible good was done. I don't mean the fetish, the fable Christ, but that great, wise, serious, most suffering man. Read Brace's *Gesta Christi,* and you'll get at it all.

How soon shall I have the whole book? I must begin the Study by the 25th.

Yours ever,
W. D. HOWELLS.

To S. L. Clemens

Mt. Auburn Station, Cambridge,
Oct. 22, 1889.

MY DEAR CLEMENS:

My wife is not well, nor likely to be well all winter, but she says I may go to you for Sunday next, and it will be a great joy for me. I'm getting good out of your book, the whole way along, and I guess I can fetch it for the Jan'y (the next) Study. It's a mighty great book, and it makes my heart burn and melt. It seems that God didn't forget to put a soul into you; He shabs most literary men off with a brain merely.

We were both so sorry for dear Mrs. Clemens' suffering.

Yours ever,
W. D. HOWELLS.

Howells was moving into a flat at 184 Commonwealth Avenue, where he lived for the last two years that his son was at Harvard.

"The Charioteers" was his name for the United Charities.

To Mrs. James T. Fields

Boston, December 27, 1889.

DEAR MRS. FIELDS:

As I don't belong anywhere yet, I have to trouble you with my slight token for the Charioteers.

My call last night was like a foretaste of heaven, where there shall be large-leisured angels appointed to hear us talk about ourselves, world without end.

Yours sincerely,
W. D. HOWELLS.

Clemens was indignant over the indifference of the American republic to the new Brazilian republic, which had overthrown the monarchy there by a military revolt in Rio de Janeiro on November 15, 1889. He wrote to Sylvester Baxter, of the Boston *Herald,* that another throne had gone down and that he was swimming in oceans of satisfaction, but to Howells he must have dwelt on the American indifference.

To S. L. Clemens

184 Commonwealth Avenue, Boston,
Dec. 29, 1889.

MY DEAR CLEMENS:

I have just heated myself up with your righteous wrath about our indifference to the Brazilian Republic. But it seems to me that you ignore the real reason for it which is that there is no longer an American Republic, but an aristocracy-loving oligarchy in place of it. Why should our Money-bags rejoice in the explosion of a Wind-bag? They know at the bottom of the hole where their souls ought to be that if such an event finally means anything it means *their* ruin next; and so they *don't* rejoice; and as *they* mostly inspire the people's voice, the press, the press is dumb.

I wish I could go to West Point with you, but I can't, or rather I won't; for I hate to shiver round in the shadow of your big fame, and I guess I hate the sight of a military-factory too, though I'm not sure; I suppose we must have 'em a while yet.

As for the Hartford end of your invitation, any and every time! We'rc all glad you're coming here.

Yours ever,
W. D. HOWELLS.

END OF VOLUME I